WALKING IN THE
CEVENNES

D0770403

ABOUT THE AUTHOR

Janette Norton has lived in France (near Geneva) for over 30 years with her physicist husband, Alan, raising four children and working in the marketing field. Her love of mountain walking dates from the time she was a guide in her twenties, and the proximity of the Alps and Jura to her home has enabled her to continue her passion. Now her family has grown up, she has branched out to explore other areas of France.

Other Cicerone books by the author:
Walking in the Haute Savoie – North
Walking in the Haute Savoie – South
Walking in Provence
Walking in the Dordogne

WALKING IN THE CEVENNES

by
Janette Norton

2 POLICE SQUARE, MILNTHORPE, CUMBRIA, LA7 7PY
www.cicerone.co.uk

© Janette Norton 2002

Reprinted (with updates) 2010

ISBN-13: 978 1 85285 336 6
ISBN-10: 1 85284 336 5

A catalogue record for this book is available from the British Library.

ACKNOWLEDGEMENTS

I would like to thank my gang of faithful friends and family, who have come to walk with me many times over the past few years from Geneva and England. Without their support, advice and criticism this book could not have been written: Josephine Andorfer, Loulou Brown, Lynn Mermagen, Janet Locke, Ann Nicholson, Jill Robinson, Lorraine Ruffing, Alexa Stace and my sisters Hilary Birch from Nassau, Bahamas, and Julia Jamison from Paris.

My husband, Alan, accompanied me on many of the walks and read it all before it went to the publishers. My grown-up children, Rebecca, Joanna, Angus and Tanya, gave me the space to get on with it!

I am especially grateful to the tourist offices of Le Vigan and Florac, and particularly the offices of the Parc National des Cevennes in Florac, for advice and documentation.

Advice to Readers

While every effort has been taken to ensure the accuracy of this guidebook, readers are reminded that changes may occur rapidly in any area, which could make some information inaccurate. It is advisable to check locally on transport and accommodation. The author would be glad to hear of any important modifications, such as new signposting or diverted trails. Please write or email Janette via the publisher at Cicerone, 2 Police Square, Milnthorpe, Cumbria, LA7 7PY, UK. Further information on walks and updated walk directions where applicable are available on the author's website at www.janettenorton.info.

Front cover: St-Chély-du-Tarn (Walk 21)

CONTENTS

KEY TO MAPS

 WALK ROUTE

 GITE/ ACCOMMODATION

 OTHER FOOTPATH

 VILLAGE

 SURFACED ROAD

 FLORAC TOWN

 JEEP TRACK

 WOOD Deciduous

 RAILWAY

 WOOD Evergreen

 RIVER

 PEAK over 1000 m

 LAKE

 PEAK under 1000 m

 CLIFFS

 SPECIAL VIEWPOINT

 MENHIR

 BRIDGE

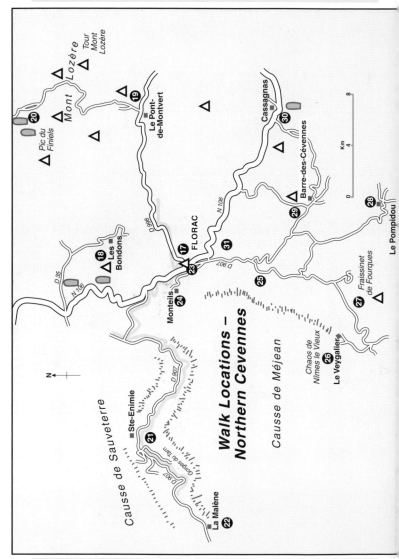

**Walk Locations –
Northern Cevennes**

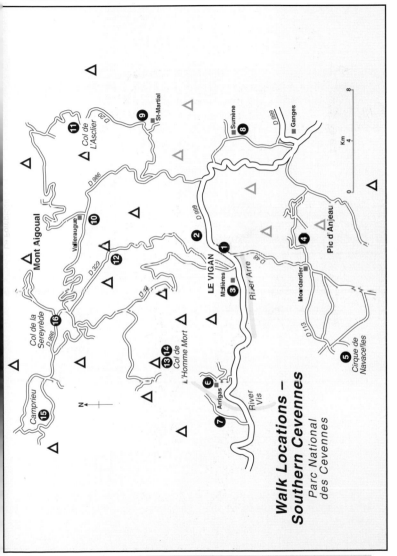

Walk Locations –
Southern Cevennes

Parc National
des Cevennes

INTRODUCTION

In my bedroom in the large rambling house where I grew up was a shelf full of an odd assortment of books, old and new. It was not until my early teens that I noticed a small, insignificant book entitled *Travels with a Donkey in the Cevennes* by Robert Louis Stevenson. This was my first introduction to a mysterious region of wild rolling hills and gorges in southern France. At the time I cared little about the Cevennes, but was more interested in the antics of a stubborn small donkey called Modestine, who sometimes consented to carry the few belongings of a then unknown Scottish student as he wound his way up and down dale.

Much later in life I reread the same little book, and it was then that I decided to explore the region on foot and visit some of the places so vividly described by Stevenson. Of course much has changed: roads have been built, towns have grown in size and tourism is now the main economic resource. Yet most of the landscape remains hauntingly wild and desolate. Many of the villages Stevenson walked through are now crumbling ruins, as many of the people, unable to survive by agriculture, left at the turn of the 19th century. In 1879 Stevenson encountered more people on his travels through the Cevennes than I did on mine!

My first Cevennes experience was a four-day circular walk in February. Although I got lost and very cold – not knowing how winter lingers in this rough upland country – the subtle magic of the area, steeped in historical conflict and economic hardship, fascinated me, and I knew I would eventually return to find out more.

It was not until many years later that I could go back and write a walking book, basing myself in two little towns, one to the north and the other to the south of the Cevennes National Park. The two areas are quite different – the south gentler and covered in chestnut trees, the north bleak open moorland and deep gorges. Insidiously the fascination of walking and discovering this remote countryside became an obsession and a pleasure, shared as always by my faithful team of walking companions.

THE CEVENNES

When I tell people that I am walking in the Cevennes they often look rather puzzled – some fish for the exact location by pretending they know where it is; others know the Cevennes is somewhere in France; the less inhibited come straight out and say 'Where on earth is it?'

The Cevennes is on the southern end of the Massif Central area of France, to the west of Provence and north of the coastal town of Montpellier, but where the area begins and ends is not clear because it is not a definite *département* (county). The southern part belongs to the Département d'Herault, the east to the Rhône-Alpes and the Gard, and the whole region, which extends from north of the Lozère to the Spanish border, is called Languedoc/Roussillon. The real Cevennes is such a criss-cross of narrow valleys and wild upland country that it does not even have a large town at its centre. Alès, in the southeast, is the administrative capital, but is on the very perimeter of the Cevennes proper. The two dominant mountainous regions are Mont Aigoual and the more northern Mont Lozère, both part of the newly created Cevennes National Park. They are bounded in the west by four upland plateaux called *causses:* (from north to south) Sauveterre, Méjean, Noir and Larzac; these are separated by deep gorges, the most northern being the famous Gorges du Tarn. To the south is the leafy Arre valley and the Mediterranean.

Why the Cevennes is so little known is something of an enigma, as only the Rhône valley separates the region from Provence, the most visited area of France. But the Cevennes is so different that it could be worlds away. In place of cosy hilltop villages, the Cevennes landscape is harsh, mountainous and deserted. The weather is more extreme – the winters are cold and windblown, snow often covering the higher slopes, and the summers are dry and hot. This is not a place to appeal to the well-heeled retirement crowd or the casual tourist. The Cevennes attracts those who have a taste for a more rugged and subtle landscape – the mysterious emptiness of its endless hillsides that look like the blue crests of waves rolling to a misty horizon, the deep dark gorges and flat, stark plains resembling the Russian steppes. The Cevenese people are dour and taciturn until you get to know them but also independent and tough, with a devotion to a Calvinistic faith that sets them apart from neighbouring regions.

In the guidebook I have split the walking areas into two – north and south of the national park, the boundary being the Mont Aigoual. In the south I stayed in a tiny huddle of houses called Loves, set in a dense chestnut forest 3km up a winding road near the town of Le Vigan. Florac on the river Tarnon was my centre for the northern walks and the starting point of my tour of Mont Lozère.

Most of the walks undertaken are within one hour's drive from the towns of Le Vigan and Florac and are well signposted. There are no paths going across private land (so walkers avoid being diverted by irate landowners), and fewer habitations mean fewer farms with yappy dogs! When you walk here you rarely meet other people or stumble on habitation – you get mesmerised by the emptiness of the country, by the endless hills stretching into nowhere and the wonderful feeling of being really alone – a rare pleasure in this constantly growing bustle of Europe.

SOUTHERN CEVENNES (WALKS 1–16)

The southern region, known as the Cevennes Meridionales, with the small town of Le Vigan in the Arre valley, has a Mediterranean character. Olives, vines and a variety of fruit trees are grown on the lower south-facing slopes, and the once useful mulberry trees still flourish, together with the chestnut trees at a higher altitude. The main town is Le Vigan, with 4500 inhabitants, situated on the southern side of the Mont Aigoual. It is an authentic, lively little town, the centre for a large rural area which has happily escaped being smartened up and given over exclusively to tourism. Although it, too, suffered from the decline in the silkworm industry at the end of the 19th century, it managed to continue the tradition by producing stockings, scarves and other textile products thanks to the installation of a large factory. The river Arre meanders through the town, spanned by a magnificent old Roman bridge, and in the vicinity is the Musée Cévenol, which gives a fascinating insight into the rural industries and culture of the region (see Walk 1 for opening times and further information).

A few kilometres southwards is the Blandas Causse (upland plateau), which always comes as a surprise, as the switch from green hills to arid limestone plain is unexpected. It has a curious ring of stones rather like a mini-Stonehenge. These are unprotected and unpublicised, but if you see them you can just stop the car and wander around! Further on this flat region is cut in two by the winding Vis river (see Walk 5 for further information).

Mont Aigoual

North of Le Vigan are the mountainous, mainly tree-covered slopes of Mont Aigoual (alt. 1567m), on the summit of which is a Victorian edifice housing one of the last high-altitude meteorological stations in Europe. It is worth visiting for the wonderful extended view of the surrounding mountains and the Causses, as well as, if the weather is clear, the Alps, Mont Ventoux in Provence and the sea!

Mont Aigoual, consisting of schist and granite, is the most southern upland area of the Massif Central and is a bulwark between the gentler climate to the south and the harsher temperatures of the north. For this reason it is often covered in cloud as the humid air of the Mediterranean meets the colder air of the Atlantic. The name Aigoual comes from the word 'aigualis', meaning water, which is very appropriate, as this is one of the wettest regions in France. It is also on the 'water dividing line' – its streams flowing north to the Atlantic and south to the Mediterranean. This area is known for its extreme climatic changes and can be covered in snow for many of the winter months, which makes it a popular place for downhill and cross-country skiing.

The whole region is now a protected national park, created in 1970 and consisting of 230,000 hectares of rolling upland covered in moorland and forest. Unlike other French national parks, however, it has a permanent population of around 600 people, mostly sheep farmers, in its central zone. Every year in June there is a Fête de la Transhumance (sheep-droving festival) when the shepherds bring up their enormous flocks of sheep to graze on the upland pasture – the sheep are decorated with balls of wool and look very colourful. There are three main *drailles* (sheep paths) in the Cevennes, all going northwards – the Aubrac from Le Vigan or village of Valleraugue; the Margeride from St-Hippolyte-du-Fort; and the Gevaudan from St-Jean-du-Gard and Alès.

A hundred years ago Mont Aigoual was completely treeless and suffered from acute erosion; it was only thanks to the heroic efforts of one particular man, M. George Fabre (1844–1911), Director of Forestry, that the slopes are now covered with 15,000 hectares of forest. Not far from the summit is an arboretum and research station (called l'Hort-de-Dieu) created by the botanist Charles Flahaut from Montpellier (1852–1935), who, with the collaboration of M. Favre, planted a wide variety of species, some now over 100 years old and of impressive stature.

Starting in 1875 George Fabre cajoled various owners to sell their land and, despite opposition from the shepherds who often burnt the young saplings, he slowly started the tremendous task of replanting, using out-of-work local labourers. He finally handed 12,000 hectares to the state in 1914. The work continued with the building of roads over the mountain, but was interrupted during the First World War and through lack of funds. It was finally completed in 1939.

Although there are no walks in the book around the immediate summit, Walks 12–15 are in the Mont Aigoual vicinity. L'Abîme de Bramabiau is a vast underground cave, which is worth a visit (see Walk 15 for further information).

NORTHERN CEVENNES
(WALKS 17–31 AND TOUR OF MONT LOZERE)

The reason why Robert Louis Stevenson was attracted to the Cevennes is that the northern area, especially around Mont Lozère, resembles the highlands of Scotland – wild heather-clad slopes, rocky outcrops, flocks of sheep, herds of cattle (though quite different from the Scottish variety), stunted coniferous trees and rushing mountain streams. The region is cold and often covered with snow in winter, though hotter in summer than its northern counterpart – all that is missing is the squelch of bog!

Sandwiched between the upland regions of Mont Aigoual to the south and Mont Lozère to the north is the isolated small town of Florac. At the confluence of three valleys on the northern edge of the Cevennes National Park and the entrance to the famous Gorges du Tarn, it is dominated by the rocky crags of the Rocher du Rochefort, the edge of the Causse Méjean to the west; north is the Mont Lozère, with the larger town of Mende beyond. To the southeast is the scenic Cevennes ridge (Corniche des Cevennes). The D106 winds through the Mimente valley (Walk 30) linking Florac with the large town of Alès to the southeast, but it takes at least an hour to get there!

The pink rocky walls of this valley especially impressed Robert Louis Stevenson – he said that 'steep rocky red mountains overhung the stream', but he couldn't find a spot to tie up his donkey because the valley was so narrow. Apart from the road it has not changed!

Chapel St Cyprien (Walk 8)

Formerly under the sovereignty of the Bishop of Mende, Florac was constantly revolting under the yoke of its oppressors and then, in the 16th century, it became one of the centres of the conversion to Calvinism (see 'A Short History of the Cevennes'). Now it serves as the administrative centre of a large rural region and also lives off tourism.

With a rushing mountain stream flowing through the town under picturesque bridges, the narrow, flower-decked streets of Florac draw the holiday crowds, especially for the lively weekly market, but its main claim to fame is that the château, which dominates the town, is the administrative headquarters of the Cevennes National Park.

Corniche des Cevennes (Walks 28 and 29)

Linking Florac to St-Jean-du-Gard in the southeast is the dramatic Corniche des Cevennes, which is a long upland shoulder between the Vallée Francaise and the Vallée Borne, punctured by narrow twisting gorges and ravines (*serres*). At first a mere track used by the shepherds taking their sheep to upland pastures (a *draille*) it then became a mule track for traders going from the Mediterranean plain of Languedoc to

WALKING IN THE CEVENNES

the Gevaudan area in the north. It is now a scenic route much appreciated by tourists, as the views on all sides are magnificent. The little
town of St-Jean-du-Gard at the eastern end at the confluence of the
two valleys has a interesting cultural museum; once a flourishing centre for the silk, leather and wool cottage industries, it is now mainly
a tourist centre.

Mont Lozère

Mont Lozère is a huge area of high granite plateaux at the north of the
Cevennes region surrounded by rivers: to the north the Lot, to the east
l'Altier and to the south the Gardon and the Luech. What little habitation there was has mainly disappeared, though, according to records,
there is still a population of 500 people who live from sheep farming,
cattle breeding and forestry. Formerly thousands of sheep made their
way from the Languedoc plains in the south to these northern uplands
along the well-trodden *drailles,* but now fewer than 3000 make the
journey each year.

Until 1795 the knights of Saint John of Jerusalem owned much
of the land and installed their headquarters in the isolated village of
l'Hôpital. Their territory was marked by stones with a Maltese cross
engraved on them, some of which can still be seen today, especially
on the ascent of Pic du Finiels (alt. 1699m). The tour of Mont Lozère
should not be taken lightly, though there are no technical difficulties
and the path is well signposted. It is a remote upland region and there
are no villages or friendly cafés to help you on your way should you
feel in need of comfort and refreshment. Neither did the author meet
many people, though this could be different at the height of the season. Even so every landlord seemed to know who we were and where
we had come from, so there must be a bush telegraph in operation!
It is advisable to book your accommodation in advance in case the
establishments are shut or full.

In an effort to promote the region, the tourist department has created a rather ugly ski station at the foot of the Pic du Finiels, and there
are some ski lifts and cross-country ski trails. In high summer there are
quite a number of tourists who drive here to make the relatively short
walk to the summit of Pic du Finiels (see Walk 20).

A small limestone area to the southwest of Mont Lozère called the
Can de Bonbons (a *can* is a small *causse* or plain) is marked by huge
granite standing stones called menhirs (see Walk 18). It is not known

whether they were erected as markers or had some sort of religious significance. What is amazing is that early man could drag these enormous stones and erect them in such an isolated, high area. Many of the stones have now been bedded in concrete to preserve them.

Causse Méjean

To the west is the high, sparsely populated limestone plain of the Causse Méjean (30km by 20km) which lies at an altitude of approximately 1000m, surrounded by the 500m-high cliffs of the Gorges du Tarn and the Gorges de la Jonte. Freezing in winter and extremely hot in summer, it would not be an easy place to live, and the few isolated hamlets are mainly deserted. Since there are few trees (though in some places conifers have been planted) the wind whistles across the bare fields. The limestone absorbs the spring rain and, though it has hollowed out underground rivers and gorges, little water remains on the surface except in shallow depressions called *lavognes*, which enable the flocks to drink and the farmers to grow wheat, corn and barley. The sudden extreme changes in temperature have caused the rocks to crack and created *clapas*, piles of rocks and stones, which are often used to make low stone walls.

After walking up the side of the gorge, with its fascinating rocky outcrops and vertiginous cliff face, it is always something of a shock to arrive at this flat upland landscape at the top (see Walk 23). It is as though you have suddenly entered another world, with its silent windswept slopes, some dotted with boulders and bushes, small isolated fields and the occasional fir plantation, but little else. The few farms still occupied concentrate on cattle, sheep raising or making cheese. This is also the home of the rare Prezwalski horse, which is threatened with extinction in the wild but flourishes here in a protected area of 300 hectares. On the western edge, where the Gorges du Tarn meets the Gorges de la Jonte, the bald-headed vulture can be seen, its huge wings cruising the air currents among the high, dramatic cliffs. These birds were reintroduced to the region in the 1970s.

Although there are roads, to get the feel of this unique country you have discover it on foot, and one of the most interesting walks is to a strange rocky area called the Chaos de Nîmes (see Walk 26). There is also a long-distance walk around the Causse Méjean, which takes about six days.

Solitary graves at Moulin des Geminards
(Walk 29)

Gorges du Tarn

The Tarn rises near the Pic Cassini in the Mont Lozère region. In its infancy a narrow, rushing, rocky stream, it widens and grows calmer as it flows west through the village of Pont-de-Montvert to join the river Tarnon at the Pont du Tarn, north of Florac. Here the cliffs are already high, but as the river sinuously carves its way like a huge snake through the Causse Sauveterre to the north and the Causse Méjean to the south, the cliff walls become even higher and more dramatic. The rare villages and habitations that cling to the riverbanks are completely overshadowed by these daunting walls of rock, often pitted with caves and small bushes.

The river continues westwards and then turns south to meet the Jonte river. All along are impressive cliffs and look-out points, and in summer the D907, which follows the river, is clogged with cars and tourists. One of the best ways to experience the gorge is to go down on a boat, if you don't mind the odd rapid! Seen from above the water is a deep translucent green, which contrasts with the silvery sheen of the pebble beaches, dotted with bikini-clad sunbathers in high season. After the Corniches de Méjean cliffs, the river opens up and turns southwest towards the town of Millau.

A Short History of the Cevennes

Like other areas of southern France, in prehistoric times the Cevennes was a melting pot of different tribes and cultures, although it seems that early man took longer to penetrate the narrow upland valleys of this remote region. The earliest traces of civilisation have been found in caves and overhanging grottos where primitive man sheltered in order to survive by hunting and fishing.

During the Bronze Age hundreds of megaliths – standing stones called menhirs and dolmens – were constructed and placed in prominent places on tops of ridges and passes (see Walks 5, 18 and 23). Why they were put there, and how, is still a mystery – they could have been used for religious purposes, as waymarks for travellers or even for early scientific experiments regarding the solar system. In any case, the size of some of them and the fact that they were dragged to these remote summits is a tribute to the ingenuity and courage of our ancestors.

Two tribes of Celtic origin occupied the Causses and the Cevennes regions around 6000 BC, the Gabales in the north and the Volques in the south. The conquest of France by Julius Caesar and the arrival of the Romans did not affect the remote areas of the Cevennes to any great extent, although archives have shown that in order to penetrate the Massif Central, 'Caesar did not let winter hinder him from crossing the Cevennes on foot', probably taking the *drailles* already in use by the Celts. Vestiges of a Roman road linking Nîmes to Millau can still be seen (Walk 3). Mention is also made that the most popular cheese in Rome came from the Lozère region. The Romans were also the first people to exploit the mineral riches of the region, and evidence has been found of early mining of iron, copper and silver, especially in the Tarn Gorge, where remains of Roman settlements have been discovered.

When the Roman Empire fell, confusion reined as the Visigoths and other barbarian hordes invaded southern France. The Saracens (Moors from north Africa) penetrated as far as the Vallée Français, but were driven off by Roland, nephew of Charlemagne. Little is known about historical events at this time, but by the ninth century the Cevennes was integrated into France proper and free from invasion.

Christianity was slower to penetrate the Cevennes than the other regions of France, and the first records indicate that the area was divided into two bishoprics, that of Mende to the north and Nîmes to the south. Monasteries and rural priories sprang into existence, such as the one in Ste-Enimie (see Walk 21). This was also the epoch of the local *grand seigneurs,* who ruled over different regions and who built their castles strategically overlooking the valleys and gorges of their domains. Together with the clergy they ruled the area militarily, politically and economically.

In the unstable environment of the 11th and 12th centuries the monasteries were often welcome havens of peace and stability. In the wild upland area of Mont Lozère the knights of the order of Saint John of Jerusalem established themselves in the village of l'Hôpital and founded the Commanderie (garrison) de Gap-Francès. They acquired vast tracts of land, and their boundaries were marked by large stones engraved with the cross of Malta, which are still standing to this day (see Walk 20 and Tour of Mont Lozère). Their benevolent rule lasted until the start of the French Revolution.

The War of the Camisards

The Cevennes only really entered the pages of history in the early 15th century, when much of the population was converted from Catholicism to the ideologies of Luther and Calvin. Preachers and settlers entered the region spreading the word of this new way of thinking. It fell on fertile ground, and such was the zeal of the local inhabitants that a message was sent to Geneva from the town of Le Vigan in October 1560 asking for a minister. By 1563 twelve ministers were preaching in the region. The reaction of the authorities was to send punitive expeditions into the area, but the inhabitants fled into the countryside and there was little bloodshed.

The Edict of Nantes was issued in 1598, wherein it was stated that religious liberty was permissible throughout France. The Calvinist faith flourished and chapels were built where the population could openly gather and hold services. However, in 1685, Louis XIV revoked the Edict of Nantes and the massacre of the Protestants began. Chapels were burnt, whole villages massacred and those that were not killed were imprisoned or sent to the gallows. Instead of deterring the people this seemed to harden their faith and they gathered secretly in isolated farms and caves to conduct their services, including marriages, baptisms and funerals. Many of the richer and more educated families fled to Calvinistic countries such as

Switzerland or Germany; some emigrated to Canada and America. Others decided to stay and fight it out.

The War of the Camisards lasted for only two years, but many innocent people, both Catholic and Protestant, were killed as a consequence. The word Camisard comes from the word 'camisa', meaning *chemise* (shirt) in the Occitan language, signifying the special shirts worn by the adherents.

The war began with the murder of the Abbot de Chaila, who was harbouring prisoners in his house in Pont-de-Montvert in the Mont Lozère region (see Walk 19), by a group of insurgents led by Esprit Séguier, who was subsequently burnt alive a few weeks later. Surprisingly few of the noble families were involved, and it was mainly a war organised by the peasants, the four commanders being Roland Laporte from Mailet and Castanet from the Aigoual region, who were both wool carders; brickmaker Jouany from Genolhac; and a baker named Cavalier from the southern Cevennes. A number of skirmishes took place, with villages fighting against other villages, the burning of churches on both sides and families torn apart.

Finally the forces of authority led by the Maréchal de Villiers managed to seriously wound Cavalier after discovering his arms depot. He then capitulated and was accused of treachery by his compatriots. Fleeing to England he eventually became Governor of the island of Jersey. In the autumn of 1703 the Maréchal de Montrevel, the chief of the royalist forces, decided to burn 32 parishes loyal to the Camisard cause. Roland continued to fight but was betrayed and killed near Uzzes in 1704. After that the Camisards lost heart and the war fizzled out.

In 1787 the Edict of Nantes was reinstated and the Protestants were free again to lick their wounds and rebuild their chapels. When walking in the Cevennes it is not unusual to come across isolated small graveyards; since the people did not wish to bury their dead in the official Catholic cemeteries they buried them on their land or, in many cases, in their basements so they would not be discovered by the royalist soldiers!

The War of the Camisards has become a legend of Cevenese pride and endurance, but has permanently marked the mentality of the people, who tend to be uncommunicative and self-contained. Although many villages, particularly in the north Gevaudan, reconverted to Catholicism, the majority of the region has remained strongly Protestant; it has taken until the Second World War for the tensions to really heal so that both religious communities can live together in harmony.

Every first Sunday in September some 15,000 protestants and descendants of those that fled the country in the 15th century gather in Le Mas Soubeyran, near Mailet, at the Musée de Désert (so called in memory of the Hebrews who crossed the desert). Here, in the birth-place of the Camisard chief Roland, which has now been turned into a musem, they commemorate the hundreds of Cevenese who died for their belief. The museum is worth a visit and is open from 1st March to 30th November from 9.30 to 12.00 and 14.30 to 18.00, and all day from 1st July to 1st September.

Robert Louis Stevenson (1850–1894)

No book can be written about the Cevennes region without a mention of the renowned writer Robert Louis Stevenson, who wrote his classic *Travels with a Donkey* in 1878. A young, penniless Scottish student, he walked from Puy-en-Velay southwards, over Mont Lozère to Florac, and continued down the Mimente valley to St-Jean-du-Gard. His adventures and tribulations with his donkey, Modestine, have enchanted readers the world over and put this remote mountainous region, in many ways so like Stevenson's native Scotland, firmly on the map.

Walking the Stevenson Trail, which takes around five days (though it took Stevenson longer), is still very popular, and on some walks in this book (Walk 31 and the Tour of Mont Lozère) you will see sign-posting indicating that you are on the Sentier Stevenson.

CEVENESE LIFE

The Bible, the tree of bread and the tree of gold: these were the three mainstays of Cevenese life – the Bible their source of culture, the chestnut tree their source of food and the mulberry tree fed the silk-worms providing economic stability. Through these three resources the Cevennes people emerged from obscurity in the 16th and 17th centuries.

The Chestnut Industry

The origins of the chestnut tree forests are obscure but could date from the Iron Age, when the religious orders penetrated the region and began to clear the land and create the farms and villages that remain today. Chestnut trees were never part of the natural vegetation of the Cevennes, which was mainly oak, green oak and beech, but were planted on the slopes between 300m and 900m. In order to prosper the trees required constant maintenance, as they hate the cold and fog, needing a deep, rich soil with long periods of sunshine to ripen the nuts; they also need constant pruning, thinning out and manuring (they particularly like iron deposits) – all time-consuming and manpower-intensive activities. Indeed the Cevennes population could not cope alone, and itinerant workers came every year from surrounding regions to help with the chestnut harvest, and special markets were held to recruit these labourers (see Walk 29).

Until the end of the 19th century the cultivated chestnut trees were the main source of food for the Cevenese population. The nut, the wood, the leaves – every part of the tree was utilised. The nuts, collected in the autumn by special wooden rakes called *gratto*, were eaten fresh or dried and also ground into flour to make bread. The drying process took place in a stone building called a *clède*, which was built next to the *mas* (farm) or in the chestnut wood itself. The chestnuts were funnelled in from the outside and spread on a wooden grating hung underneath the beams. A fire was lit underneath and kept going for several weeks until the constant smoke had dried the nuts. They were then shelled, which was achieved by walking on them with special spiked shoes! The wood was used for building and for making furniture, beer barrels and fencing – even the traditional Cevenol beehives are made out of chestnut trunks. At the end of the harvest the flocks of sheep, goats and pigs grazed in the woods to fatten up on the leaves and remaining nuts.

In 1871 the chestnut forests were hit by disease called 'la maladie d'encre' and this, together with the exodus of the population, was the death knell of this noble tree. Two-thirds of the splendid chestnut woods have disappeared, cut down for their excellent wood, but have been replaced by other species, such as the Austrian pine, which do not need looking after. However, hundreds of chestnut trees still remain, most of them untended and some of magnificent size; they are a symbol of the Cevennes and of a tree that can nourish a whole population.

The Silk Industry

The other tree that is a symbol of the Cevennes is the mulberry. Again it was planted for a specific reason – to feed the silk worms whose cocoons furnished the silk thread to make clothes and stockings, the main economic resource of the region. Sericulture, or the art of making silk, started at the end of the 13th century but was at its height in the 17th.

Mulberry trees were planted at altitudes of up to 600m beside the roads and fields in convenient places where the leaves could be easily picked. Two tons of leaves were required to nourish 33g of eggs when they hatched into worms. Before special incubators were constructed in the 18th century, the eggs were kept warm in special sacks hung under the blouses and skirts of the women!

Once the worms had hatched they were kept and fed in the huge high buildings called *magnanerie* which are still seen in the Cevennes today, many of them in ruins. These buildings were constructed so that the rooms were kept at an even temperature with constant ventilation – hence the rows of small windows and many chimneys. After one month, when the worms had ceased eating and started to weave their cocoons – which took around three days and yielded 1500m of silk thread, it was imperative that the cocoons remained dry and did not rot. The thread was then spun off the cocoons, mainly by the nimble hands of women and young girls, to be made into bolts of silk, garments and stockings in the local factories.

In the middle of the 19th century the silk worms were struck by a disease called *pébrine*, and a remedy was not discovered until 20 years later in 1870. By this time cheap silk imports from China and India were entering the country, and the industry never recovered – the last silk-producing enterprise closed in 1965.

Decline of the Region

When the chestnut and silk industries failed, many of the Cevenese could no longer survive and the exodus began. Rather than emigrating to Australia, the United States or Canada, the people tended to move to the coalmining area around Alès, in the southeast, at the start of the Industrial Revolution. Between 1846 and 1896 the population of this area tripled, but the age of prosperity was short-lived, and one by one the mines closed. Many of the population then moved to other areas such as Marseilles and Montpellier.

*Traditional beehives made of chestnut logs
at Moulin des Geminards (Walk 29)*

The First World War is the main reason why the Cevennes became one of the least populated areas of France. Because there was no work for the young men they signed up in droves and died likewise. During these years the population declined drastically, as in some villages all the young men were killed, leaving women and children to survive as best they could. Many of the villages were abandoned and remain in ruins to the present day. The Second World War had a less catastrophic effect, and the decline in population was only 10 per cent. In fact, during this period the area became a place of refuge, harbouring many exiles including Jews, who were fleeing persecution; the wild isolated areas of the Cevennes made a good hiding place. The Resistance (Le Maquis) played a role in dispersing and hiding the exiles in isolated villages and farms, the farmers being glad to have extra help with no questions asked!

Present-day Cevennes
Although the towns around the Cevennes, such as Alès, Mende and Montpellier, offer employment, economic opportunities for the isolated villages in the high upland regions now lie in tourism and in the sale of houses for conversion into secondary residences. Tourism

is expanding as more and more people are looking for areas which are unspoilt and offer space and quiet. Some villages which, a decade ago, were silent and falling into ruins have now been renovated and brought back to life. The Cevenese who left their land in order to survive are now coming back, even if it is only to renovate the family farm and live there a few weeks a year. Painters, writers and other artisans are moving into the area, lured by relatively cheap property.

Perhaps the very fact that the Cevennes does not have an obvious agricultural or industrial future means it has a different role to play – as a refuge for those seeking a respite from the increased hussle and bustle of life in the big cities. In a world where roads and buildings are spreading everywhere, and the once green fields are covered in urban sprawl, we need the Cevennes to remain as it is – wild, empty, mysterious and forgotten!

Using the Guide

At the start of each walk details are given of the walk difficulty, time, height gain, maps, depart point and signposting.

Walk Difficulty

Most of the walks in this book are within the capacity of a reasonably fit person and are graded 'strenuous' (rather than difficult), 'moderate' or 'easy'. The Cevennes region does not have high mountain peaks, so there are few sudden steep height gains and vertiginous places. Further details after the grading should give a good indication as to whether the walk is suitable for your abilities.

Time

The timings correspond to the average walking pace of a reasonably fit person, but this is only a rough guide, as everyone has a different rhythm. It is also important to leave plenty of time for stopping to look at the views, taking photos and for a picnic. Generally, you can expect to walk 3km in one hour if there are no excessive gradients. Four centimetres on a 1:25,000 map equals 1km (for quick measurement put three fingers sideways on the map – this equals roughly 4cm, which is 20mins walking). Appendix A gives a table of walk times.

Height Gain

When reading the walk details look carefully at the altitude gain. Extra altitude equals extra walking time, and steep gradients, whether up or down, can tire you if you are not used to it. Only a few walks in this book have a significant altitude gain; as a guideline, with a light rucksack (6–7kg) you should be able to climb 400m in one hour (250–300m with a weight of 15kg). The descent should be quicker, namely 500m in one hour. When walking, especially in southern climates, the heat and humidity will slow you down (see 'When to Go').

Maps

Although each walk is accompanied by a sketch map it is recommended that you buy the listed 1:25,000 IGN maps, which are available in local shops. It is easier to buy them when you are in the region than to try to get hold of them in the UK. They cost around 9 euros (exchange rate is about 1.6 euros to £1 at the time of publication). Sometimes the local supermarkets sell them cheaper.

The numbers on each sketch map show key reference points, especially where there are major changes in walk direction, and correspond to a numbered section in the text. However, please read the instructions carefully, as there may be additional turnings that are not numbered but where the path is not clearly indicated, even on the IGN map. Unfortunately many IGN maps are out of date or inaccurate, and the jeep tracks and paths taken on the walks are not always shown.

Departure Point

In the text directions to the start of each walk ('How to Get There') are given from a specific town (Le Vigan or Florac). Where possible the walks start from points where there is a car park or good roadside parking.

Signposting

This gives an indication as to how well the walk is signposted and whether you are following a Grand Randonnée (long-distance footpath), a local path with its own different coloured splashes or wooden signposts.

If you see white and red horizontal paint splashes on your route you are on one of the Grandes Randonnées, which go all over

GUIDELINES FOR WALKING IN THE CEVENNES

- Read the walk description carefully and look at the IGN map and the sketch map before you go.

- Make sure the walk is within the capacity of you and your companions.

- Give yourself plenty of time by setting off early. If a walk gives a time of 5 hours, allow at least 2 hours extra for looking at things, reading the walk description and eating.

- In the Cevennes, especially in the summer, you will need to take **plenty of water and sunscreen** – wear reliable sun glasses and a floppy hat.

- Never deviate from the marked path – if there is a short cut it is usually shown. If you are lost go back the way you came, if possible.

- If you are climbing be careful not to dislodge stones or boulders – they can gather momentum as they roll down the slope and hit other walkers.

- Never walk alone, even if you know the route, and always tell someone where you are going.

- Do not pass beyond any barrier indicating 'Proprieté Privée' unless the walk description indicates that this is permitted.

- Even if the day looks hot and fine take waterproof clothing, as the Cevennes often has sudden storms.

- Take your litter home with you. Do not pick the wild flowers but leave them for others to enjoy.

- Do not light matches or make a fire, and take particular care when it has been dry.

- Remember to shut all gates and barriers you go through.

- When walking on roads, face oncoming traffic. Remember that in France this means on the left-hand side of the road.

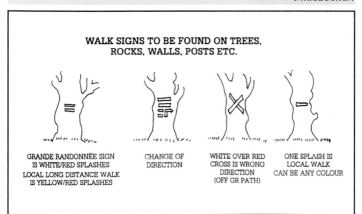

**WALK SIGNS TO BE FOUND ON TREES,
ROCKS, WALLS, POSTS ETC.**

GRANDE RANDONNÉE SIGN
IS WHITE/RED SPLASHES
LOCAL LONG DISTANCE WALK
IS YELLOW/RED SPLASHES

CHANGE OF
DIRECTION

WHITE OVER RED
CROSS IS WRONG
DIRECTION
(OFF GR PATH)

ONE SPLASH IS
LOCAL WALK
CAN BE ANY COLOUR

France and are usually well maintained. Please remember that a cross instead of a splash (of the colour you are following) means that you are about to go in the wrong direction! Some of the local walks join these paths for a while and then break away to circle back to the starting point. Local walks have different coloured splashes, but in some areas these are rather arbitrary and can suddenly disappear for no reason. In others there are so many colours that one gets bewildered!

Many of the walks in the Cevennes region are newly signposted, and great strides have been made by the local tourist offices to make the walks clearer. However, it is a wild, remote area, so it is wise to stick to the signposting and splashes and not try to do shortcuts or take other paths indicated on the map – if you are lost you will meet few, if any, other people to ask directions from!

Observations
The initial italic paragraph in the walk description gives useful additional information, which might help the reader to decide whether he or she wishes to do the walk. It also includes historical background of the town or village the walk is starting out from, as well as anecdotes about the countryside or things of interest to be seen on the way.

TRAVELLING TO THE CEVENNES
The official French Tourist office in the UK is:

> Atout France, Lincoln House, 300 High Holborn
> London WClV 7JH
> Tel: 090 68 244 123 (60p per minute)
> http://uk.franceguide.com
> info.uk@franceguide.com

They will answer enquiries and send information and brochures.

By car
It is not possible to reach many of the walks in this book without a car. If you arrive by train or air and want to hire a car, all the major hire firms operate from stations and airports. Information about rental can be obtained from your local travel agency.

If you take your own car, the easiest route to the Cevennes is to take the motorway via Reims, Dijon and Valence, which avoids the traffic around Paris. To reach the Cevennes exit at No. 19 (direction Pont St Esprit) and take the N86 to Bagnols followed by the D6 to Alès. From Alès you take the N106 to Florac (northern Cevennes) or follow signs to Le Vigan (southern Cevennes). Another option is to continue on the motorway to Nîmes and take the N106 through Alès to Florac or the D999 to Le Vigan.

The motorways are refreshingly empty in France compared to Britain, except on some busy holiday weekends, and have excellent stopping areas. However, there are motorway tolls to pay, which can add considerably to the cost of motoring. For route planning: www.viamichelin.com.

By Rail
For information on travelling by rail contact:
> Rail Europe Ltd, 34 Tower View, Kings Hill, Kent ME19 4ED
> (UK representative for all SNCF and continental rail travel)

There are 5 departures per day to Montpellier which is the nearest station to the Cévennes.

For online booking: www.raileurope.co.uk. For information about rail travel from the UK to France: www.seat61.com/France.htm.

The river in the centre of Florac

By Air

The nearest airports to the Cevennes region are Nimes (for Florac) and Montpellier (for Le Vigan). It takes about an hour to drive to Le Vigan from Montpellier.

For information on flights and times contact: www.ryanair.com, www.easyjet.com and www.britishairways.com.

WHEN TO GO

The Cevennes, because of its geographical diversity, has a much more extreme climate than its neighbour Provence.

The high mass of the Mont Aiguoul is the most southern part of the Massif Central and creates a barrier between the Mediterranean climate to the south (around Le Vigan) and the more rigorous climatic conditions further north. It catches the high winds and cloud coming off the Mediterranean and has one of the highest rainfalls in France – winter can be bitterly cold and snowy. Further north, around Florac and the Mont Lozère, the climate is more continental – hot in summer and cold in winter.

The best time to go is in the spring, early summer or autumn; for the southern area April and May can be glorious and the best time to see the spring flowers, but you run the risk of a certain amount of rain, especially in the narrow Cevennes valleys, where it can be quite intense.

If you travel to the Mont Aigoual and the Lozère region in May there are carpets of alpine flowers, but be prepared for colder weather. June and early July are usually pleasant, as are September and October, when you get the extensive autumnal colouring.

The summers are usually hot and dry, especially on the upland plains, where there is little shade for walkers and no water; in the Mont Lozère region there may be irritating flies in the wooded areas. Mid-July to August is the height of the tourist season, and anywhere in France should be avoided!

Do not attempt to visit the northern Cevennes in the winter months unless you want to cross-country ski!

ACCOMMODATION

Although the Cevennes is a tourist area and does offer hotels, *gîtes*, bed and breakfast establishments and a wide range of camping sites, it must be remembered that the villages and towns are widely dispersed,

The old Roman bridge at Le Vigan (Walk 1)

Looking down the Arre valley from Roc de L'Esparon (Walk 3)

The restored Moulins de la Foux, La Cirque de Navacelles (Walk 5)

so the choice of places is limited. It does not have as many places at the top end of the market as you would find, for example, in Provence.

The walker has the advantage that it is really too hot to walk in July and August when most places are full and the camping sites are cheek by jowl. It is much easier to find accommodation in May, June, September and October, when there are fewer people about and prices are lower. It is always advisable to book in advance, though this is not essential.

Hotels in France are typically less expensive than in England and are great value – the only things missing are the tea-making facility in the bedroom and, of course, the hearty breakfast – you pay extra for this in a French hotel. Most rooms have en-suite bathroom or shower and WC. The choice is wide, and below are some recommended hotel chains.

Logis de France: This is a nationwide network of hotels which offers comfortable accommodation and excellent food at reasonable prices. The hotels are graded from one to three star according to their degree of comfort (look for the distinctive logo which consists of a yellow fireplace on a green background). For information on the Logis de France hotels in the Cévennes area look under the section Languedoc-Roussillon on the website www.logis-de-france-languedoc-roussillon.com.

Campanile Hotels: These tend to be on the outskirts of towns rather than in villages. They are usually modern and impersonal, catering more for the family market rather than the discerning tourist. For a list of hotels visit www.campanile.com.

Châteaux and Independent Hotels: If you want to go up-market there is a book published with a list of lovely looking châteaux (often with the owners acting as hosts) and independent hotels available all over France. There is a description in English and a photo of each establishment. Prices of the rooms and meals are clearly marked. Some of them are not at all expensive for what they offer! For further information visit their website: www.chatotel.com .

Gîtes de France: Very popular with the English, these are country cottages which are available for a weekly rent all over the French countryside and are good value. They can vary from extremely comfortable to quite basic so read the explanation beside the photo carefully!

It is a good idea to pick an area of the book that appeals to you and then rent a gîte in a central position for the walks indicated.

For a list of gîtes in the Cévennes area visit their website: www. gitesdefrance.fr and look for the section 'Languedoc Roussillon'.

Gîtes d'étape: These are youth hostels of a particular type, usually without a warden, but open to people of all ages. They can be reasonably comfortable with good beds, showers and a well-equipped kitchen, but they can also be quite basic and are mainly intended for cheap overnight stops by walkers and cyclists. If you prefer not to cook your own meals there is often a café/restaurant in the vicinity.

In the high season they can be uncomfortably full, but are a wonderful way to get to know fellow-travellers and share a convivial evening. Out of season you often have the place to yourself. The only snag is that you may have to hunt for the person responsible in the village or nearby (usually posted on the door) to get access to the *gîte*.

For a list of gîtes d'étape in the Cévennes area visit the website www.gitesdefrance.fr.

Chambres d'Hotes: This is the French equivalent of bed and breakfast, though often the breakfast is not included or, if it is, is limited to coffee and bread (croissants if you are lucky). The number of these establishments is increasing all over France (look for the Chambre d'Hôte sign or enquire in the local café or shop).

The degree of comfort varies tremendously, and, unlike in British establishments, you will rarely get a TV or beverage-making facility in your room. Most rooms have their own shower/toilet, but you could be sharing with the family.

For a list of Chambres d'hotes in the region visit the website www. gitesdefrance.fr.

Camping: The Cevennes region is particularly favoured with camping sites, especially in the Gorges du Tarn area. Camping sites are graded from one to five star, and range from those offering a shop, hot showers and a swimming pool to sites providing only basic washing facilities.

Camping à la ferme is cheap and popular, though the facilities are minimal – remember some toilets in France, especially on camping sites, are still of the squat variety!

The local tourist offices (see Appendix C) have a complete list of camping sites. Most of them speak English and will gladly send the information. Visit the website www.gitesdefrance.fr which also publishes a list of camping sites.

Clothing and Equipment

When you think of southern France you imagine that the sun never stops shining and it is always agreeably warm in summer and winter. This is not the case in the Cevennes, which has a harsher climate and more defined seasons. In spring and autumn it can get cold and rainy, and in the summer it can be unbearably hot, especially on the Causses (high plateaux) where there is little shade.

The best solution is to dress in light layers and, even if the weather looks good, take a windproof jacket; choose the breathable type to avoid getting hot and sweaty. When the sun shines the rays are more intense than in Britain, so sun protection is important, as is a shady hat. The type of trousers which zip down into shorts are very practical as on many of the walks there are prickly gorse and broom bushes which scratch bare legs.

The most suitable footwear for walking in the Cevennes is a lightweight pair of sturdy boots with plenty of ankle support and soles that grip well on rocky terrain.

As none of the walks described is long, a light- or medium-weight rucksack is quite adequate. An outside strap for a water bottle is useful in this region, where you must take lots of water. It is wise to carry a compass and altimeter, provided you know how to use them! They are not essential for these walks, but can be helpful in bad weather. A mobile telephone is also useful, but note that they do not work in all areas of the Cevennes.

The following is a suggested list of essentials for your rucksack for a day's walk:

- map as stipulated on the walk description
- compass
- basic first aid kit including insect repellent
- survival blanket (useful if you get lost or hurt)
- high-factor sun cream and lip salve
- sun hat and sunglasses

- woolly hat and gloves (winter only)
- glucose tablets and/or chocolate (useful if your energy flags)
- Swiss Army knife with as many attachments as possible
- waterproof cape or poncho which goes over everything including your rucksack (useful when pouring with rain and for sitting on)
- lightweight sweater
- lightweight wind and waterproof jacket
- water bottle – **note it is essential to take lots of water if the weather is hot; do not drink from streams or dubious village fountains**
- picnic (buy a crusty baguette at the local bakery before you set off and eat it with fresh cheese or ham – much nicer than sandwiches!).

Optional extras include: altimeter, camera, binoculars, mobile phone and reference books.

FLOWERS AND VEGETATION

Due to the different geographical and geological areas of the Cevennes, the flora is very diverse and many species are endemic to the region. The Causses are limestone, and the water drains away into underground grottos and rivers. The upland regions of the Mont Aigoual and Lozère are shist and granite, with plenty of water, where temperatures in winter and summer are extreme. The southern Cevennes has a Mediterranean climate.

The leafy Arre valley around Le Vigan is where spring arrives first, with flowers such as primroses, violets, periwinkles, snowdrops, crocuses and daffodils making their appearance long before the snow has left the upland heights of the Aigoual and Lozère – in June and July the slender catkins and white flowers of the chestnut trees which cover many of the hillsides are very attractive. This is an area with a southern flavour, and up to 500m the Mediterranean vegetation prospers. The air is alive with the smell of herbs such as thyme, and there are clumps of blue flax and aphyllanthes. There are various species of evergreen trees, such as the kermes oak (often called scrub oak, with prickly leaves), holm oaks, (which have glazed, water-retaining leaves), juniper bushes, boxwood and species of pine. Higher up are the chestnut forests (see Introduction, 'The Chestnut Industry').

On the summit of the Rochers de la Tude (Walk 4) are stately asphodel lilies and tall white heather in May. Here the difference in vegetation between the northern and southern slopes is quite marked – the south smelling of herbs and creamy rock roses, while the north is colder, with species of orchids, the charming blue columbines (aquilegia) and, lower down, the yellow laburnum trees.

Up to an altitude of 1000m the Mont Aigoual is covered in trees (see Introduction, 'Southern Cevennes', for an explanation of the reforesting of the area). It is a young forest consisting of pines and beech, and is often rather dark; this prohibits the growth of many varieties of flowers, with the exception of the white wood anemones which cover the slopes in early spring while the trees are still in bud. However, in the open glades you can find different species of crane-bill, amongst others, and the beautiful pink martagon lily which flowers in July. In a boggy area on the Cascades d'Orgon walk (Walk 16) the author was excited to see for the first time fragile looking, hairy-stemmed orange tulips. There is also a species which is rare outside the high Cevennes, called Arabette des Cevennes, which looks rather like a species of sweet pea. It flowers in the summer on riverbanks.

The higher grassy slopes of both the Aigoual and Mont Lozère have carpets of daffodils, narcissi, hairy anemones and crocuses in the early spring, and even in the Alps I have never seen so many varieties of orchids, sometimes covering whole fields. Later tall yellow gentians, arnica, pink willow herb, blue monkshood and various species of daisy replace them, but in many places the sheep have cropped the grass clean.

Above 1500m both mountains, but particularly Mont Lozère, are covered in heather, myrtle bushes, gorse and broom; in some areas, peat bogs hosts their own species of feathery grasses and delicate white wind flowers.

The vegetation that has grown swiftly in the last 50 years is broom – the dense bushes cover the slopes in June with their yellow flowers and peculiar smell. For many Cevenese this brash yellow symbolises the gradual decay of the region, as it grows on the slopes which were once used for pasturing cattle and sheep – now, with the huge flocks disappearing, the persistent broom has taken over, and the only way to get the land back to pasture is to burn the bushes.

The stony nooks and crannies of the limestone *causses* and gorges turn into flowery rock gardens as the pink moss campion, the creamy rock roses, white saxifrage and blue violets create a kaleidoscope

Village of Les Bondons
(Walk 18)

of colour. Lichens and mosses cling to the more vertical slopes of the gorges. The *causses* have their own species of white potentilla and also an orchid called Ophrys d'Aymonin, which resembles a fly orchid – hunted for unsuccessfully by the author! Often used as barometers and attached to doors of houses, because their flowers open and shut according to the humidity, are the huge Carline thistles which grow on the upland steppes; unfortunately they are so often picked that they are becoming rare. The only bushes that survive the onslaught of the herds of sheep are the prickly blackthorn (sloe bushes), which tend to circle the shallow water-filled depressions called *lavagnes*.

If you want to discover orchids then walk up the rocky Gorges du Tarn (Walks 21 and 22) in May when it has just rained – the author saw more species in one day than ever before, including red and white helleborines, purple broomrape, birdsnest orchid and the rare spiky lizard orchid.

Suggested books: *Mediterranean Wild Flowers* by Marjorie Blaney and Christopher Grey-Wilson (Harper Collins). This is a complete guide with over 2000 illustrations. It includes illustrations of the different pines and deciduous trees to be found in the southern area.

Flore du Parc National des Cévennes – obtainable at the park shop in Florac (French only). Lots of photos of the flora to be found in the national park and on the Causses.

WILDLIFE

The Cevenese people have always been great hunters and probably needed to be in order to survive. The new ecology movement has been slow to get off the ground amongst the older farmers, though an awareness of the need for conservation is growing amongst the younger generation.

With the setting up of the Cevennes National Park in 1970, certain species have been reintroduced to the area, such as the Grand Tetras (capercaillie) (see Mont Lozère walk), the mouflon (a type of sheep originating from Corsica), black woodpecker and the bald-headed vultures on the edge of the Causse. As all the animals are protected the numbers of deer, mountain hares, badgers, foxes, squirrels, pine martens and wild boar have increased, as have birds such as owls, thrushes (once trapped) and woodpecker.

Weathervane in Pompidou village
(Walk 28)

Wolves have, as yet, not been reintroduced, probably because of the flocks of sheep, but in the 17th century a certain wolf became a legend. The Beast of Gévaudan, as it was called, took a liking for the tender flesh of young girls and killed over 50 people, striking terror to the whole region before being shot by a local hunter.

On the windswept Causses I have seen hares, weasels, stoats and small deer, though there seems precious little for them to eat and very little cover. There is a wide variety of bird life; you can hear the larks and the cries of the pipits and see the hawks hovering overhead. On the cliffs surrounding the gorges are birds of prey such as buzzards, eagles and the bald-headed vultures, the latter recently introduced – it is a moving experience to watch these enormous birds with a tremendous wingspan floating, seemingly effortlessly, round and round in the thermal currents like a crowd of paragliders! There are also swifts, swallows and crows; by the river banks are kingfishers, dippers, wagtail and inoffensive grass snakes which live off the fish.

On the lower slopes on the Mediterranean side of the Cevennes, where it is hotter and drier, one is frequently alerted to rustling in the undergrowth. This could be attributed to the thousands of tiny lizards, which abound everywhere, a grass snake or a viper, which are rarely seen, or one of the huge iridescent green lizards which at 60cm long are the largest in Europe. The air is alive with the rasping noise of the crickets and other insects. One of the more fascinating is the preying mantis, which does look as though it is praying but has the reputation of eating its mate!

But the most curious creature I have seen in the Cevennes was when I was walking round the Mont Lozère in the pouring rain; suddenly at my feet slithering across the path were four lizard-like creatures, black with big bright yellow spots. These are called spotted salamanders, and they only come out when it is raining hard, normally preferring to rest in swamps and ponds.

Walk 1

CIRCUIT DE L'ARRE

Difficulty:	Easy short walk with no height gain
Time:	1hr 45mins (plus time to look round the museum)
Height gain:	None
Maps:	Cartes IGN 2641 ET Top 25 Mont Aigoual/Le Vigan
Start point:	Central square – Le Vigan
Signposting:	Yellow splashes on the first half but not very obvious
	Red/white splashes of the GR after the bridge at Alvèze

This is a very pleasant, easy walk along the Arre river and could be combined with a visit to the interesting Cevenole Museum installed in a former silk-weaving factory. It enables the visitor to see what life used to be like in the Cevennes region. One of the rooms is dedicated to traditional crafts, such as basket- and barrel-making, gold prospecting in the rivers, pottery and ironwork. There are informative displays concerning the chestnut industry, silk making, sheep raising and bee keeping, which were the sources of income until the end of the 19th century. Also shown are models of the different styles of architecture – the farms in the Causses area being quite different from those in the mountainous regions.

The Arre river rises in the St-Guiral area of the Mont Aigoual and flows down the mountainside through the town of Le Vigan. It is joined by numerous other mountain streams before itself joining the Herault after 25km. Like other rivers in the area the water level can suddenly rise dangerously high if there has been a lot of rain. For information concerning the town of Le Vigan see Introduction, 'Southern Cevennes'.

HOW TO GET THERE (FROM LE VIGAN)

The walk is from the town itself. Park behind the town hall (Mairie) where there is a lot of space and make your way to the main square.

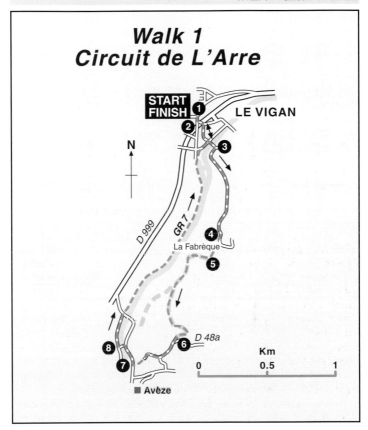

Walk 1
Circuit de L'Arre

DIRECTIONS

(1) From the western end of the square with the church up on the right, go down the Rue Pierre Gorlier, where there is signpost indicating 'Musée Cevenol' (with a bookshop on the corner). Follow this narrow street over a bridge, then cross the road to the right signed 'Musée et Vieux Pont' (still the Rue Pierre Gorlier). Go along here and turn left on the Rue des Calquires, passing the museum on the right.

Musée Cévenol, Rue des Calquières, Le Vigan. Tel. 067 81 06 86.

Open times: November to April – Wednesdays only, 10.00–12.00 and 14.00–18.00; May to October – every day except Tuesdays, 10.00–12.00 and 14.00–18.00

(2) Turn left on the Rue du Pont just before going under the bridge and then take an obvious hairpin back onto the bridge. There is a lovely view to the right of willow trees and the river Arre rushing over rocks when the water level is low enough; there is a weir on the left, but a new bridge further on mars the view. On the other side of the bridge take the first turning right on the Rue Cap du Pont ignoring a yellow cross (10mins).

(3) The narrow road passes a large rock and continues with houses up left and open fields with the river beyond on the right. At a pillar (where is the other one?) keep on the road and then straight ahead at a crossroads – you are now going through woodland. Go past gates on the right and then you can see La Fabrèque, a big run-down, ugly-looking house which used to belong to the Count of Sporta of the nearby village of Montdardier. There are no yellow splashes here (20mins).

(4) Turn right on a narrow paved drive, which goes to the left of the building and then continues down over a dry riverbed by an aqueduct covered with vegetation. On the left are dilapidated gates and sinister tall pines surround the whole area. There is a partially hidden blue splash on the aqueduct wall (25mins).

(5) Do not continue up the overgrown jeep track but go right and then immediately left on a narrow path through the pines with a moss-covered wall to the left. Continue upwards (the wall goes off to the left) through mixed woodland and then chestnut trees, going up man-made log steps. The path meets a wider track (to the left is 'privé'). Continue right on the main track which zigzags up the hill. At the top ignore the track going left but continue round the contour of the hill on a flatter path which then starts to descend. On the corner, there is a gate and a sign on the right saying 'Sentier Communale de Vigan/Avèze' (40mins). The path goes into the open and narrows as it continues through bushes with a vegetation-covered wall left. There is now a good view of the Roc de L'Esparon over on the right (see Walk 3).

The walled narrow track continues down past an orchard into a shallow little valley with a stream flowing through and a number of vegetable gardens, each with its own wooden hut. The path becomes a grassy jeep track and continues over the pretty little stream at the Pont de Mousse and up to the right along the other side of the valley. It is interesting to note that these allotments are well irrigated as the water from the stream has been diverted into narrow channels between them.

(6) The track meets the D48A (50mins), which goes up left to the hamlet of Loves. However, go right and continue on the road round a corner (ignore the junction right signposted 'Le Caila') past some houses to a T-junction at the main road to Avèze.

(7) Go right on the road (you can see the village of Avèze left) for a few minutes and then left on a quaint stone bridge across the river where there is Camping Municipale on the other side (1hr). The red/white splashes of the GR7 now appear.

The river here is very attractive as it flows over stones, and there is a stony beach which is a good place for a picnic – beware of broken glass though!

(8) Turn right after the bridge onto a narrow road, which soon reaches the main bridge from Avèze. Do not cross the bridge but go straight over onto a narrow path, which follows the river all the way to Le Vigan. This is a pleasant flat path where bushes and willow trees border the riverbank – you can hear the traffic over on the left. It crosses a number of watercourses coming down into the river, passing orchards and a pylon opposite a high weir. The river becomes more rapid, and stretches of the cobbled path are raised and man made.

The path continues under a metal bridge where there is a sluice gate and an old mill on the other side. The river becomes calmer now before going over another weir. The main river flows to the right round an untidy island of willows, and there is a wide channel beside the path which leads to a dam – the water has obviously been channelled off here to use for some former industrial process.

Follow the path into Le Vigan, with a disused factory on the left, then go ahead at a crossroads past the Centre Culturale and a swimming pool – on the right is a school. Continue on, crossing a bridge over the road, and turn right onto the Rue Barris, following signs 'Centre ville' to the church and into the main square (1hr 45mins).

Walk 2

CIRCUIT DES MAURES

Difficulty:	Easy – some medium steep uphill to start
Time:	3hrs 15mins
Height gain:	306m
Maps:	Didier & Richard Top 25 2641 ET Mont Aigoual/Le Vigan 1:25,000
Start point:	Parking at the Hôtel de Ville (Mairie) of Le Vigan
Signposting:	Excellent – the GR60A goes to the col where it meets the GR60. Continue on the GR60 until you turn down the mountain. There are also wooden posts with PR21 on them and yellow splashes all the way round the walk – you can't go wrong!

A relatively easy walk up to a low pass above the town of Le Vigan and then along a delightful ridge before dropping down to walk along the river. According to legend, when the Saracen hordes invaded this area at the start of the eighth century and destroyed the town of Le Vigan, they came by way of the Col des Maures (Maures meaning 'moor' in the ancient Occitan language), which is now indicated as Col des Mourèzes on the IGN map.

Le Chevalier d'Assas was born in Le Vigan in 1733 and belonged to a bourgeois family. He became a captain in the Auvergne regiment and died in battle in Hanover at the age of 27. His claim to fame is that when his regiment was ambushed in a wood he led with the fabled battle cry 'A moi Auvergne, ce sont les ennemis', which has gone down in French history thanks to Voltaire who wrote about the incident in 1768.

How to get there (from Le Vigan)

This walk is from the town itself. Park behind the town hall (Mairie) where there is a lot of space.

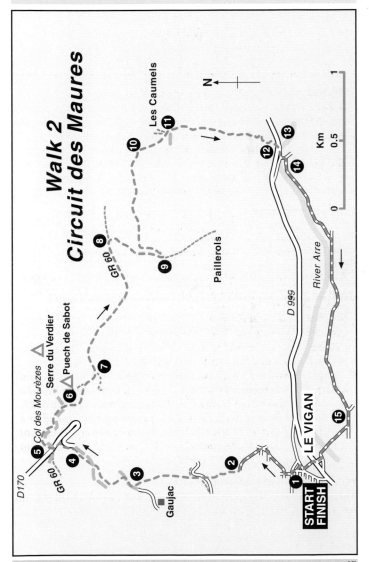

Walk 2
Circuit des Maures

Directions

(1) Take the road up to the right behind the Mairie called Rue de Mareilles where there are red/white signs of the GR60/60A and yellow splashes. After 5 minutes, at a crossroads, continue straight on the Chemin de Gaujac, which narrows where there is a red/white splash on a wall.

(2) A few metres further on look for another GR splash and a wooden PR21 (PR means *petite randonnée* – small walk) post indicating Col de Mourèzes and take a rather overgrown grassy path to the right. It goes up medium steep on an attractive sunken mule track through old stone walls and shady woodland to reach the road again by a small water pumping station (20mins). Cross the road and continue on a stony path upwards through tall bracken and chestnut trees until you reach a jeep track (35mins).

(3) Turn right and then 30m further on turn up left on a narrow path where there are GR and yellow splashes. You get your first open view of tree-covered hills with the three peaks of the Pic d'Anjeau on the skyline. Continue upwards, passing a ruin to the left and walking along the top of old stone terraces which were previously cultivated.

(4) The path rejoins the road going up to the pass (40mins). Turn right (look for markings on a telephone pole). On the second corner after a house, turn up left on another slightly rockier path, which again meets the D170 5 minutes later at the Col de Mourèzes (45mins).

There is a stone here saying that this path is part of the 'sentier André Chamson 1900-1983', Chamson being well-known as a writer of books about the region. The tourist bureau of Le Vigan inaugurated the stone in 1993. They have created a special Chamson walk from the centre of town to the Serre de la Lusette, which was the subject of one of his books, L'Aigoual, published in 1930, and an area in which the author loved to walk in.

(5) Turn left on the road (avoid a track up left signed DFCI G-43) and go right on a jeep track signposted DFCI G-41 where there are GR signs, a wooden PR21 post and yellow splashes. Keep on this pleasant track, which soon comes to a fork at an open field where there are lovely views; if you look back you can see two antennae on the tops of the tree-covered hills.

(6) Go right; there are crosses on trees left (55mins). The track undulates along the summit through kermes oak and box bushes (avoid path to left) and for a time there is a steep slope to the right.

(7) Careful – when the track turns a corner go straight on a narrower path where there are GR markings and yellow splashes (1hr 5mins). Walk beside an overgrown orchard and then keep straight past a path on the left with a no entry sign. The path narrows as it goes through woodland and open spaces. It gets rockier in places and at one stage there are extended views on both sides and over the outskirts of Le Vigan down on the right. As the landscape opens out the vegetation changes to heather and stunted bushes such as juniper, this change being caused by a geological fold. Keep on the main path, which starts to go down with a crumbling wall initially on the right – there are glimpses of hamlets through the bushes left.

(8) Take the path down right off the ridge (1hr 25mins) where there is a wooden PR21 post and yellow splashes. Here you leave the red/ white splashes of the GR60, which continues along the top. The terrain is initially steep and rocky and would be slippery and difficult in wet weather. Crossing some scree, you get your first view of the hamlet of Paillerols, which is perched on a shoulder below. It looks neat and restored with some cultivated terraces. A rivulet appears from nowhere and trickles down the path itself before veering off to the left. Shortly after there is a small building housing a water tank. Continue round the top of a narrow tree-covered ravine and then join another path by a high wall (1hr 40mins).

(9) Go left. (The path straight ahead goes to the hamlet of Paillerols and then down to the road. This is an alternative way back and takes half an hour less: not done by author.)

The path goes along the side of the hill (ignore a fork down right), crossing three rivulets – there are old terraces and walls, remains of cultivation and habitation in the past. It reaches a rocky area where there are open views again and later passes an attractive miniscule pool of water in the rocks.

(10) You reach the top of a rocky shoulder where the path bears round to the right by a wooden PR post (2hrs) – there are magnificent views of the surrounding hills and you can see the valley of the Arre river over on the left. The path leads down the front of the mountain and

Bridge over the river Arre

suddenly reaches a *mas* (huddle of houses) called les Caumels on the IGN map (2hrs 5mins) – it consists of one big ruin and an unusually tall renovated house. It is quite a shock to cross mown grass, dotted with cherry trees, and you feel an intruder as you walk between the house and the large ruin.

(11) Bear to the left at the end of the lawn – there is a yellow splash on a tree (do not go straight where there is a red splash). Wend your way down through chestnut trees and tall bracken. The path becomes a mule track between two defined walls – on the left there is a large area of cleared land. This leads to a jeep track, which looks new and is not marked on the IGN map (this clears up the mystery as to how the people reach their renovated house at les Caumels).

Cross the jeep track and continue on down the mule track (yellow splash on tree) through woodland – you can now see the river Arre down on the left. The path becomes rockier and descends quite steeply through chestnut trees.

(12) Careful, before the path reaches a road it branches to the right in front of a house by an iron post (2hrs 35mins). It goes underneath a bridge where there is a concrete irrigation canal right and reaches the D999.

(13) Turn right on the road (yellow arrow) for about 50m and then bear down left at a wooden PR post. This is a narrow slip road, which goes down and then turns left over a very unusual old arched bridge with a water aqueduct flowing over the top of it. The river beneath looks delightfully cool and clear – there are sandy banks that look as if they make good swimming places for the people in the camping site on the other side.

(14) Turn right on the narrow road after the bridge (2hrs 40mins) and follow this all the way into Le Vigan. It is a pleasant setting with the river on the right and houses with large gardens on the left. There is a delightful old restored mill on the other side of the river by a weir and, further on, a large factory called Well, which makes a popular brand of stocking. Ignore a new bridge to the right and continue straight by another camping site and, further on, a small waterfall where the river seems to be flowing more rapidly. There is a sign saying 'Le Vigan' (3hrs) as the road enters a small industrial site and passes low blocks of flats.

(15) Cross the next bridge by a large supermarket (here the yellow splashes stop). Follow the sign 'Centre ville' and turn right on a bridge over a road. This takes you into the main square with the church up on the left. Turn right down here, continue past the fountain at the end and bear up left. This road passes the statue of the Chevalier d'Assas (see above) and at the top turn left towards the Hôtel de Ville (3hrs 15mins).

For information on Le Vigan see Introduction, 'Southern Cevennes'.

Walk 3

ROC DE L'ESPARON

Difficulty:	Moderate walk – uphill to start and a short scramble to the Roc de L'Esparon
Time:	3hrs 30mins
Height gain:	378m
Maps:	Cartes IGN No. 2641 Top 25 Mont Aigoual/ Le Vigan 1:25,000
Start point:	Village of Molières-Cavaillac
Signposting :	Good – follow PR20 posts and yellow splashes which are very clear most of the way round

This is a delightful walk through three lovely villages with a spectacular view down the valley surrounding Le Vigan.

There is an interesting legend concerning three brothers who came from the Château de L'Esparon, called Alban, Loup and Guiral. On her deathbed their mother begged them to marry into local families and produce heirs. Unknown to each other each of the three fixed his sights on the same beautiful girl, called Irène, and played court to her. Unable to choose between them she decided she would tell them they had to go to the Crusades to prove which one was the bravest. This they did but on arriving home they found to their consternation that in the meantime their loved one had died. United in their grief they decided to become hermits and exiled themselves to live on the summits of three local peaks – Saint-Alban, Pic Saint-Loup and the Mont St-Guiral (Walk 14).

HOW TO GET THERE (FROM LE VIGAN)

From Le Vigan take the D999, direction Millau, for 4.1km. At Cavaillac turn up right on the D272, signposted Bréau-Salagosse/ Molières-Cavaillac, and then shortly after left on the D790, which takes you to the village (7km from Le Vigan). Pass a little park bordered with rosemary bushes and turn up left and park in an open area at the top.

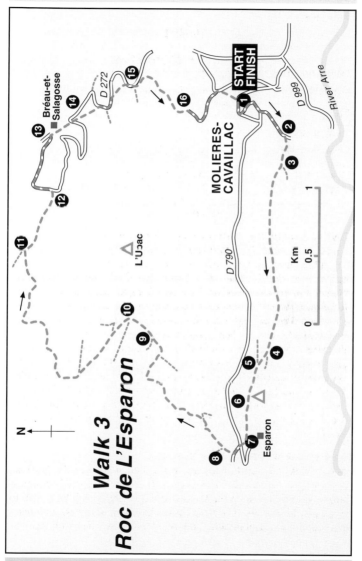

Walk 3
Roc de L'Esparon

N

START
FINISH

River Arre

D 999

MOLIERES-
CAVAILLAC

D 790

Bréau-et-
Salagosse

D 272

L'Usac

Esparon

Km

0   0.5   1

DIRECTIONS

(1) Follow the road up from the parking (Chemin de la Filature) and then as indicated by yellow splashes bear up right towards the church (Place de l'Eglise). Go down on a narrow road to the left of the church (not the Rue de L'Eglise right beside the church) and then left again on the Rue Mènard where there is a yellow arrow. Follow the road round right which goes under an attractive stone porch to the Place Bellevue (ancient gateway to the village) where there is a good view into the Arre valley.

(2) The yellow splashes direct you down out of the village, and after about 270m, where there is a small iron cross and a post with 'PR.20 (3)' on it, go up to the right (10mins).

This is a wide stony track along the top of old terraces with a wall on the right, which goes gently upwards. There are cherry trees (delicious to eat if you do the walk in early June) and some old olive trees; otherwise it is an open path, so there are sweeping views into the valley below and later on you can see the outskirts of Le Vigan.

(3) The path bears up to the right initially between stone walls (15mins) and then continues climbing steadily along the top of former terraces. It narrows and becomes stonier as it enters scattered oak woods, continuing along the side of the hill, and eventually flattens off. It goes through a wooden barrier and starts gently climbing again.

(4) Where there is a yellow cross on the path ahead and a low barrier of stones, bear up to the right by a wooden post, PR20(4) – (the straight path does in fact go directly to the village of Esparon but has been closed because of rock falls). The path is narrow and climbs up quite steeply. Follow the yellow splashes carefully. Bear left at the top by a wall and go over a smart new stile to reach a wider track.

(5) Bear left here (yellow cross on tree right) and a few metres later bear left again at another intersection. The wooded area is scattered with rocks. Where the path turns a corner you get your first view of the rocky outcrop of the Esparon, which looks unusual as it appears to be a pile of jumbled boulders with trees on the top – and looks tricky to get to the top of!

Follow the yellow splashes along the path which initially goes through stone walls and then, after veering left, climbs steeply upwards – there is a short rocky scramble over some boulders and you arrive at a flat spur (1hr 5mins). From here you can see the valley coming in from the right and opening out as the Coudoulous river (not visible) comes down from the north to join the waters of the Arre. The scattered buildings are the outskirts of Le Vigan – all around are rolling hills covered with forest.

(6) Bear right on a defined path which goes underneath a big rock and round the bottom of the Esparon hump where there are some stately cedar trees – there are lots of yellow crosses telling you not to go to the left and attempt to climb it, though it is surely possible. At a fork go right down the side of the hill. You can see a big farm down on the right and, shortly after, the village itself on the left as the path meets the narrow road going into the hamlet (1hr 15mins).

It is worthwhile exploring the short winding streets of Esparon to admire the ancient houses, which have been tastefully renovated.

(7) At the little Place du Village turn down right just before the low wall of the half-renovated bakery. (Note: this shortcut is easy to miss because of the renovations, so if you cannot find it continue down on the road – you can see the col below quite clearly). The grassy shortcut path soon crosses the road and continues down to reach the Col de L'Esparon (1hr 25mins) at an intersection.

(8) Cross the road to meet a signpost at the Col de L'Esparon. Take direction La Dernadette 3.8kms, Bréau-et-Salagosse 4.9kms. The jeep track passes a house up on the left and soon enters cool chestnut forest. Ignore any turnings off and keep to the main track, which is wide and flat – just after the turning DFCIG-59 look for a bevy of white beehives in a small clearing to the right.

(9) Where the track meets pine trees look for a signpost indicating right down a narrow path. There is a red/yellow cross on the track ahead. The path goes down medium steep through tall grasses and pines to reach a jeep track in a clearing.

(10) Go down right on the jeep track. **Careful** – do not take the track immediately after to the right. Further down go through a barrier (sign here indicating 'Fôret Dominale de L'Aigoual'). When the jeep track veers to the right, go straight on to a narrower track. Continue round a wide tree-covered gully, where you can distinguish on the surrounding slopes the bright green chestnuts from the more muted oaks and, sticking out like pylons, the darker pine trees. The path crosses a rivulet, which runs through the gully and eventually goes out into the open through a grassy area with lots of broom and heather.

(11) At a junction (2hrs 20mins) where there is another post, PR20(8), turn right as indicated and descend gently to reach the village of Bréau-et-Salagosse. The view opens out and you get a beautiful view of the valley and surrounding hills.

(12) At the top of the village in the Place Prisonnière go left following yellow splashes (ignore red/yellow cross) which take you down the long quaint village street. Go right at an iron bench just before entering the Place de la Mairie, where there is a charming auberge, Les Quatres Saisons (2hrs 35mins).

(13) Go left in the Place and then right down the Ancienne Voie Romaine which turns into a narrow cobbled track with high walls each side. This is part of an ancient Roman road, which went from the town of Nîmes to Millau. It reaches the D272 after a few minutes.

(14) Walk a few metres to the left and take a path down right just before the road turns (2hrs 45mins). This is another wide, shady sunken mule track, which joins the road again.

(15) Go right and cross a bridge over a dry riverbed. Turn a corner and take the second turning to the right at a new signpost Les Vignes indicating Molieres-Cavaillac 1.3kms.

There is a warehouse left and further up a number of new houses. At the end of the houses the road becomes a jeep track. Continue up keeping to the right and where it goes into a field take a narrow rocky path right (there are yellow splashes here). Shortly after keep left (right goes up over a field to a half-finished house). The narrow balcony path is undulating along the side of a hill in and out of woodland, past a ruin to the left. You have completed a circle and the rocky Esparon hump is now straight ahead.

(16) The path goes down between high banks to a road. Go right to reach a signpost. Following yellow splash go up right on to a wide jeep track. A few minutes after, on a wide corner, go straight ahead on a narrow path and follow signs on left which take you up by a small park to the entrance of the village. Retrace your steps to the parking (3hrs 30mins).

Walk 4

PIC D'ANJEAU/ROCHERS DE LA TUDE

Difficulty:	Moderate – on the longer way there is a short scramble up a rock
Time:	Shorter walk – 2hrs 45mins round the Pic D'Anjeau
	Longer walk – 4hrs 20mins including the Rochers de la Tude
Height gain:	189m and 279m; start 617m
Maps:	Didier & Richard Top 25 2642 ET St-Guilhem-Le-Désert
Start point:	Parking on the D113 300m from the village of Montdardier
Signposting:	Good – no signs but follow yellow splashes. This is one of the cases when the markings on the IGN map are not in accord with those on the ground so follow the instructions carefully on the path down from the Rochers de la Tude.

This is a lovely walk around the rocky peaks of the Pic d'Anjeau (alt. 862m) and the Rochers de la Tude (alt. 896m) – the contrast between the northern and southern sides of the mountains is very marked. The northern side is lush and green with many species of orchid flowering in springtime, while the southern side is dryer with Mediterranean vegetation.

The rocky limestone peaks of the Pic d'Anjeau stand out as a landmark in the continuous rolling hills of the southern Cevennes. According to legend the Rochers de la Tude have always served as a weathervane for the local shepherds – if they are covered in cloud in the morning then the weather will be bad.

The picturesque but shabby village of Montdardier is situated at the foot of an ancient fortress dating from the 12th century which sits on top of a rocky crag. The château used to command the pilgrim route towards St-Jacques-de-Compostelle between Le Vigan and Lodève. Destroyed many times it was finally rebuilt at the end of the 19th century by the famous architect Viollet-Le-Duc. The château is now in private hands.

The area around Montdardier was known for its quarries of fine limestone used in the preparation of lithographs. At the turn of the century the largest of these quarries, called Pouget, employed 120 workers. It was closed in 1930. There are still one or two limestone quarries in the region. Until recently there was an important zinc, silver and lead mine at Les Malines.

How to get there (from Le Vigan)

Take the D48 from Le Vigan to the village of Montdardier (9km) on a winding road. At the entrance to the village turn left on the D113 signposted St Laurent Le Minier.

Leave your car 300m along this road on the left in a parking area for an adventure camp. There used to be a large map here showing the two walks of the Pic D'Anjeau and the Rochers de la Tude but in 2009 this had disappeared.

Directions

(1) Cross the D113 and take the obvious wide track going up on the other side bearing right. There is a sign 'DFCI. G-54' (Défense des forêts contre l'incendie) and a number of different coloured splashes. Follow the yellow ones unless instructed otherwise.

The track goes gently upwards through the Vis Forest bordered by stately pines and oak. In spring the yellow blooms of the numerous laburnum trees add a splash of colour and the banks are dotted with orchids. Keep straight and ignore three junctions back to the right. As you gain height winding round the side of the hill the jagged rocky summit of the Pic d'Anjeau comes into view above the tree-covered slopes – there are, in fact, three peaks, namely the Anjeau, the Roc Castel and the Roc Peyras.

(2) After 2km the track reaches a wide clearing at the Col de Baraquette (alt. 745m) (30mins), which divides the Pic d'Anjeau from the the Rochers de la Tude. Go forward across the stony clearing, bearing right through a green gate in a fence where there is a yellow splash (straight ahead is the path along which you will return).

Note: It is also possible to take a path that goes over the top of the peaks, but is advisable only for those who enjoy scrambling and do not suffer from vertigo (route not done by author).

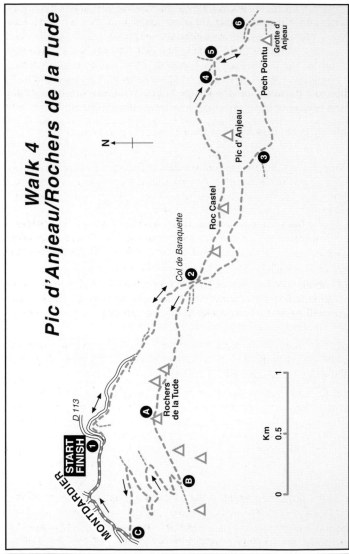

Walk 4
Pic d'Anjeau/Rochers de la Tude

The narrow path goes down round the southern flank of the Anjeau mountain. Here the vegetation is very Mediterranean, with box, juniper and the prickly kermes and holm oaks; the smell of wild thyme is overwhelming. The brilliant blue aphyllanthes and the stately white asphodel lilies flower in May. There are extensive views of rolling tree-covered hills which become blue and hazy as they merge with the horizon; the farms and the village of Caucanas, perched amongst the green, look rather forlorn and isolated, and one wonders who lives there and what they do to scratch a living! Many of the houses are probably holiday homes and shut for the best part of the year.

(3) This is a delightful path going down moderately steep to join a wider track (1hr), where you turn left and continue round the mountain. Down on the right is an interesting rocky area backed by the impressive stone rock face of the Vis river gorge. You can see your own path continuing round the mountain flank.

The track reaches a disused barrier (1hr 10mins). Just before a second rusty barrier there is a rocky path up left which can be taken to reach the summit of the Pic d'Anjeau – this way is less difficult than the path straight up from the Col de Baraquette.

(4) About 40m beyond the second barrier take careful note of yellow splashes indicating a narrow path to the left (1hr 15mins). This is where you will return to directly after you have visited an impressive prehistoric grotto.

(5) Continue straight for a few minutes until you meet a jeep track, where you turn right to the Grotte d'Anjeau. The wide track goes to the left of a tree-covered hill called the Pech Pointu.

(6) **Careful because there are no signs or splashes.** Watch for a narrow rocky path to the right going up into bushes (1hr 25mins). After 30m keep to the more defined path which branches off right (green arrow on a rock further on). A few minutes later you suddenly come to an impressive grotto at the base of a tall cliff face. The ground slopes down to the huge opening so take care if it has been raining.

There is a notice explaining that prehistoric man used the grotto as a dwelling, and ancient bones and pottery have been unearthed here. The Protestants also used the grotto as a clandestine meeting place in the 16th century when they were being persecuted (see Introduction, 'The War of the Camisards', for further information).

From the grotto retrace your steps to the path before the barrier (no. 4 on map) that will head up right on the return – there are clear yellow splashes (1hr 40mins).

This is a fairly steep walk, winding up the side of the hill to a rocky slab (1hr 50mins). From here there is an extensive view – to the left the craggy summit of the Anjeau and down in the valley ahead the quarry-like traces of the Malines mine.

The Malines mine was formerly an important site in France. For around 100 years zinc, silver and lead were extracted, and until as late as 1960 it was a source of employment for the surrounding villagers.

Following the yellow splashes on the rock go down the rocky path, which then starts to go up round the north flank of the Roc Castel – you are gaining the height you lost on the south side. Here the vegetation is greener, with deciduous trees and tall pines, and the mountain slopes down sharply. The narrow path climbs quite steeply for about 20mins with some broken terrain and concealed tree roots before levelling off with excellent views ahead of the three Anjeau peaks. You then arrive again at the Col de la Baraquette (no. 2 on map) (2hrs 25mins). There is a bench on the right under the trees where you can take a welcome rest while contemplating the valley below.

SHORTER WALK
From the col (pass) take the same wide track you came up, back to the car park (2hrs 45mins).

LONGER WALK – ROCHERS DE LA TUDE
Cross the clearing of the col, making for a small stone shelter partially hidden by undergrowth, and take a narrow path to the right of the building – white, yellow and orange splashes. This goes upwards quite steeply for 150m to the first rocky outcrop of the three Tude peaks (795m), from where you get a particularly good view of the Pic d'Anjeau and the valley below.

After a dip, the path continues upwards and the still visible clearing of the Col de la Baraquette already looks a long way below. There is a scramble up a pitted rock face, but it is not high or difficult, to the second summit (alt. 843m) (2hrs 45mins). Look back at the superb view of the Anjeau peaks. The path dips, then climbs up again through

The author on Pic d'Anjeau

attractive woodland, dotted with asphodel lilies and orchids in May, to the third rocky hump (alt. 890m) (2hrs 55mins). The panorama is breathtaking and there is a good view of the town of Le Vigan to the north.

(A) Bear left here (yellow cross on a stone ahead). The path goes gently round the back of the third hump through wood, grassy clearings and rocky places. It passes a low wall to the right and tall pine trees.

(B) Just after an uphill stretch, look carefully for a narrow path off to the right which is easy to miss. There is a yellow splash on a tree further along the path (3hrs 5mins). Follow right around a large rock and then, at a brow, go straight ahead through a clearing in the trees. Note – because of tree felling there could be diversions to the route. The path now starts to drop fairly steeply to a junction where you turn right following a yellow splash and, careful, right again after about 20 metres.

The path takes you back along the flank of the hill and goes around a sharp hairpin left, continuing steadily downwards to meet a jeep track (3hrs 25mins). Turn left and go up for about 20m, then off down right on a narrow path with yellow splashes and a PR sign. The path loses height steadily, making several traverses back and forth before joining a wide track.

Turn left, following a PR sign on a post, and continue down to a wide intersection. Just before the intersection there are good views through the trees on the right of the fairy-tale château which dominates Montdardier. Bear round hard right following yellow splashes. Continue to the next intersection, turn hard left and follow the yellow arrow downhill (3hrs 55mins).

(C) After a few minutes, ignore a track going back down right to an aerial, and when the path meets a narrow tarmac road turn down right. This soon meets a wider road, where you turn right again and pass the sign Montdardier (4hrs 5mins). Walk into the village and down the main street, which looks completely deserted as most of the houses are either shuttered or unoccupied. At the end of the village turn right on the D113 and walk 300m to the parking area (4hrs 20mins).

Château de Montardier, standing above the village of Montardier (Walk 4)

View of the Cirque de Navacelles from the Blandas Causse (Walk 5)

Planting onions at St-Martial (Walk 9)

Flock of sheep on the Draille de la Transhumance (Walk 11)

Old houses at Les Bondons, Sentier des Menhirs (Walk 18)

The church at Bédouès, near Florac (Walk 17)

Walk 5

LA CIRQUE DE NAVACELLES

Difficulty:	Moderate – some up and down to reach the bottom of the gorge; somewhat airy on the scree crossings
Time:	4hrs 15mins – leave extra time for looking into the gorge and exploring the mills
Height gain:	290m down and up
Maps:	Cartes IGN Top 25 2642 ET St-Guilhem-le-Désert 1:25,000
Start point:	The village of Blandas (17km from Le Vigan)
Signposting:	The red/white splashes of the GR7 until Navacelles. Then red/yellow and blue splashes until the Source de la Foux. Blue only on the Sentier Botanique and yellow from the lip of the gorge back to the village.

The Cirque de Navacelles is a popular tourist area, so in high season there are lots of cars and people. The walk is full of interest – a descent into the ancient oxbow lake down the steep cliffs of the gorge, a look at a quaint little village, a lovely walk along the winding river to reach some old mills by a dramatic water fall and then a climb up out of the gorge – it is worth the effort!

The Blandas limestone plateau or Causse is high (1000m in some places) and rocky the rocks being formed from ancient marine deposits. Here the Vis river has hollowed its way through the rocks creating cliffs of over 300m. In places the water has eroded the rock creating numerous underground cavities and caves.

How to get there (from Le Vigan)

Take the D48 from Le Vigan, direction Avèze, Montdardier, Cirque de Navacelles. Go through the village of Montdardier (ignore the D113A right to Navas) and then turn right on the D113, direction Blandas, Cirque de Navacelles. You are now driving through the Causse de Blandas, a plateau of pasture and rocks; look on the right as you drive

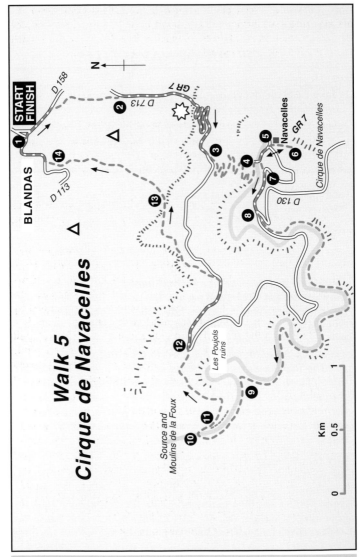

Walk 5
Cirque de Navacelles

along and you will see a curious ring of stones called a dolmen (a sort of Celtic ring – see Introduction, 'A Short History of the Cevennes', for further information). Park in the centre of Blandas, which is a small village with a wide main street.

DIRECTIONS

(1) Take the D158 out of the village, signposted Cirque de Navacelles 2km, and follow the red/white splashes of the GR7. After a few minutes turn right at a GR sign where there is a cross on a concrete plinth.

The contrast in scenery from the area around Le Vigan is striking – the ground is flat, and although there are green fields they are strewn with boulders. There are cattle and horses in some of the fenced-off pastures.

This is a grassy shortcut, which narrows to a bushy path and then has walls either side. You get your first view of the tall cliffs surrounding the gorge.

(2) When you reach the road again (15mins) turn right where there are GR markings on a telephone pole. The road passes a large parking area on the right with a café and on the left is a viewpoint (20mins) – you are looking down into a dried-up oxbow lake caused by the river Vis. It looks like a green arena surrounded by cliffs, with a hill in the centre crowned with a statue. There is a small village with the river running at the foot of it and a waterfall – the river comes from a wide gorge bordered by cliffs and winds its way back into another. You can see the road snaking below the cliffs on the other side and an aqueduct further down – it is a fascinating and unusual sight.

There is a large notice board with an explanatory map and interesting information concerning the site: '145 thousand years ago at the time of the Dinosaurs the whole of the Languedoc area was covered by sea. By the year 3000 a plain rose up (the Causse) and the river Vis forged a gorge through the hills and in its meandering created an oxbow lake. By 4000 BC the river had rejoined its original water course creating a waterfall, leaving the curious bowl-shaped imprint of its original passage for future generations to marvel at.'

Continue down the road past four hairpin bends.

(3) Just before the next corner look for a narrow track down the side of the gorge to the left by the second pine tree and a telephone pole (35mins) – there is a GR7 sign on a stone. The path is initially steep and narrow and you have to watch your feet. It soon becomes stonier and wider, descending in big zigzags. As you get nearer the bottom it becomes bushier as it widens and narrows – you get even lovelier views of the river, the village and the horseshoe area with the tall cliffs around it.

(4) The path meets a narrow tarmac track (not wide enough for cars) with some houses built into the side of the gorge (1hr 5mins). There is a low wall on the other side, with the rushing river beyond. The track traverses a delightful rustic arched bridge and then bears left through a parking area to where the river becomes a dramatic rushing waterfall flowing over large flat rocks. Go out left to a man-made lookout to fully enjoy it. Opposite is a rather charming hotel called Auberge de la Cascade (1hr 10mins).

(5) Leave the auberge on the right and turn into the lower end of Navacelles village, which consists of a huddle of beautifully restored houses – there is even a discreet souvenir shop.

(6) Bear right again by a water pump and walk to the end of the short street where there are steps upwards past a small grotto with a statue. Go up past two houses. Keep right at the next two junctions and then left as the path winds up to the tall statue of the Virgin Mary (1hr 20mins).

Take a good look at the beautiful surroundings – around the bottom of the hill is a green swathe of grass, which looks like a moat; in fact thousands of years ago it was the bed of the Vis river. Below is the village and the road curling round the tall cliffs of the gorge.

Retrace your steps through the houses to the auberge and then straight across the road and over a wide field which seems to separate the two parts of the village. From here follow red/yellow and blue splashes until you reach the mills at the Source de la Foux.

Go up the narrow road (not wide enough for cars) by a small church through this delightful huddle of houses (there is a *gîte d'étape* to the right) and under an archway to the main road at the top of the village (1hr 35mins).

Celtic ring of dolmens on Causse de Blandas

(7) Go right and walk along the road with the river hidden below in the trees until you reach a junction.

(8) Straight-ahead is signposted Blandas and up left St Maurice Navacelles. Instead take a grassy path between the two roads with red/yellow splashes and indicated Resurgence de la Vis/Moulins de la Foux.

It becomes a level balcony path high above the river along the side of the cliffs. Bushes cling to the lower gorge walls and there are innumerable rocky landslides and scree beds – high above are solid walls of rock. Go under a rock and over a dry riverbed before passing above a small dam (1hr 50mins) and then descending all the way to the river's edge in a short steep scramble – keep left and ignore a path down right.

Keep to the main path which undulates beside the river on the right, sometimes near the bank sometimes quite high above it, over patches of scree, dry stream beds and through dense bushes (if you look on the IGN map the river makes three big curves at this point).

When you are right beside the water there are some delightful grassy glades where you can have a picnic and watch the water which is flowing strongly – at times rushing over boulders, small waterfalls and rapids – it must be superb for white water rafting and canoeing.

The gorge cliffs tower higher as the path cuts across a big bend in the river and you can no longer hear the sound of rushing water.

(9) Where there is a ruin ahead (2hrs 35mins) keep to the main path bearing left (right goes past the ruin and round the grassy promontory) – there are majestic cedar trees nearby and on the other side of the river. Continue over scree and a dry riverbed before reaching yellow signposts (2hrs 45mins).

(10) Go down right towards the river signposted La Foux/Blandas. Stay on the path, which is fairly steep with a notice that you are on a dangerous site with steep cliffs, slippery rocks and landslides. Ignoring steps to the right continue to the mouth of an enormous gaping cave, which looks really sinister. When you have taken your fill of this go back and left down the steps to the Source de la Foux, an incredible sight of tons of water gushing out of the rock from an underground spring. There are two old buildings here, which used to be mills and have been partially restored. You can enter and see the big round mill-stones – it is interesting to imagine how these water mills functioned in the days before other sources of power.

Cross the river on a natural rocky bridge and climb up the other side on a steep and narrow path.

(11) A few minutes later turn up left where there is a blue splash on a tree which is difficult to see. This path is called a 'Sentier Botanique' on the IGN map but there is little sign of special vegetation except for some lovely cedar trees and tall Austrian pines.

You are now half way up the side of the gorge. Far down on the right you can see the river snaking along and there is a good view of the Poujols ruin, which must have once been an old farm, standing alone on its green peninsula of land. The path crosses patches of scree, which are rather vertiginous, and reaches the road at a hairpin bend (3hrs 20mins).

(12) Go left up the road and up left again at the next bend on a narrow steep path where there is a sign and a yellow splash (3hrs 30mins). You are now high enough to see the horseshoe cliffs of the cirque and the village although you cannot see the hill in the middle. The path traverses the side of the gorge below a dramatic vertical cliff face before reaching the top (3hrs 55mins).

(13) Here the terrain is suddenly flat which is quite a shock after all the climbing up – take your last look at the gorge before choosing between two paths, which join up later on. Further on there is a yellow splash.

The flat path goes beside a fence and through a green gate across fields. The land on either side is open and grassy, interspersed with rocks and bushes. After rising slightly you can soon see Blandas ahead. It is a curious village in that it is quite spread out rather than huddled together like other Cevennes villages – this could be because it is on a plain and not in the hills.

(14) Go right at yellow sign marked with a PR (or if you prefer continue until the road and turn right), past a round pond on the left and down a short grassy mule track to the road where there is a green signpost saying Foux/Navacelles. Turn right and walk into the village (4hrs 15mins).

Walk 6

SENTIER DE LA TRESCOULADE

Difficulty:	Moderate but long; there is quite a height gain but it is gradual
Time:	4hrs 45mins
Height gain:	750m
Maps:	Cartes IGN No. 2641 ET Top 25 Mont Aigoual/Le Vigan 1:25,000
Start point:	Main square of Arrigas village
Signposting:	Follow wooden posts until La Condamine – intermittent yellow and purple/white splashes from then on

A long walk round a semi-circle of mountains – lots of lovely extended views and interesting rocky summits. This walk is best done in springtime when the wonderful slopes of yellow broom can be fully appreciated!

The word 'Trescoulade' derives from a verb of the old Occitan language meaning 'going behind a high place, crossing a pass'.

The area around Arrigas used to be famous for its copper mines, which were closed at the turn of the century. Although there was a railway line to Arrigas a station was never built, and people had to walk to the neighbouring village of Aumessas to get on the train!

According to legend the tumbled rocks of St-Peyre are the site of an ancient Druid altar, and there are vestiges of former habitation in the form of a man-made canal and holes where there was a bridge. Now overgrown vegetation makes it impossible to reach the summit.

HOW TO GET THERE (FROM LE VIGAN)

Take the D999, direction Millau, for 14km, through the villages of Bez and Arre. After Arre look for the D929 right, signposted Arrigas, and continue for 2.2km to arrive in the village. Park in the main square by the church.

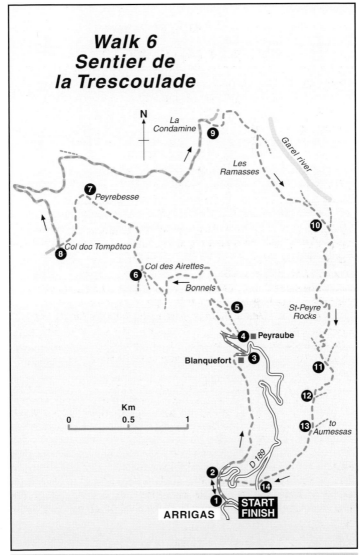

Walk 6
Sentier de
la Trescoulade

N

La Condamine

9

Garel river

Les Ramasses

7 Peyrebesse

10

8 Col des Tompôtoo

6 Col des Airettes

Bonnels

5

St-Peyre Rocks

4 ■ Peyraube

Blanquefort ■ **3**

11

12

Km

0   0.5   1

13 to Aumessas

D 189

2

1

14

START FINISH

ARRIGAS

DIRECTIONS

(1) From the main square take the D189, signposted Peyraube, where there is also a sign saying 'Sentier de la Trescoulade 5hrs'. The road goes up and underneath the old railway line. Take the second turning left where there is another sign. The path is a sunken grassy mule track with old walls each side (it is called a *calade*, which is the local word for a walled path to stop erosion). A few minutes later it reaches a paved road (5mins).

(2) Go straight up the paved road (yellow splash on a post). Note: according to the map this is a track, but it has since been paved. The road goes up medium steep and then deteriorates to a jeep track – you can see the hamlet of Blanquefort above. The track becomes a balcony path curving around to the hamlet – over on the right is a wooded gorge with a river running through it. If you look up you will see that all around is a semi-circle of tree-covered hills, many of them crowned with rocks. The wide grassy path goes over a stream and curves round the top of the gully reaching the road (D189) at Blanquefort (30mins).

(3) Go left on the road following the yellow PR sign, ignoring a bridle path going off left on a corner and continuing to a fork at the entrance to the hamlet of Peyraube.

(4) Bear up left and take the first turning left again, opposite the garage of the first house, where there is another yellow sign. This is a wide track winding round the top of the gully northwest (you can clearly see the path you took coming up over on the left). It is going gradually upwards, initially through woodland and then out into the open where you get good views of the surrounding hills.

(5) Careful – at a small crossroads turn up left where there are yellow, purple and white splashes (50mins). This is not easy to see when you are walking on the open bushy hillside. The path goes steadily upwards and is rather boggy with lush vegetation (you can see the pass you are aiming for up over to the left). It reaches a delightful stream flowing down over boulders with yellow broom bushes in clusters on the banks. Cross the stream and around the next corner you can see the isolated farm called Bonnels. The path goes round the back of the building passing a lovely arched water trough and then a ruined barn to the right (1hr). The place looks uninhabited although the roof is new – how anyone could survive up here when there appears to be no access road is a mystery!

Continue on the track, which is very overgrown with tall grass and cow parsley, past the ruins of another big building (could this have been a *mas*?) through chestnut and pine trees. It then winds up the hillside over open bushy country, and if you look back you can see the farm below at the head of a bushy valley. On the horizon is the unmistakable serrated silhouette of the Pic d'Anjeau. Below is the hamlet of Blanquefort, where there are some huge buildings of a holiday camp.

The path zigzags fairly steeply up to the Col des Airettes (alt. 970m) (1hr 25mins). This is a lovely open pass covered with broom, and from here you can see the route you will be taking round the head of another wide gully up to another pass.

(6) Turn right following wooden post and purple/white splashes. The path crosses the top of the pass, which is delightfully flat after the climb up. It continues through shady woodland, crossing a stream which flows down into a beech-covered gully to the left as it curls round west. It goes across a number of subsequent rivulets and then over another stream before going up to meet another track and a GFCI-50 sign at a place called Peyrebasse (1hr 40mins).

(7) Bear left following a yellow PR sign and walk on round the side of the hill until you come to the Col des Tempêtes 5 minutes later at a wide forest track. There is a sign here saying 'Chemin Forestière de Cazebonne'. From this col there is a superb view of the Arre valley, the Blandas Causse and on the horizon the Pic d'Anjeau.

(8) Turn right (post) on this forest track which goes through tall Austrian pines, winding up round the contours of the hill and slowly gaining height.

It circles round another wide gorge, and where the path winds up right and into the open you can see down to the Col des Airettes and the path you came up – you are now winding back but higher up! Ignore a turning to the left signposted 'Mont St-Guiral' by an attractive waterfall and continue on, crossing more streams. Keep straight at a second turning left just after a stream, where the frontiers of the Cazebonne and Barrière forests meet (2hrs 25mins).

The forest track goes by an interesting pile of rocks jutting out of the hillside right. It is worthwhile to go round it to appreciate the extended view, especially of the nearby rocks of St-Peyre and the village of Peyraube below. The track rises gently to a large sandy area called La Condamine (alt. 1240m), where there are beautiful slopes of yellow broom covering the rock-strewn hillsides – a really incredible sight when the flowers are in bloom (2hrs 50mins).

(9) Careful here: turn down to the right as indicated on the wooden post a little further on. Where the sandy track bears to the left (the way down to Arrigas by jeep track) keep straight going through a break in the fence, where there is a yellow sign and arrow to Arrigas.

   Careful: again do not go straight as indicated by the arrow – there are in fact no more yellow posts until much later in the walk; maybe they will be put up shortly. Look for an old wooden post to the left and a stone with purple/white splashes. Take this path down the hill through attractive broom bushes, and follow it carefully in an easterly direction – there are occasional yellow splashes and some cairns. To the left is the bushy gorge of the Garel river and to the right broom-covered slopes with jumbles of rocks on top (Les Ramasses on the IGN map). The path continues round the side of the hill, where there is an attractive shallow dip in the hillside right and lovely extended views.

(10) At a junction bear down right at yellow splashes (3hrs 15mins). On the left you can see a ruin and the corrugated roof of a hut in the bushy gorge. Continue south on a more sunken path with high broom bushes, bearing round a hill and into woodland. The path goes through a barrier (the edge of the Fôret Dominale de L'Aigoual) and there are lots of large rocks through the trees right. It goes along the top of an old wall out of the woodland where you can see the fascinating jumble of rocks called Rocher de St-Peyre (for more details see above) up on the right (3hrs 35mins).

   The path continues past these rocks and huge boulders and descends the side of the mountain in wide bends so that you do not feel you are descending steeply. It goes in and out of oak, and lower down chestnut wood, crossing open spaces. Much of this hillside has recently been ravaged by fire. Later on you can see the shoulder of the hill down on the right and a pass which separates the villages of Aumessas and Arrigas. Keep on the main path following the intermittent purple/white and yellow splashes.

(11) Where a path comes in from the left there is a yellow PR sign (not seen since the Condamine) which indicates to keep right along the line of the shoulder. It is an easy grassy path by crumbling ancient walls and through bushes reaching signposts at an intersection.

(12) Keep straight (right says St-Guiral and back where you have come from Col de L'Homme Mort). This is a bushy narrow path going down the hill – you can see Peyraude and Blanquefort hamlets up the valley right.

(13) A few minutes later you come to another grassy intersection. Go right following the PR sign (left goes to Aumessas). The bushy path becomes irritating, with grass hiding stones beneath, and descends down the front of the shoulder. At times you are walking along the tops of overgrown terraces with low walls, and at others through oak woods and young chestnut trees. Follow the yellow intermittent splashes carefully, as the way is not always clear. Keep to the main path right at a fork by an old wall.

(14) The path reaches the D189, where you cut across and down a rather steep shortcut. When you meet the road again turn left past a shrine and round the corner to a PR sign and a narrow path left, which is a steep shortcut down to the village – tricky at the end of a long walk! At the road turn left and walk into the main square of the village (4hrs 45mins).

Walk 7

SENTIER DES RUISSEAUX

Difficulty:	Easy walk, mainly through woods with one river crossing which could be tricky if the water level is high
Time:	2hrs 45mins
Height gain:	190m
Maps:	Cartes IGN No.2641 ET Top 25 Mont Aigoual/Le Vigan
Start point:	Parking on the side of the D231 just before the Cazebonne forest track goes up left
Signposting:	PR wooden posts – not always evident

This walk starts from a narrow wooded valley, which goes to the small isolated hamlet of Le Villaret. Although much of the walk is in woodland there are also magnificent open views. It would be a good choice for a hot day in summer as there is plenty of shade and an opportunity for a refreshing dip in the Cazebonne stream, which is also a trout reserve. All the rivulets crossed in the gullies flow into the Vis, which widens, creating a gorge, as it flows southwards.

This region has a Mediterranean climate with hot summers and rainy autumns, which is why irrigation canals were built to divert the river water to the crops. Now most of the area has turned back into forest.

HOW TO GET THERE (FROM LE VIGAN)

Take the D999, signposted Millau, to the village of Alzon (18km from Le Vigan). Go through the village and turn right on the D231, which enters a charming wooded valley. Drive on a narrow road for 3.8 km, past the Château de Mazol on the left (a hotel) and under a railway bridge. Park on the left-hand side just after the third bridge. There is a large sign 'Fôret Dominiale de L'Aigoual' and a forest track up left indicating 'Col de L'Homme Mort' and 'Chemin Forestière de Cazebonne' (marked on the IGN map as Coste Gineste, the name of a nearby house).

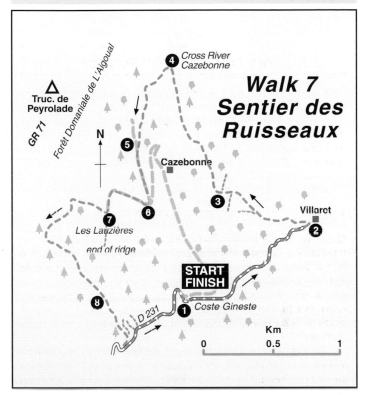

DIRECTIONS

(1) Walk up the road signposted Villaret 1.5km, where there is also a wooden post indicating Sentier des Ruisseaux (Path of the rivers) 8km, the walk you are doing. This is a delightful narrow road fringed with trees with the Vis river down on the right – after a few minutes it crosses a bridge by a little waterfall before rising gently to reach the hamlet of Villaret where the road ends (15mins).

(2) At the entrance of the village, opposite a parking area, climb up a flight of steps left (post with an arrow) through the huddle of houses, mostly unoccupied and in ruins.

Villaret consists mainly of a large muddy farm with chickens, geese and ducks scratching around; there are small cultivated fields with some grazing cows. It is a pleasure to see a working farm in such a remote area instead of silent shuttered, renovated houses. There is delicious goat's cheese for sale here.

At the top of the hamlet the path bears left by a ruin and becomes rocky as it turns round the front of the hill, climbing gently through oak trees. Soon it becomes grassy, flanked by large bracken, broom, brambles and hawthorn trees, which make a lovely splash of white colour in springtime (when the author did this walk the vegetation had been cut back to create a path and someone had obviously been the whole way round clearing the way). There are lovely views of wood-covered slopes and ridges.

(3) At a T-junction (40mins) where there are cedar and pine trees ahead turn right (north) and shortly after left into a forest by a big atlas cedar tree – this is clearly marked by posts with arrows. At a fork a few minutes later bear up right and continue upwards, meandering round the hill through deciduous and pine trees, some of which have white and red splashes – this does not mark a route but the limits of the Aigoual forest.

Continue on this track, which is poorly defined, along the side of a bushy valley and over two rivulets. You can hear the river Cazebonne as the path starts to turn round the top of the valley and into open country. It reaches some magnificent beech trees in a stony area with two cairn-like rocks (both dabbed with red) and an old wall with a sort of leafy ditch alongside – this is an ancient irrigation ditch (see above).

(4) Be careful here to follow the path left down to the river, which rushes attractively over flat boulders at a sort of ford (1hr). It is easy to cross at this point when the water level is low, but it is not obvious (some additional signposting would be appropriate!). On the other side of the river, follow the rather undefined path, which passes a tiny clearing and turns into an overgrown jeep track. There is a lovely waterfall down on the left.

Continue along the jeep track. Follow PR wooden posts and ignore any signposted paths to the left. After crossing a stream at the end of a tree-covered gully, the track starts to wend its way down the other side and there are tall Austrian pines to the left.

(5) The path arrives at a wooden barrier across the road and joins a wide forest track (1hr 20mins). Go left and continue down to a hairpin bend where there are open views. **Note –** if you continue down the track it is a shortcut back to the car.

(6) Go right, as indicated by a PR wooden post, and down a grassy path with views over another wooded gully – the path goes into the open and there are delightful views on either side before again plunging into woodland and across another rivulet. Walk up a fairly steep path out of the gully to a very attractive open ridge (1hr 40mins) where there is a ruin (Les Lauzières on the IGN map). This is an excellent place for a picnic as there is a lovely view of rolling tree-covered hills in all directions; if you look back above the ruins you can see the jumbled rocks of the St-Peyre (Walk 6).

(7) The path goes over the ridge at a crossroad and down (marked by a post) into another wooded gully, crossing a stream. **Be careful here,** as it is easy to cross before you should and lose the path – keep the stream to your left and cross where you see the wooden post. I lead up once again through an oak forest, swinging left round the side of the hill before bearing down right through chestnut trees to cross a number of rivulets in another gully – this is the fourth!

The path continues down the side of the main valley, widening into a track which becomes narrow and stony, and then grassy. At a fork go down right (indicated by a post). There is a small cairn just before the path bears to the right by a wooden PR post. The path becomes stony again as it descends through oak wood – here you are walking along a wooded shoulder and you can see both sides.

(8) At a grassy fork turn left (post) and walk down the front of the hill – you can hear the stream again. At a T-junction (post) bear right, and shortly afterwards you reach the road (2hrs 30mins).

(9) Turn left along the road crossing two bridges to reach the parking area (2hrs 45mins).

Walk 8

CIRCUIT DES CAMISARDS

Difficulty:	Strenuous – though not technically difficult; there are two ascents and descents, the second one being the steeper. Do not attempt this walk in wet weather and take plenty of water.
Time:	5hrs 45mins
Height gain:	Two ascents and descents of around 300m
Maps:	Didier & Richard Top 25 2741 ET St-Hippolyte-du-Fort
Start point:	Village of Sumène
Signposting:	There are wooden posts with numbers on part of the way. Yellow splashes (also blue and red), but not always obvious.

The first part of the walk is straightforward, but the second part is challenging and should be attempted only by fit walkers when the weather is settled. The Ranc de Banes ridge dominates the town of Sumène and has a distinctive, interesting shape. Halfway up it is surrounded by a high cliff wall, which looks like a frill. The views on this walk are stunning and give the walker an idea of the vast and remote wilderness of the Cevennes countryside.

This walk is called the 'Circuit des Camisards' because the rebels used the many caves in the high cliffs of the Rieutord Gorge to store supplies of ammunition and food during the War of the Camisards (see Introduction, 'The War of the Camisards').

The village of Sumène is amazingly unspoilt, with the Rieutord river running through it and a narrow main street ending in the square. During the Camisard war the town remained Catholic, but was attacked by Roland and his troops. There are two versions of the outcome of this attack. One is that the inhabitants hid in the church and managed to repulse the invaders, even killing two of them. The other is that the villagers were disarmed and deprived of food, and the Camisards continued on their way south to the town of Ganges.

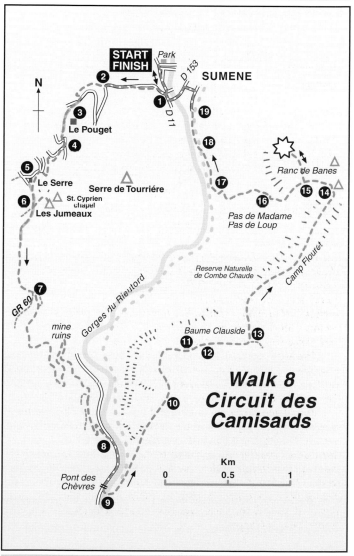

Walk 8
Circuit des
Camisards

How to get there (from Le Vigan)

Take the D999, direction Ganges/Nîmes, for 9.5km and then turn left, direction Sumène, on the D11 for 4.5km (14km from Le Vigan). At the entrance to the village ignore a sign to the left for 'Centre ville', but go straight ahead down the narrow main street and park in the car park left in the centre.

Directions

(1) Walk down the main street to the little square and go right, signed Le Pouget. Go up this narrow road past the Hôtel de Ville, rising gently out of the village with vegetable gardens down left.

(2) On a corner at a sort of bridge, bear up right on a jeep track (yellow splashes) – there is a shallow woody gorge on the right. At a fork go up left (down right leads to a large house) on a wide unmade track bordered by chestnut trees, which soon reaches the road again. Cross the road and continue up steeply until you come to the first house in Le Poujet (20mins).

(3) Turn right through the attractive hamlet, with houses on the left and their gardens on the right, past a telephone box.

(4) Where the road forks (cross down right) bear up left. Then look for a rough jeep track bearing up left where there is a post indicating PR.22.l. Keep on this track, which rises steeply and bears round to the right to meet the road at an intersection (35mins).

(5) Take the first jeep track left, following the yellow splash and signpost 'Le Serre' (greenhouse). You are now on the GR60, which winds round towards a tall dilapidated house with 'Le Serre' written on it, situated in a beautiful position overlooking the valley. Here the landscape opens out and there are rolling hills in all directions. Go straight through a sort of carport in front of the house and continue past an orchard to the right. Over to the southwest is the distinct silhouette of the Pic d'Anjeau

You are heading towards two tree-covered humps called Les Jumeaux ('The twins'). Where another path crosses keep straight on until you come to a large open clearing (45mins).

(6) At the clearing you can go straight ahead, following the yellow splashes and GR markings, if you are feeling lazy! However, to see the renovated ruins of the chapel of St Cyprien, take the first turning left

and walk up a stony jeep track until you arrive at the ruins just below a TV mast at the summit of the first hump (1hr).

There is an altar in the ruins with the following inscription on it: 'Hermitage St. Cyprien, patron de L'Affrique [a village in the region]. Built around year 1000 on the ruins of a Roman "oppidum" [fort]. Destroyed in 1558 and restored in 1989'.

From here there is also a beautiful view of Sumène in the valley below, backed by the Ranc des Banes mountain where you will be walking later. It has a curious white wall of rock going up its side. The hamlet of Le Poujet is higher up left but looks a long way down!

Retrace your steps to the clearing (no. 6 on map) and bear left (splashes on tree). You are now on a balcony path, which undulates through typical Mediterranean vegetation, namely boxwood, kermes and holm oak (1hr 10mins).

The path becomes reddish and stony. Looking back you can see the two-rounded humps of the twin hills, one of them with its TV aerial on the summit.

(7) Where the path forks by a wooden post with PR3 on it, bear down left towards the Rieutord Gorge with its dry riverbed. Here the GR60 goes off to the right. There is a sign advertising La Maison de Combe Chaude, which is an information centre and nature reserve. The path narrows after the turning, still descending. Ignore any paths to the left, crossing a mini-gorge, which is easy to miss, occasional landslides and man-made walls.

Be careful at one spot to bear to the left and not go straight on (1hr 45mins) – there is a small cross on a rock but it is not easy to see.

At the ruins of a mine, the path bears down to the right (1hr 55mins). If you want to examine the mine closer ignore the yellow cross and continue straight to see an old wall with metal hooks in it and two round towers. Return to the path and continue down in large loops – on the other side of the road below you can see an old arched viaduct clearly, which used to carry the railway line.

(8) On meeting the road (2hrs 15mins), turn right and walk for 350m until you see a bushy path left over the dry riverbed by an old grass-covered stone bridge, the Pont des Chèvres ('Goats' bridge'), which looks distinctly fragile. **Careful** – there are no yellow splashes, though there is one on the bridge.

Ranc de Banes from the village of Sumène

(9) For a few minutes the path is flat as it goes above the dry river, left, and then underneath one of the arches of the unused railway. After that it starts to climb through scattered stunted trees, bushes and long grass (direction northeast). There are welcome patches of shade as you climb steeply upwards for about 300m. You can now see clearly where you came down on the other side of the gorge.

At a rocky area (2hrs 45mins) do not go straight (yellow cross) but bear right. As you gain height there is a bit of a scramble over boulders where you may need both hands – look carefully for the infrequent yellow splashes.

(10) The path reaches a glade and later a small pass (2hrs 55mins). It then turns round the mountain, direction north, through bushes and rocks. Now you can see the village of Sumène far down in the valley on the left, the two twin hills up above and the long hill to the road in the gorge. Beyond are the high ridges of the national park, with Mont Aigoual on the skyline.

(11) The path passes a large cave in the bushes, right, and then round a corner into the large opening of the Baume Clauside (3hrs 5mins). It looks incredibly dark at first but there is a bend in the middle after which you can see the exit clearly – it is a good idea to have a torch in case you slip on the uneven rocky cave floor, but you can easily manage without one if you are careful.

Soon after the cave there is a rocky area where the yellow splashes seem to peter out, but there are cairns, so follow them carefully – you are now on the top, with Sumène (north) down left and Ganges down right (south).

This is a very rocky area of limestone lapia, covered with boulders (3hrs 15mins). There is one yellow splash on a tall boulder and then they temporarily disappear

Instead rely on the cairns and pale blue splashes which lead you down near the front of the rocky escarpment on a narrow path – eventually the yellow splashes appear sporadically.

(12) At a junction (3hrs 30mins) keep to the right (yellow cross left on rock). You are now off the tricky rocky area and the going becomes easier through stunted trees and bushes; you turn away from the edge along the wide, flat grassy top of the mountain. Over on the left there is a fenced-off area with signs later on saying it is a nature reserve.

(13) Five minutes later at a T-junction (post) turn left on what is initially a rather undefined path but later becomes clearer. The way along the top is quite flat and easy as it continues westwards through grass and bushes (if you are wearing shorts you can get quite scratched!) – you can see the rocky ridge jutting out as you approach the Ranc de Banes.

(14) At a large patch of scree go up the slope to the right (blue splash) onto a more defined path. Be careful to look for a yellow cross ahead and take a turning by a rock with splashes indicating left (4hrs).

There are sweeping views as you continue round the front of the Ranc de Banes, direction northwest, crossing several slopes of scree.

(15) The path reaches a post and red splashes going up right (4hrs 15mins). Follow the red and then green splashes upwards for a few minutes and you arrive at one of the rocky outcrops (*corniche* in French) of the Ranc de Banes. The view is magnificent in all directions – Sumène is far below in the valley in front and all the surrounding mountains rise in waves, with the higher ridges of the Cevennes National Park on the skyline. Retrace your steps to no. 15 on map (4hrs 30mins).

Continue on down over a long, rather difficult scree slope where you have to watch your feet very carefully – the red splashes outdo the yellow ones here!

After this exhausting 10 minute descent there is some relief as the path goes into stunted woodland. However, it is still rocky and difficult as it descends steeply down the front of the mountain through scattered stunted trees and bushes – care is needed all the way!

At a rocky promontory, you can look back and see how far you have come down and how far you still have to go to reach the road and river below – you are roughly half-way. From here you can appreciate this curious cliff wall that goes right up the mountain like a frill.

(16) Continue down left and ignore a narrow turning right. The path now drops down between high rocks as it negotiates the cliff wall – there is some scrambling through the Pas de Madame and the Pas de Loup (passages between rocks).

(17) At a T-junction turn right (5hrs 10mins) and continue down steeply. Soon abandoned terraces come into view on the left with a sewage plant in the valley below. Some 10 minutes later go left (cross on the right) and, as the path nears the road, there is a high wall on the right. You are now off the slope of the mountain heading along the side of the wall with the unused railway viaduct coming in on the left; you can hear the water of the river beyond.

(18) Keep to the path as it bears left underneath the viaduct where there is a final post (5hrs 30mins) – bear right and a few minutes later you arrive at a house and then a paved road – what a relief!

(19) Keep going along the slightly raised road – on the left are vegetable gardens by the side of the river. At a fork go down right (left goes to the old railway station). Continue past an abandoned factory, left, to reach the village at an avenue of sycamore trees. Turn down left and then left again at the bottom by a Casino store.

Bear right, then go over a bridge to reach the main road of the village. Turn right again and into the square with the sign to Le Poujet. Continue up the main street to the parking on the right (5hrs 45mins).

Walk 9

LE SENTIER DES ANES

Difficulty:	Moderate – one short steep slope from the Col des Bes
Time:	3hrs 30mins + time to visit the church
Height gain:	280m
Maps:	Cartes IGN 2741 ET Top 25 St-Hippolyte-du-Fort 1.25,000
Start point:	Village of St-Martial
Signposting:	Generally poor – red/yellow splashes and then nothing. Blue splashes on the way down but not at the Col de la Tribale or Col des Bes when needed!

This is a jewel of a walk with no great height gains and voted by my husband as his favourite! It goes over three passes and round unspoilt valleys. The little village of St-Martial is a huddle of houses set on a hill surrounded by bright green terraces planted with onions. It boasts a 12th-century church which has been tastefully renovated. Le Sentier des Anes means 'donkey path', which suggests that before roads were built this was a mule track and an important means of communication between the two valleys.

How to get there (from Le Vigan)

Take the D999, direction Ganges/Nîmes, for 9km and then turn off left direction Sumène on the D11 for 4km. At the entrance to Sumène turn sharp left on the D20, direction St-Martial, and continue up this road for 9km (22km from Le Vigan).

Leave your car in the parking area on the left before the village and walk into the village centre.

Directions

Follow the sign to the 12th-century Romanesque church which is worth a visit. It has been beautifully renovated inside and there is a stained-glass window above the altar dedicated to St-Martial, who is

Col de Bes

6

5

Le Bes

N

Walk 9
Le Sentier
des Anes

7

■ **La Marre**

8

D 20

La
Bastide

4 *Col de la Tribale*

D 420   *D 20*

Baldet

3

D 20

D 290

La
Coulisse

9

△   **ST-MARTIAL**

P | **START**
      | **FINISH**

1

Col du
Dévinayre

2

Km

Le
Coudonnier

0   0.5   1

not a local saint as there are hundreds of villages all over France dedicated to him! (Visit not included in the timing.)

(1) Walk back down the way you arrived on the D20 and look for a road up right signposted Le Coudonnier/Gîtes de France (5mins). There is a yellow splash higher up.

The narrow road goes underneath the high wall of the cemetery towards a statue of our Lady (you get a lovely view of the village from up here). There are a number of terraces around this village planted with *raiolettes* (a special type of onion grown in the Cevennes), potatoes, tomatoes and other vegetables. It is a refreshing change to see agricultural activity, as most of the terraces in the Cevennes are no longer in use. The wide path follows the contour of the hill, with the road below left and the valley beyond.

After 10 minutes you arrive at Le Coudonnier, which is a Gîte de France in a beautiful position, with a cherry orchard below and a vineyard. Continue gently upwards on a clear track (yellow splashes) with an old wall to the right. Soon you can see the renovated buildings of Mas Goutanière over on the right (a *mas* is a large farm) and, on the skyline south, the rocky silhouette of the Pic d'Anjeau. Cross the new tarmac road which leads to the Mas and continue straight on the path by a wall on the right. On the terrace above are vineyards by a shuttered house, and on the left olive trees. Here you see the first yellow/red splash on a telephone pole.

At a fork keep left (right goes to an onion terrace) and continue past two interesting old arched water cisterns before entering chestnut woods. There are infrequent yellow/red and blue splashes. The path climbs gently up the side of the little valley and then around a jutting-out hill through more chestnut trees. It goes in and out around the contours of the hill, where the vegetation changes to holm and kermesse oak, and juniper and broom bushes interspersed with lots of bracken. There are also masses of attractive white rock roses in springtime. You can see the impressive cliffs of the Ranc de Banes above Sumène, left, and some small villages in the valley. At a fork go up right 40m to reach a T-junction at an open bushy area with a giant chestnut tree. This is the Col de Dévinayre (50mins).

Note: Just beyond the chestnut tree is a large fallen rock with some holes in it, which is a menhir (see walk 18 for details).

(2) Turn right at the col and you will soon see a yellow splash on a tree. This is a flat, shady path through holm oak trees on the northwest side of the hill, so it is cooler in summer. Up left you can see a cluster of houses called La Coulisse in an open area. Ignore a tarmac road leading to a house down left and continue straight on a recent tarmac road, past another house left (Le Péze) and down a sunken lane to reach the D420 (1hr 15mins).

(3) Go right and continue to the crossroads at the Col de la Tribale – there are no splashes at this turn-off but a yellow splash further on. As you walk up the road there is a good view left of four little hill villages, with the village of Notre Dame de la Rouvière in the valley and the nearer farm of La Bastide.

(4) At the col (1hr 20mins) take the rather undefined eroded path ahead, half-left up the bank behind the sign to Col de Tribale and past two iron posts (no splashes here, nor is it indicated on the official map). The path soon becomes clearer, with a low wall right and a fence left. This leads to a new wooden gate and a sign 'Col de Bes'. Continue up this steep path, which turns into a built-up rocky mule track (direction east) which is also a *draille* (sheep path) going through delightfully shady holm oak forest as it undulates round the hill and through another smart wooden gate (1hr 35mins).

You are now going round the other side of the hill (north), with views through the trees, right, to a valley below – there is a clearing where someone has gone mad marking the stones and fallen logs with red splashes! Keep straight on this delightfully wooded *draille*, which rises gradually to a wide wooded ridge. It then starts to wend downwards on a narrower path to the right of the ridge (if you look closely you can see it is still a *draille*, as there is an old wall hidden by undergrowth). There are no splashes here. Up ahead you get a clear view of the Col de L'Asclier, with a solitary house on it (Walk 11), and the pylon on the Liron mountain. The woods peter out into bushes and heather as the path descends to meet the road, which you can see nearby on the right.

(5) At the road go up left for 500m to reach the Col de Bes (2hrs 20mins), with another menhir stuck on a promontory dominating two valleys. There is a magnificent view here of two valleys and the Liron ridge on the skyline.

The village of St-Martial

The valley you have been following down on the left, with the Valnierette river running through it, is fertile with a mild climate, in contrast to the valley to the east, which is wilder and less welcoming. Two different worlds separated by a pass! This is an interesting col in that the grassy surroundings are dotted with round stones containing the ashes of campfires. It looks as though some pagan ritual has taken place here, which could be associated with the nearby menhir!

(6) Careful – ignoring the jeep track (which you will cross below), walk down from the menhir to the road and turn left for a few metres. On the other side of the road (direction southeast) there is a concealed path down right just before a ring of campfire stones and a small rocky area. It is initially hidden by bracken, with a wild rose bush on the left, and is difficult to locate, as there are no splashes. However persevere and it soon becomes clearer, going steeply down, at first parallel with the road – blue splashes appear when the terrain becomes rockier.

Soon you can see a beautiful *mas* (farm called Le Bes) over on the left, which the path traverses above through scattered chestnut trees. There is a stately poplar and a large cedar tree nearby – it looks an idyllic spot! The path continues down and makes a couple of mini-zigzags (blue splashes) to reach the narrow paved road going to the farm (2hrs 40mins). There are a number of uncultivated terraces and some vineyards.

(7) Turn right and continue down into the beautiful valley, which is partially wooded with stately chestnut trees and has a little river running through (L'Elbes). On the other side is a huddle of houses called La Marre. Go by the turning left to La Marre and keep on the paved road. After passing a ruin up on the right (Les Vernedes), the road crosses a small stream and bears left.

(8) **Careful here** – after about 40m take the narrow path up right which is opposite two telegraph poles, one with a blue square on it (3hrs). There are no splashes, so it is difficult to see. This is a stony former mule track going fairly steeply upwards, with an old wall on the right and bordered by stunted holm oak. It levels out after 10 minutes, but shortly after climbs upward again. There is a lovely view of St-Martial as the path continues, passing houses to the left before reaching a T-junction and wider track.

(9) Turn left and take the zigzagging track downwards through old stone walls, with farms over on the right. When it reaches a paved road coming in from the left continue down past a small vineyard, right, to reach the outskirts of the village. At the Mairie keep left and go across the D20 road and into the main village street (3hrs 30mins).

Walk 10

TRUC DE MONTAIGU

Difficulty:	Moderate – an initial climb of 290m through chestnut forest. The path along the front of the mountain needs some care.
Time:	3hrs 30mins
Height gain:	356m
Maps:	Cartes IGN No. 2641 ET Top 25 Mont Aigoual/Le Vigan 1:25,000
Start point:	Valleraugue – parking at Place du 19 Mai
Signposting:	There is no signpost at the start of the walk or at the col – red/white GR markings to the Col de l'Elze and then yellow splashes

This walk is relatively easy except for the stiffish climb at the start and some slippery stretches on the narrow path round the front of the hill. The Col de L'Elze gives a splendid view of the surrounding mountains and particularly of the Mont Aigoual, best seen from a distance.

The attractive village of Valleraugue is situated at 350m at the foot of the Mont Aigoual in the Herault valley and was once the centre of the silk industry. As you drive up the valley you will notice the huge, tall houses or magnanerie, where the silk worms were raised on the top floors and fed on the leaves of the mulberry trees (see Introduction, 'The Silk Industry', for more information). Many of these tall buildings have fallen into disrepair since the silk industry disappeared. Now the valley is known for its apple and cherry orchards.

The well-known 'Walk of 4000 steps' to the top of the Mont Aigoual starts behind the church – it takes a full day to go to the top and back by the same route.

How to get there (from Le Vigan)

Take the D999 signposted Nîmes/Ganges. At Pont d'Herault turn up left on the D986, signposted Valleraugue, and continue up this valley until you come to the village (22km from Le Vigan). Go through

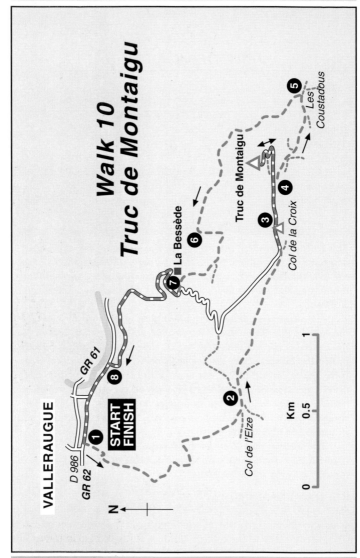

Walk 10
Truc de Montaigu

VALLERAUGUE

D 986
GR 62

GR 61

START FINISH

Col de l'Elze

Col de la Croix

Truc de Montaigu

La Bessède

Les Coustadous

N

Km

0   0.5   1

Scenery around Pont-de-Montvert, on the Mont Lozère (Walk 19)

The banks of the Tarn near La Malène (Walk 22)

One of the old streets in Ste-Enimie, Gorges du Tarn (Walk 21)

the main street to the parking in the Place du 19 Mai, just before the Information Centre – always useful!

DIRECTIONS

(1) From the parking walk up on the D986, direction l'Espérou, past the Information Centre – there is a little public park on the right with the river beyond. A few minutes later turn left by a red/white GR splash. You are on the GR62C to the col, called the Chemin de Cagnel.

This is an initially narrow, steep concrete path with a wall on the right and a stream down amid trees on the left. It passes the back of a *gîte d'étape* with a lovely view down the valley. Becoming rocky, the path winds upward through chestnut woods by the side of a small tree-covered gully, passing an old stone building. It circles round the top of the gully, crossing some rivulets, before entering denser woodland where there is a *clède* – a small stone hut where you can still see the fireplace and the racks above where they used to dry the chestnuts (see Introduction, 'The Chestnut Industry'). As the path traverses the hillside there are glimpses of the valley below before it climbs up fairly steeply over some rocky patches to reach the col. Do not turn right just before the summit but continue straight on (1hr).

This is a pleasant wide grassy pass with a *bergerie* (sheep shelter), certainly still in use as you can smell the sheep, and two fenced fields. There are several GR splashes here but no signposts – to the right goes to the Col de la Lusette on the GR62C. Further down right is the path to Valette.

From this pass you get a very good view north of the Hérault valley below. On the horizon is the ridge of Mont Aigoual, crowned with its ugly building and two satellite towers. South is the Serre de Rouas, and to the southwest is the Pic de Barette, also with its satellite tower, and the Lusette ridge. This is a delightful spot to stop for a picnic.

(2) Go left past the two sheepfolds with fenced fields beyond. Shortly after, at a fork keep right (yellow splashes), although the two paths meet up later. There is a lovely extended view northwards from this ridge, and you can see three narrow valleys going down to meet the main Herault valley. After a few minutes bushes on either side hide the view and there are tree-covered hills ahead. The path goes down gently and you can see the pylon on top of the Truc de Montaigu.

(3) It reaches the Col de la Croix at a paved road (1hr 20mins). Turn up right, and after 5 minutes pass the sign down to the right DFCI. G23, which you will take later. Continue up the road to the Truc de Montaigu (alt. 740m). As you go higher you can see another valley down on the right, with the pretty village of Taleyrac surrounded by cultivated fields. When you reach the pylon (1hr 40mins) you have a panoramic view including Valleraugue, nestling in the valley below, and La Bessede, the hamlet you go through on the way down. It is worth the effort and it is interesting to note the groups of cedar trees on the slopes – were they planted or did they grow there naturally?

(4) Retrace your steps and take the path with the yellow splashes marked DFCI.G23 (1hr 50mins). This leads down round the south flank of the hill with interesting rock plants on the stony bank to the left and a line of young larches planted on the right.

(5) Ignore the first turning back down right (no signpost). Shortly after the path reaches a crossroads at a clearing called Les Coustadous. Ignore the track going down right and continue straight for about 100m. **Careful:** look for a small signpost left indicating Valleraugue/ La Bessède which is not easy to see (right goes to Campredon (2hrs).

This narrow path is well indicated by yellow splashes but in poor condition, and you have to watch your feet as you wade through deep piles of chestnut leaves.

When the author did this walk for the first time she saw a long grass snake draped across the path. It looked bloated as though it had just eaten a good meal and was too tired to move. When prodded it slithered gracefully away!

Continue round the mountain, losing height gradually – the slope on the right, though tree covered, is quite steep. You have to watch your feet! The path crosses rivulets, and at a specific spot where it seems to curve left round a small shoulder keep an eye out for the yellow splashes, as they are not obvious on the trees.

You are now on the north flank of the hill and the terrain becomes quite mossy in places, which is a relief from the piles of leaves. There is a short open stretch where there has been a landslide. The hillside right is covered with trees but is steep in places. At one particular spot be careful, as the slope is eroded and you cannot see this because of the leaves. Watch out for rare yellow splashes and stay on the main path as it meanders right and left and is not easy to follow.

(6) Careful: where there is a low wall in front, go right and then abruptly left round the fold of the hill into a gully (2hrs 40mins). Now you can see the buildings of La Bessède in front with some neat grass-covered terraces, but although it looks near it is over the other side of the tree-covered gully. Continue down over three little streams (three small indentations) before going round the other side and coming to a rocky area. Then the terraces of the village appear and an attractive large stone water cistern rather like a pond – this is marked on the IGN map as a *source*. Down on the right is an orchard. The grassy path reaches the hamlet of La Bessède, which is a charming huddle of old houses (with one quite modern-looking) and is obviously being renovated.

(7) Go through the houses and at the end is a jeep track (3hrs) which shortly reaches a wider road. Turn down right, initially with fields either side, towards Valleraugue – there are a number of mulberry trees here which were planted to feed silk worms, silk production having been an important Cevenese industry.

The road goes round the side of another tree-covered gully, in which you can hear a stream running, with a large ruin that could have been a mill. As you turn a corner the village is spread out before you with the river running through and a weir. The road goes by a cemetery and the fire station.

(8) Turn left on the Avenue des Cevennes and walk through this attractive village until you get to the parking at the Place du 19 Mai (3hrs 30mins).

Walk 11

LA DRAILLE DE LA TRANSHUMANCE

Difficulty:	Easy ridge walk with magnificent views
Time:	3hrs 45mins
Height gain:	600m
Maps:	Cartes IGN 2741 ET Top 25 St-Hippolyte-du-Fort
Start point:	Col de L'Asclier (26km from Le Vigan)
Signposting:	Good – red/white markings of the Grande Randonnée all the way round

A really lovely ridge walk along one of the famous drailles de la transhumance (sheep trails), which is surrounded by wild uninhabited Cevennes countryside that makes you feel you are on top of the world. There are no difficult ups and downs and no worries about directions, as the path follows the Grande Randonnée all the way round. The huge old chestnut forest is fascinating and makes you wonder how the farmers scraped a living in such an environment.

How to get there (from Le Vigan)

Take the D999 (signposted Ganges/Nîmes) from Le Vigan to Pont d'Herault. After 5km turn left onto the D986, signposted 'Peyregrosse 6km'. At Peyregrosse turn up right on the D420 in the direction of Col de Tribal. This is a winding narrow road, which reaches the col at a crossroads after 8km. Go straight across (signposted 'Col de L'Asclier'), and continue twisting and turning for a further 7km until you come to the col by a house and a bridge. Go under the bridge, and just beyond is parking to the right before a sign reading 'Route Forestière du Liron (Forêt Dominale de la Vallée Borgne)'.

Directions

(1) Go back under the bridge, which is called the Pont Moutonnier, and look for a GR6/67 sign to the right indicating 'Bonperrier 1hr 45mins' (there is also a sign pointing in the other direction – GR60C Source 100m, Notre Dame de la Rouvière 2hrs). Up on the left is the

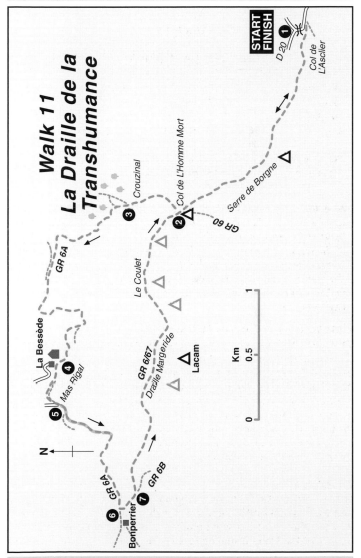

Walk 11
La Draille de la
Transhumance

START
FINISH ❶

D 20

Col de
L'Ascler

Serre de Borgne

❷ Col de L'Homme Mort

GR 60

Crouzinal

❸

GR 6A

Le Coulet

GR 6/67

Draille Margeride

Lacam

La Bessède

❹

Mas Rigal

❺

N

GR 6A

❻ Bonperrier

❼ GR 6B

Km

0   0.5   1

TV aerial on top of the Montagne de Liron, and later on you will see the path going all the way up.

Following the GR6/67 the rocky path goes up and along the ridge of the Serre de Borgne. After climbing gently for about 50m there is a magnificent view south of rolling tree-covered hills with hardly a building in sight. A little later you can see the same type of scenery northwards; wave upon wave of mountainous landscape and the only evidence of civilisation is the odd sinuous road snaking through the green ridges.

The track goes round the ridge on the right-hand side (northeast flank) on an open, undulating path down to the Col de l'Homme Mort. Over to the left is a lovely wood with majestic tall beech trees. Ignore a path to the left, which is the GR60 coming up from village of Notre Dame de la Rouvière, but continue straight until you reach the GR6A, clearly signposted 'La Bessède', going down to the right (40mins).

(2) This is a narrow path winding down fairly steeply, direction northeast, through broom and bramble bushes and a short rocky area. It reaches tall chestnut trees and a small fenced sheep enclosure before passing a ruin called Crouzinal on the IGN map. Afterwards the path enters a magnificent chestnut forest where the trees are tall and look very old.

When chestnuts were a viable crop, the peasants lived off the trees (they ate the nuts every day, fed them to their pigs and sold the wood). The trees were coppiced, which means that the main tree trunk was cut down so that the side shoots could grow up. Since the decline of the industry the trees have been neglected, and now the once small shoots, so carefully tended, have grown up into huge tree trunks (see Introduction, 'The Chestnut Industry', for futher information).

(3) Bear left at a fork, with plenty of signs in red paint to tell you so (55mins). The wide path winds through the forest and crosses two rivulets before passing by walls and some ruins. It starts to go round the hill going slightly downwards. Ignore a branch to the right with a yellow arrow and picture of a squirrel (there are also pictures of birds in other places so these must be local walks). Shortly after the trees thin out the path comes into the open.

Down on the right is a narrow road and there are some pockets of habitation – clusters of farm buildings called *mas* formerly occupied by extended families, many of them now in ruins. The road goes to the hamlet of La Bessède, which has small cultivated fields and vineyards around it.

The path turns into a rocky mule track, curling round the horseshoe-shaped hillside towards La Bessède on the other side of an attractive bracken-covered gully, crossing three streams. The hamlet is fascinating in that it is an inhabited working farm, unlike many of these remote places, and there is also a *gîte*.

(4) Walk through the village (1hr 40mins) and go up left at a sort of crossroads by a chestnut tree and a GR sign on a building – down on the right is a long, new white shed probably used to house sheep.

Ignore a branch down to the right with a red/white cross. The path goes up again towards Bonperrier bordered by a smart fence; as you climb higher you notice that much of the land is fenced off.

(5) Where the path meets a jeep track go straight on past a concrete water tank and trough, crossing the top of the small valley where a rivulet goes under the track. There is a small dwelling to the left as you climb higher. Many of the trees on the mountainside are dead, and the broom bushes are all burnt. There is a constant sound of bells from the flocks of sheep grazing on the hillsides.

(6) At the top go left at a T-junction (2hrs 15mins).

To the right are the interesting ruins of the mas Bonperrier, now marked 'Propriété Privée'. Apparently sizeable dwellings are rare on the tops of mountains, as people preferred to build in the valleys where they could belong to a community. At Bonperrier the GR6/67 joins, and to the left is the GR62. Return to the T-junction and go straight on.

You are now walking on part of the well-known Draille Margeride, which goes from the town of Lasalle to Florac. In the past thousands of sheep were driven along here in spring time on their long journey to higher pastures, accompanied by shepherds and dogs who stayed with them for the summer months and then drove them back to lower altitudes in the autumn.

(7) Continue straight on the wide track of the Draille Margeride, which is also the GR6/67 to the Col de L'Asclier. Ignore a path down to the right (the GR6B to the village of Notre Dame de la Rouvière) and continue straight on the wide track by a fence. The only vegetation is burnt broom bushes, perhaps being cleared to make fresh pasture for the sheep. The path comes to an aerial and small electricity building. Down on the left is a good view of the village of Le Bessède – so you have circled right round the flank of the mountain; you can see the path you came up clearly. There are more ruins on the slopes on the left and it looks as though there must have once been a small farming community in this region. After the aerial the path narrows and reaches the turn-off you took on the outward journey at the Col de l'Homme Mort (3hrs 5mins). From here you follow the same path (unfortunately the return path is upwards which is not so convenient at the end of the day) and then return to the Col de L'Asclier (3hrs 45mins).

Walk 12

LES CASCADES D'ORGON

Difficulty:	Moderate – there is one steep descent and two streams to scramble over if the bridges have not been repaired. It is best to avoid this walk after heavy rain.
Time:	3hrs 15mins
Height gain:	150m down to the stream and up the other side
Maps:	Cartes IGN 3641 ET Top 25 Mont Aigoual/ Le Vigan 1:25,000
Start point:	Parking at Cap de Côte on the D329 (20km north of Le Vigan)
Signposting:	Posts with yellow markers and arrows (not always pointing in your direction); red/yellow splashes for some of the way; red/white splashes of the GR60, then red splashes only

This is a walk in the national park through impressive beech woods and open areas with dramatic views – the waterfalls are worth visiting. The only difficulty is one steep descent and a river crossing made by jumping from stone to stone, which is not for everyone! It could be that the destroyed bridge a little further down will soon be repaired. In springtime this area is popular with 'canyonists'.

HOW TO GET THERE (FROM LE VIGAN)

From the centre go up beside the church to the large public park. Turn left and then up right on the D170 signposted Mandagout for 11km. Just before entering the village turn up left on the D329, signposted 'Le Souliers/Les Vieilles'. This road winds up the hillside for 9km (do not go off left on the D232 to Les Vieilles). Watch for a parking area on the left called Cap de Côte just above a *gîte*. You are now in the Cevennes National Park.

DIRECTIONS

(1) Walk down in front of the *gîte* and take the upper path to the right (not the higher one indicating WC) – you will return on the lower path, which is signposted 'Cascades d'Orgon 4km'. This open track (called Sentier de Cap de Côte on the IGN map) follows the contours of the hill and there is a magnificent view over the Cevennes countryside – rolling hills in all directions and, down in the valley, the village of Bréau-et-Salagosse. You can already hear a waterfall on one of the innumerable streams tumbling down from the wooded hillsides.

The beautiful view disappears as the path goes over two scree beds and undulates along the side of a tree-covered rocky valley through impressive beech forest. It continues through beech woods, crossing a delightful stream (20mins) and then three rivulets all close together (the stream could be dried up depending on the weather). If you look carefully you can see two waterfalls crashing down the other side of the valley. The path widens into a jeep track (40mins).

There is a delightful picnic spot down the path to the left into a glade, with a little hut and a stream burbling over rocks – nothing could be more perfect on a hot day! (5mins each way)

Stay on the jeep track for a few minutes until you come to a wide clearing with paths in all directions.

(2) Go straight across (do not follow the red splash to the left). Shortly after, at another clearing with many intersections, take the second turning left following a post with a yellow marker. You are now on a VTT track (mountain bike trail) marked with a blue triangle and two dots; according to the map this is also a *draille* (long-distance sheep track). This is the GR60, but the red/white splashes do not appear until later. The path is straight, with short grass on either side and fir plantations beyond.

Go gently down to a stream, which is easy to cross, and then slightly up again through the fir plantation, with the stream down on the right. Pass a small concrete hut which looks like a refuge before reaching a crossroads a few minutes later. Go straight across and continue to a narrow tarmac road, D329 (1hr).

(3) Go left down the road (GR cross on tree to right) and look for a track to the left just before going round a corner where there is a wooden post and a sign reading 'Chemin Forestière No.13'. This is

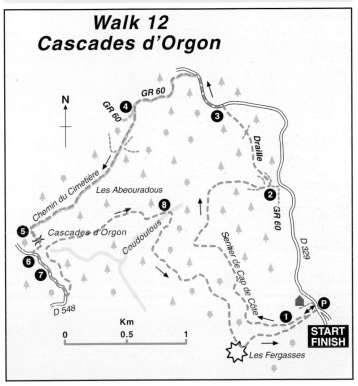

**Walk 12
Cascades d'Orgon**

still a jeep track bordered on both sides by fir and beech trees – ignore any branches off.

(4) Keep left when the VTT and GR60 path go up to the right. At a further clearing and crossroads (1hr 20mins) go straight on the 'Chemin Forestière No. 15' (on the IGN map also ominously called Chemin du Cimetière ('Cemetery road', which must have some historical meaning; there is a stone marker here). The track is heading slightly downhill – keep to the main path.

(5) A stream appears on the right-hand side (1hr 30mins). Do not go across but stay on the left-hand side through a delightful clearing and picnic area with a large beech tree in the middle. The path narrows as it continues beside the river, passing a small concrete weir to the right, through beech trees to reach a pretty little green bridge over a waterfall. There is a lovely view down the tree-covered ravine and beyond as you cross the bridge and climb up a bouldery path to the D548 (1hr 35mins).

(6) Turn down left and pass three small parking areas.

(7) Just before the fourth parking and a sign 'Parc National des Cevennes' there is a narrow turning down left, originally marked 'Sentier de Recolin' (**careful** – the sign was not there when the author did the walk for the second time so the turning was difficult to locate; it could be that this section is to be rerouted). This is a very steep narrow path down into the ravine through tall beech trees, and care should be taken as there are steep drops. Further down it becomes rocky with some scrambling. Follow the faded yellow/red splashes on the rocks. You can hear the stream running through the bottom of the ravine and, as you turn a corner, you can see the dramatic waterfall rushing down from the little bridge you walked over at the top.

After some more scrambling you reach the stream, which has to be crossed (the suspension bridge has been washed away). **Be careful** here as you jump from rock to rock, but it is actually far easier than it looks (2hrs 5mins). Look for the red/yellow splash which indicates the path the other side, not immediately evident. It climbs up quite steeply and continues through beech woods. At a T-junction keep right and continue round the ravine, crossing two rivulets – at times there are steep drops on the right.

(8) The path comes to another rushing stream, the Coudoulous (2hrs 30mins), which you traverse on helpfully placed logs. It then continues round the contour of the same hillside on which the walk started, but lower down. The vegetation has changed to a more southern aspect, with numerous gorse and broom bushes. Enter beech wood again, crossing more rivulets, before going gently upwards into open country.

The path reaches a small promontory with a low fence. A magnificent view of the southern Cevennes unfolds ahead with the unmistakable silhouette of the Pic d'Anjeau on the horizon and the rocky cliffs of the Ranc de Banes to the left. Continue on this balcony path (in front you can see the road you drove up) until you reach the Cap de Côte parking (3hrs 15mins).

Walk 13

LAC DES PISES

Difficulty:	Easy walk with no great height gain Note: this walk can be combined with Walk 14 to Mont St-Guiral, making an overall timing of about 6hrs.
Time:	3hrs 10mins including 20mins to walk round the lake
Height gain:	Some up and down – nothing significant
Maps:	Cartes IGN 2641 ET Top 25 Mont Aigoual/Le Vigan
Start point:	Col de l'Homme Mort (northwest of Le Vigan, not the same one as in Walk 11)
Signposting:	Follow the red/white splashes of the GR 66/71 which are not always obvious. There are no signs from the lake back to the parking, but the path is defined.

A delightful walk on a high plateau where there is no significant climbing to be done – you have already done that on the car journey! The track is varied as it passes through coniferous and beech woods, but it is never enclosed for too long, as there are plenty of open spaces where the views to the south are magnificent. The lac des Pises is an added bonus, and as the walk is relatively short there is plenty of time to dawdle and enjoy the landscape.

You will see signs indicating 'Partage d'eau' (watershed) at various passes on the Aigoual mountain. The waters to the north flow to the Atlantic and those south towards the Mediterranean.

How to get there (from Le Vigan)

Take the D48, direction Mont Aigoual, and go up this winding road following signs to L'Esperou/Merueis/Col de Minier until you arrive at the col (23km from Le Vigan). There is a memorial to General Huntziger (commander of the 2nd army at Sedan, who was killed in a plane accident on the Col de Minier in 1941), and also a sign indicating the *partage de l'eau* (watershed). At the col turn left on a narrow forest road called the Route Forestière de Lingus and signposted 'Col de l'Homme Mort 11km'. This is a surprisingly well-surfaced road through forest and grassland. After 5km ignore a parking and picnic area with a sign left saying Lac des Pises after a bridge, and branch left after 10km where there is a sign right to Dourbies. After 11km, park in a small area at a junction with a sign reading 'Col de L'Homme Mort'. Here the tarmac ends and there are various GR signs.

DIRECTIONS

(1) Follow the GR signpost '66/71 L'Esperou' (direction south-east) on a rough jeep track going slightly uphill through tall coniferous woods. It shortly comes out into the open and there are extended views to the right.

(2) At a fork keep right (GR splashes and wooden post) – the left fork is where you emerge on your return. This is an attractive, open sandy path through broom-covered slopes which soon change to mixed woodland going gently downwards (beech, oak and coniferous trees). The track goes over a stream and becomes concrete surfaced for a while. It again reaches open ground, where there are grassy slopes dotted with boulders and rolling hills – the interesting silhouette of the Pic d'Anjeau is on the skyline to the south, with the Pic St-Loup, near Montpellier, behind. The track enters woodland again and comes to a fork (35mins).

(3) At the fork go down right by a GR splash on a tree (ignore a wooden post indicating straight on). Go through a wooden barrier ('No entry' sign for cars) and continue down through attractive widely spaced woodland. The track bends to the right and makes a loop. Watch carefully for a rock with red/white GR and yellow splashes and go down right on a narrower path (45mins).

The path becomes poorly defined down through the woods by a stream and it is important to follow the red/white GR signs; after rainfall the water may flow directly down the trail! Finally the path becomes rockier, going through another open area before entering woodland again and rejoining the original wide track (55 mins).

(4) Cross over the wide track and take a narrow path going on down – watch for signs here.

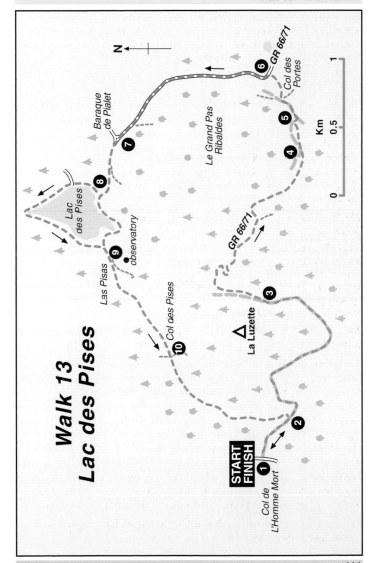

Walk 13
Lac des Pises

N

GR 66/71

Col des Portes

Baraque de Pialet

Le Grand Pas Ribaldes

GR 66/71

Lac des Pises

observatory

Las Pisas

Col aes Pises

La Luzette

START FINISH

Col de L'Homme Mort

Km
0.5
0
1

6
5
4
7
8
9
3
10
2
1

The terrain is root covered and boulder strewn, going down into pine forest again (the forest track is up on the left). Look carefully for red/white splashes on the rocks, as the path sometimes becomes difficult to follow through an old beech forest (ignore yellow splashes to right). Turn right when the path rejoins the forest track, which is now gravelly (1hr 15mins).

(5) Losing height gradually, you come to a signpost where there is another wide track coming in on the right from the village of Aumessas. Bear left, following the sign 'Lac des Pises 2km'. There are sweeping views to the south before arriving at the Col des Portes, where there is a crossroads and a rocky hillock beyond with a little house beneath it (1hr 25mins).

(6) Go straight and note that there will be no more red/white splashes or wooden posts, as the GR 66/71 goes down off to the right. This is a wide concrete track which winds north through a widely spaced fir plantation into sweeping open grassland, where it is bordered by large boulders. At a T-junction with another road, turn left towards a modern building (1hr 40mins),

(7) Turn left over a rivulet, and bear left again in front of the small building called Baraque de Pialet. Continue up an incline (there is an older building over on the right).

(8) Go right at a fork, and the path reaches the attractive Lac des Pises, surrounded mainly by grassland (1hr 55mins).

Longer route: it is possible to walk round the lake, which takes an extra 20mins. In this case turn right towards a dam and woodland. The path crosses a river behind the dam and goes through a parking area where you bear left past a yellow PR sign. Follow the obvious path round the lake, crossing boggy terrain at the end of the lake on some wooden walkways. After getting back to open grassland, fork right at a yellow PR sign, up to the observatory mentioned below (2h 20 mins).

The lake is an ideal spot for a picnic and a short siesta, but unfortunately there is a notice that swimming is forbidden – probably because of the fishing. The lake is artificial, with an area of 13 hectares and a depth of 4 metres. It was initially made in 1965 to attract tourists to the region. Since the creation of the Cevennes National Park this is also a nature reserve and sheep-grazing land.

Direct route: Turn left and walk round the southern side of the lake, crossing a stream by a clump of trees. A few minutes later the path veers left away from the water on a wide grassy path towards a house with an observatory behind – it looks like a white golf ball on top of a round building, with a retractable roof for the telescope!

This small observatory (alt. 1391m) belongs to the Astronomic Society of Montpellier and was inaugurated on 6th July 1991.

(9) After looking at the observatory go behind the neighbouring fir trees and take a narrow uphill path with a sign to the 'Col des Pises' (not easy to see). Follow this narrow path over a rivulet, through beech wood and a rocky area, and then up a grassy hill; if you look back you can get your last glimpse of the lake. The attractive path goes in and out of woodland, across an open field, through a fence and reaches a crossroads at the Col des Pises (2hrs 45mins).

(10) Go straight ahead (direction west). You are now on a wide forest track which winds round the contour of a hill with magnificent open views before re-entering woodland. Ignore two paths branching left and continue bearing right round a corner to reach the first fork on the outward journey (no. 2 on map)

Retrace your steps on the original GR path to the car park at the Col de L'Homme Mort (3hrs 10mins).

Walk 14

CIRCUIT DE MONT ST-GUIRAL

Difficulty:	Easy walk except for the climb to the top of Mont St-Guiral, which is a short but quite tricky scramble over rocks.
	Note: this walk can be combined with Walk 13 to Lac des Pises making an overall timing of about 5hrs.
Time:	2hrs 45mins
Height gain:	Negligible
Maps:	Cartes IGN 264l ET Top 25 Mont Aigoual/Le Vigan 1:25,000
Start point:	Col de L'Homme Mort (alt. 1303m)
Signposting:	Follow the red/white splashes of the GR 66/71 and wooden PR posts. Also infrquent green/white splashes.

This is an easy walk, mainly on a wide track through the forest. There are some open areas with magnificent views, even if you do not attempt the rather sporty short ascent of the Mont St-Guiral (alt. 1366m). It was on this rocky summit that one of three brothers lived the life of a hermit (see Walk 3).

How to get there (from Le Vigan)
See Walk 13, Lac des Pises.

Directions
(1) At the Col de L'Homme Mort, which is a clearing in the forest with lots of signposts, go straight for about 50m to see a map of this walk on a stone edifice (it says it takes 3hrs 30mins which is somewhat exaggerated). Go back to the clearing and take the narrow path GR 66/71, direction northwest, signposted Prunaret /Dourbies, where there are red/white, green/white and blue splashes on a rock. It goes through planted coniferous woods, though many of the trees have been chopped down, and descends gently round to the left to meet a wide forest track (5mins).

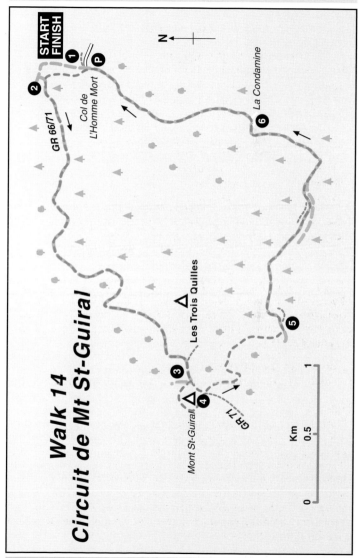

Walk 14
Circuit de Mt St-Guiral

(2) Turn left following GR signs and a PR post. This is a flat track through mixed woodland – avoid a path up left with a chain across. The track turns a corner by a stream and goes through coniferous trees along the hillside, crossing rivulets which run down under the track. There is currently logging activity in this forest, so you pass piles of logs and muddy tracks where the machines have gone in to cut the trees. The track passes a post with green/white splashes and then goes through beech forest. On a corner where there is an open patch go out to the right to admire the view of rolling hills. When you turn the corner you see a pile of rocks up to the left.

> *These are Les Trois Quilles (according to my dictionary there are two meanings for 'quilles' – one is 'skittle' or 'ninepin' and the other is 'keel of a boat'. I think the first is more appropriate.)*

There are numerous rocky boulders amongst the trees as the track continues through small open glades. Soon you can see a high rocky hill ahead, which is Mont St-Guiral.

(3) The track meets an intersection (1hr). Go straight on a narrow path round the bottom of Mont St-Guiral (GR markings) and after a few minutes take a path up to the left (splashes on rock). Climb up fairly steeply to an open grassy area with a rocky pile of boulders rearing up on the left. The GR71 continues straight ahead, but instead take the path indicating Sommet de Mont St-Guiral 5mins.

(4) Careful – this rocky path involves scrambling over boulders and is somewhat vertiginous in places, but there are lots of hand holes so it is within the capability of the average agile person.

The view from the summit is worth the effort – wave upon wave of mountains and views down into the valleys of the Arrigas and the Arre. To the south the distinctive shape of the Pic d'Anjeau sticks out, with the St Pierre peak near Montpellier on the skyline. In the foreground are the scraggy rocks of Les Trois Quilles and St-Peyre to the east (see Walk 6).

> *Enjoy the grassy glade surrounding Mont St-Guiral – it is the ideal place for a picnic.*

Retrace your steps to the intersection (no. 3 on map) and take the forest road no. 79 to the right. There is also a PR wooden post signposted Doubies (1hr 25mins). You are leaving the GR red/white splashes and from now on you follow infrequent green/white splashes. Go along this forest track (avoid a path up right), fording a rivulet and passing numerous boulders amongst the trees. Continue round a hairpin bend and shortly after there is a small stream running along on the left, eventually going under the track and down the hillside right. The track continues down through beech forest and through an open broom-covered area with lovely views. If you look back there is a good view of Mont St-Guiral.

(5) At an intersection (1hr 50mins) the track joins a bridle path (post with a horseshoe on it). Go left (leaving the forest road 79 on the right) along a fairly flat jeep track round the southern side of the hill. The woods are less dense and there are lovely open views to the right as you pass little waterfalls and rivulets, which are attractive after heavy rain. Later a wide track joins from the right at a sign 'Chemin Forestière de Cazebonne', the same path as followed in Walk 6 for a short while. The track you are on is called the Chemin Forestière de la Barrière.

Continue straight, and at a corner with an attractive pile of rocks on a promontory go right and enjoy the extended view, especially of the nearby rocks of St-Peyre and the village of Peyraube below. The track rises gently to another large open sandy area called La Condamine (alt. 1240m), where there are slopes of broom bushes, especially striking when they are in bloom in early June.

(6) Go on straight, direction north (Walk 6 turns right here). The track now enters beech forest, rising steadily as it meanders round the hillside. Go past the stone edifice with the map of the walk to reach the Col de l'Homme Mort (2hrs 45mins).

Walk 15

L'ABIME DE BRAMABIAU

Difficulty:	Moderate – a short scramble over rocks if you choose to look at the Perte de Bonheur
Time:	4hrs (add 1hr for the visit to the Abîme + 45mins for the Arboretum)
Height gain:	420m
Maps:	Cartes IGN 2641 Top 25 Mont Aigoual/ Le Vigan 1:25,000
Start point:	Opposite the Mairie in the village of Camprieu (alt. 1099m), where there are Grande Randonnée signs
Signposting:	The red/white splashes of the GR are sometimes rather difficult to see and are only applicable for part of the walk. Also wooden posts and yellow splashes. Note: A bevy of wooden posts has been put up all round this area, but do not always refer to the walk you are on!

This is an unusual region – after winding up the mountainside from Le Vigan the grassy plateau around the scattered village of Camprieu looks deserted, but is a cross-country ski area in winter. There are three interesting sites on the walk – first, the Perte du Bonheur (where the river disappears into the ground); second, the impressive Abîme de Bramabiau where the river emerges again ('abîme' meaning 'gorge' or 'abyss'); third the well-known arboretum half-way round. If you want to visit all three in one day it will take around 6 hours, so start early!

This walk is best done out of season as the Perte de Bonheur and L'Abîme de Bramabiau attract plenty of tourists.

How to get there (from Le Vigan)

Take the D48, direction Mont Aiguoul, and go up this winding road following signs to L'Abîme de Bramabiau. In the village of L'Esperou, take the D986 (signposted Mont Aigoual/Camprieu), which goes

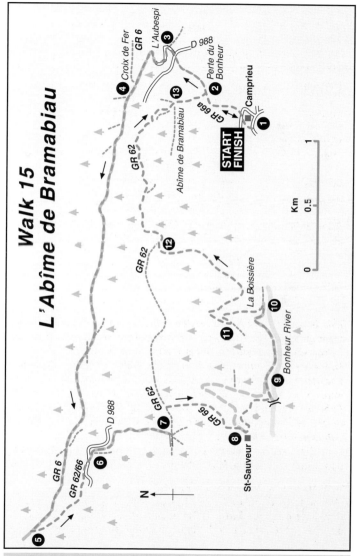

Walk 15
L'Abîme de Bramabiau

over the Col de Serreyrède. Continue left and after a few kilometres turn left again on the D157 into Camprieu (the D986 continues to Florac). Drive through the hamlet and park either near the church or further on near the Mairie where there are GR signposts (37km from Le Vigan).

DIRECTIONS

(1) Take the path up to the right beside the Mairie, signposted GR66A, round the back of houses and the church to meet a road a few minutes later. Cross the road (red/white GR splash and post) and continue down a wide path over flat rocks – you are on an open grassy plateau, which goes down gently to a shallow valley with low rolling hills all round (10mins).

(2) Careful, there is no sign here – at the bottom turn down to the right on a narrow bushy path to see the Perte du Bonheur, where a river disappears into the ground to resurface in the Abîme de Bramabiau gorge (see below for details). You arrive at an attractive grassy area on edge of the river. Follow the path over the rocks by the rushing stream – there is some clambering around here, jumping from rock to rock. Be careful through a wide tunnel, as the rocks are slippery. There are more rocky boulders at the end of the tunnel where the turbulent water disappears into the earth under a huge overhang – an impressive sight.

Make your way back to where you turned off (no. 2 on the sketch map) and turn right (30mins). A few metres along, the GR62 turns to the left – this is where you will return from the walk.

Note: if you want to visit the Abîme de Bramabiau only this is the quickest direction to take.

Otherwise continue on the GR66A through open fields – up left is an information centre and café with a parking area for the Abîme de Bramabiau. The path crosses the road (35mins).

(3) Go up a narrow paved road through L'Aubespi, consisting of one large house. Ignore a track to the right on a corner (this is the shortcut for Walk 16) and continue on with a fir plantation on the left until the paved road degenerates into a jeep track by a new house. The track bears right (northwest) climbing gently to a low pass called the Croix de Fer (alt. 1178m) (45mins).

There is a small TV antenna here and some interesting arched ruins. If you go over to an iron cross you get a lovely view over the rolling green plateau and the rocks where the river disappears.

(4) Go left by a wooden post onto the GR6 which has come in from the right – do not take another path down right (red/white cross on a gate). The wide GR track slowly gains height as it heads west into tall sombre pines (ignore a path to the right). Look back here for a good view of the rather spread-out village of Camprieu. The track is flat along a sort of balcony, with the valley through the trees on the left; it passes a new concrete water tank. Ignore the first turning to the left (1hr 15mins) and almost immediately another merging from the right in a clearing. The track starts going slightly down around the other side of the hill through beech forest, where the slope is more pronounced. It gains the ridge again, where there are views to the left of rolling wood-covered hills. Continue on the main track, ignoring a further smaller path to the left and a new logging track to the right.

(5) Watch for a sharp turn left marked 'GR62/GR66 Camprieu 7km/ Doubie 10km' (1hr 40mins). Go down through woodland to meet the D986 road 10 minutes later.

(6) Cross the road and bear down right on a wide jeep track – there is a sign 'Aboratum de St-Sauveur et sentier des arbres 3km'. Go past another water tank to a junction (2hrs).

(7) Take the left fork where there is a red/white GR splash (not the wooden post to the right) and descend gently until you meet a cross-roads 5 minutes later. **Note –** you can continue on the GR62 here, which reaches the Abîme de Bramabiau by the direct route cutting out St-Sauveur and the arboretum.

Go down to the right on Chemin 124/GR66 (wooden post) through pine forest to the buildings of St-Saveur. Turn right above the church and descend towards the château. This is an interesting cluster of buildings consisting of a church with a churchyard beside a small feudal castle (2hrs 15mins).

There is information here concerning the Cevennes National Park and also a board explaining that St-Saveur is the start of a fascinating arboretum of 2.5km. It contains blue cedars, Douglas firs, giant cypress and other exotic trees, the more magnificent specimens planted between 1886 and 1910, making it one of the oldest of its kind in Europe. The whole area is now under the auspices of the national park authorities.

St-Saveur originally belonged to a nobleman who commanded a royal regiment during the French Revolution, but managed to escape the terror by emigrating. His domain was sold to a Jean Bourzet de LaBoue and inherited by his son, who in turn left it to his two children. Because the children contested the ownership of the property it was sold in 1880 to the Forestry Commission who subsequently created the arboretum.

(8) Go past the church and down right at a fork following the red/white splashes of the GR66. This is a narrow sunken path by the side of a dank gully with a stream to the right. It is part of the arboretum and there are names on some of the trees – a Cyprus, huge Atlas cedar and a Douglas fir further down. The path crosses a rivulet flowing into the main stream and arrives at a clearing by an old bridge and waterfall.

(9) Careful – do not cross the bridge but continue straight on the jeep track indicating 'Parc auto – Sentier des arbres et arbustes', with the river on the right. **Note:** here you leave the red/white splashes of the GR, which go across the bridge. At a corner keep straight and on the jeep track, and do not follow the wooden sign up left.

This sign leads round the arboretum, which takes about 45 minutes (route not done by author).

A few minutes later there is a small dam over on the right and then a series of waterfalls and rapids. The track bears right over a small bridge at a stream (ignore the path up left).

(10) Turn up sharply left at a forest sign no. 127 and a wooden post (2hrs 35mins) through tall pines, re-crossing the stream at a higher level. There is an old building on the left called La Boissière and then a further ruin (ignore all posts to the left).

(11) At the ruin take a grassy path up right indicated by a post just beyond – there are also yellow splashes (2hrs 50mins). Turn down right where there is a post and green spot (ignore path straight on), crossing the stream for the third time. This delightful path leads up and around a rocky wooded shoulder – you can hear the noise of the Bonheur river down in the gully on the right.

There is a board indicating that this area is part of the original Fôret Dominiale de L'Aigoual – in 1989 the old pines were cut down and in 1991 new trees were planted such as the Austrian pine and Atlas cedar.

The path continues through ancient beech forest, passing an old beech tree with an enormous gnarled trunk before reaching the GR62 (3hrs 15mins).

(12) Turn right (GR splashes) and then cross several rivulets. Ignore a path down to the right (post here), which looks as if it is a shortcut to the Abîme (in fact it peters off into nothing). At a break in the trees there is a notice board and a view down right into the crevasse-like opening of the Bramabiau. You can see the lights inside to guide the people through the cave.

In 1888 Edward Martel first explored the vast underground cave between the Bonheur river and the impressive waterfall where the river emerges through a jagged opening in the hillside. He was the forerunner of the now popular sport of speleology, discovering many other underground caves in the area. It was Martel who first descended into the famous Gorges de Verdon in northern Provence.

The word 'Bramabiau' originates from 'brame du boeuf' (wailing or howling of oxen) and is apply named after the deafening noise of the water as it gushes from the tall, narrow opening in the rocky limestone cliff, which is over 100m high. The turbulent waters of the underground river have hollowed out a fascinating labyrinth of around 11km of twisting underground cavities, some of them of immense width and height. Constant erosion has created impressive stalagmites and stalactites that are now attractively lit, enabling the tourist to appreciate the beauty and complexity of their convoluted shapes. Opening hours: 9.00–19.00 Easter to mid-November. Entrance fee charged.

The track continues over more streams to a crossroads (3hrs 40mins). If you wish turn down right to visit the Abîme, there is a notice directing you to first go up left 100m to the Maison des Guides to buy your ticket. The tour through the cave takes 45 minutes – it is a guided walk of 1km above the river, very dramatic and worthwhile.

The track down to the Abîme is fairly steep (with convenient benches for visitors who have parked their cars at the top and are not used to walking).

It takes 20 minutes up and down, crossing a bridge over the stream at the bottom. You have to wait outside the entrance for a guided tour, and in the summer there could be a queue as this is a popular tourist attraction.

Add around 1hr for the walk down and up plus the tour through the cave.

(13) If you have visited the Abîme go back to the crossroads and turn down right.

Otherwise continue straight at the crossroads where there are no red/white splashes but wooden indication posts. The track comes out onto the grassy open area of the Bonheur valley and rejoins the junction (post here) to the Perte du Bonheur (no. 2 on the sketch map). Turn up right and retrace your steps to the car (4hrs).

Walk 16

VALLEE DU BONHEUR

Difficulty:	Moderate – only because of its length; there is no great height gain
Time:	5hrs (4hrs 15mins if you take the shortcut at no. 6)
Height gain:	350m
Maps:	Cartes IGN 2641 ET Top 25 Mont Aigoual/Le Vigan
Start point:	Col de Serreyrède (alt. 1300m)
Signposting:	Follow the wooden PR posts and the red/white splashes of the GR – not always obvious

The Vallée du Bonheur, meaning 'Happy Valley', is a good choice if you enjoy a long walk without any great height gain. The forest track through the beech wood can be somewhat monotonous, but the open valley is enchanting, and the disappearing river, La Perte de Bonheur, an added interest.

The Serreyrède pass is a watershed where the waters coming down from Mont Aigoual divide into those going southwards to join the Rhône and the Mediterranean and those going westwards to join the Atlantic.

Camprieu used to be a tiny hamlet, but has now been transformed into a tourist centre. There is a large sports complex and a holiday centre consisting of small wooden holiday houses, a lake with beach and restaurant. This is also a cross-country ski area in winter.

Note – if you have the time after the walk, drive to the Abîme de Bramabiau, where the Bonheur river emerges in an impressive cave (see Walk 15 for further information).

How to get there (from Le Vigan)

Take the D48, direction Mont Aigoual, go up this winding road until the village of l'Esperou and then turn left on the D986 (signposted Mont Aigoual/Camprieu) to the Col de Serreyrède (32km from Le Vigan). Park beside a building called the Maison de L'Aigoual, which

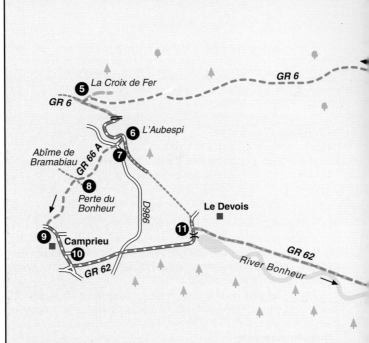

**Walk 16
Vallée du Bonheur**

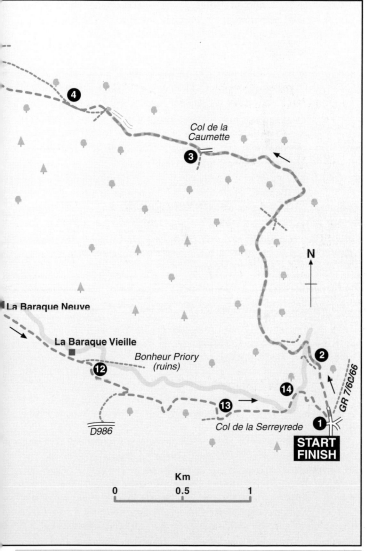

La Baraque Neuve

La Baraque Vieille

Bonheur Priory
(ruins)

Col de la
Caumette

N

D986

Col de la Serreyrede

START
FINISH

GR 7/6C/66

Km

0   0.5   1

is an information centre and shop selling local produce. There is also a notice at this pass indicating 'Partage des eaux' (watershed – see above) and a memorial cross to prisoners and workers.

DIRECTIONS

(1) Take a path on the other side of the building from the parking. After a few metres it splits into three – left is the GR62 where you will return, the middle is a wide forest track with a wooden PR post, and up to the right is marked GR7/60/66. Take the middle track, which is initially flat, and fork right after a few minutes up through beech forest. Go round a bend to the left (you can see the other path below) and then round a gully where there is a stream.

(2) At an intersection continue straight on the Chemin Forestière 71 by a PR post (15mins). The track skirts the top of another gully and continues gently upwards round the hillside.

(3) The path reaches a crossroads where there is a small round stone building like a sentry box and a sign 'Fôret Dominale de Bethuzon/ Col de Caumette Alt. 1455' (1hr). In early spring you will see carpets of small yellow daffodils at this spot.

Go straight as indicated by a PR post (you are joining the GR6) and continue downwards through fir and beech wood round the north side of the hill. Keep straight again at a further crossroads in a large clearing.

(4) Careful – after about 10 minutes take a narrow path up to the left where there is a post and a small cross on the main track – this is very easy to miss. It is an attractive sandy path criss-crossed with tree roots going down through mixed woodland and wild raspberry bushes. The red/white GR signs are infrequent and indistinct.

Note: If you miss the narrow path you arrive at a hairpin bend on the forest track. Go left by a cairn and then down to the right after a few metres.

After 10 minutes the path becomes a dry streambed as it gets steeper. It becomes less woody as it goes through a glade and then up into the open, where there are lovely views of the valley below and tree-covered rolling hills beyond. There is now a fence to the right as the path meanders round the broom-covered hill, crossing a patch of marshy land. The scattered ski village of Camprieu and a small lake come into view in the valley down on the left (1hr 30mins). Carpets of purple anemones, tiny multi-coloured violets and blue and yellow orchids can be admired here in springtime.

There are views to the north and south as the path goes gently down the grass-covered ridge, and ahead is a tree-covered hill, La Fageole (see Walk 15). There is a wooden barrier over the path, with a short diversion to the left to avoid a stretch which is clearly eroded. Another path merges from the right and the track is now wider and flat, passing a small house on the left.

(5) The path reaches La Croix de Fer (alt. 1178m), where there are some interesting arched ruins, a small TV antenna and an iron cross (2hrs 5mins).

Bear left on a jeep track following the GR62/66A and the PR post (the GR6 continues straight). Continue down, bearing left again by a new house where the track becomes paved (small fir forest right). It winds down to the hamlet of L'Aubespi, which consists of one large house!

(6) Shortcut

Note: As you go round the corner by this house, you may go straight on. This is a shortcut to the little lake, which takes only 15 minutes. At first it is a paved road, which deteriorates into a sandy jeep track; it passes through attractive grassy fields and is bordered by shrubs and broom bushes. When you reach a T-junction turn right and then left just before the bridge following the PR posts **(see no. 11 below)**. **Longer way via Perte du Bonheur:** if you wish to see the Perte du Bonheur (the river disappearing into the ground) continue round the corner.

(7) The road meets the D986, which you traverse right to a post and a track between grassy meadows covered in wild flowers. Ignore a path joining from the right, which is the GR62 (the return on Walk 15). A few metres further on take a path down to the left (curiously, there are no markings here) to meet the Bonheur river at an ideal picnic area.

Follow the path right round the rocks of this rushing stream. There is some clambering over rocks through a short, wide tunnel (care should be taken as the rocks are slippery) to reach more rocky boulders where the turbulent waters disappear into the ground under a huge overhang – an impressive sight. Retrace your steps to the original path (about 20mins there and back).

(8) Turn up left (GR markings) over flat limestone rocks which meet the main path into the old part of Camprieu and a narrow paved road. Traverse it across, right, Rue de la Cledette (PR post) and go down to the main street of the scattered hamlet and a number of GR signs by a small parking area (parking for Walk 15) opposite the Mairie (2hrs 45mins).

(9) Turn left in front of the church – there is a GR sign on a concrete tower opposite, which also happens to be the public toilets! Pass a statue of the Virgin Mary on top of a fountain and then a cross. On the meadow right is a huge, ugly building, which looks like a sports centre.

(10) When the road meets a newly built crossroads turn left (PR post). At a further crossroads go straight (signposted 'Devois', which is a holiday centre). You are walking along the bottom of the valley, where there are scattered holiday houses backed by the delightful grassy ridge of the Bonheur. The road passes a children's adventure playground and mini-golf before reaching the small lake, which is obviously part of the holiday centre (3hrs 10mins).

(11) Turn left over a small bridge, where there is a weir, and go right following a PR post **(shortcut joins here)** along the side of the lake, which is quite attractive with a small beach, a restaurant with bright umbrellas, and wooden holiday houses. The road peters out into a jeep track though the bottom of the valley, with attractive alpine meadows each side and the Bonheur river meandering on the right – beyond are sweeping grass-covered hills topped with forest. You can see the path going along the hill on the left to La Croix de Fer.

Go by the buildings of La Baraque Neuve before crossing the stream, which is then on the left. The valley becomes narrower and more attractive as it goes further away from the holiday centre (a telephone line through the middle does spoil it somewhat). The track passes the buildings of La Baraque Vieille (alt. 1146), an old farmhouse and ruins (3hrs 50mins). Cross a tiny rivulet going down to the river and continue towards the tree-covered end of the valley.

(12) A few minutes later go straight on at a fork (post). **Note:** The path left, cut off by barbed wire and a padlocked gate (although it lacks a 'No entry' sign), continues along the bottom of the valley to the ruins of a 12th-century priory before going up to rejoin the main GR track. It

WALK 16 – VALLÉE DU BONHEUR

is in principle a more attractive way, avoiding the woods, but appears to be firmly out of bounds!

Your path takes you up into the woods at the end of the valley – you can still see down into the valley, left, and later on the ruins and a house.

> *The priory of the Bonheur valley used to be a landmark and a refuge in this desolate region. When the weather was particularly bad, as it often is during the winter, the monks used to ring a bell to guide lost travellers to food and shelter.*

Continue up the side of the valley ignoring another track down left (GR cross). The track climbs slowly through woods. Be careful to take a left hairpin bend marked by a PR post and GR62 signs – the main track straight (also with a PR post) goes up to meet the road. Go through dense young mixed woods and then into beech forest again, crossing a rivulet going down into a gully left. Since you have done a U-turn you can see the priory again in the valley through the trees.

(13) Watch for a narrow rocky path up to the right (4hrs 20mins) with GR markings and a PR post. It goes up steeply through beech forest and there is an ancient man-made wall ahead with a door in it – this is probably the remains of the 'mines de plomb' (lead mine) mentioned on the IGN map.

The path meets a wide forest track, where you turn left round the top of the valley. There is a strange flattened area on the left (the remains of mining or a clearing destined to be a car park?).

(14) Soon the path narrows, with a river down on the left and an ancient archway standing alone. This is where the path from the priory should come in, but the archway is surrounded by barbed wire. It could be that the area has been fenced off because the ruins are dangerous and/or renovations are foreseen. The archway could undoubtedly be part of the priory, most likely a shrine as the rivulet runs by it.

Cross the rivulet and go up wooden steps to meet the forest track again, where you go right. There is a steep climb with possible short-cuts back to the col and the original path behind the information centre at the Col de Serreyrède (5hrs).

Walk 17

ROUND MONT PUECHERAL

Difficulty:	Shorter walk: moderate – there is a steady climb up and down
	Longer walk: moderate/strenuous – the second climb up and down is more tiring
Time:	3hrs 15mins or 4hrs 40mins
Height gain:	305m or 335m (involving a second 250m climb)
Maps:	Cartes IGN 2739 OT Top 25 Mont Lozère 1:25,000
Start point:	Above the Village de Vacances, 2km from Florac on N106
Signposting:	Excellent – follow the red/white splashes of the GR43/68 and yellow splashes – then the yellow splashes only to Bedouès. From then on follow the red/white splashes again of the GR70 and (longer walk only) the GR68. On the longer way round the splashes become patchy.

This is a walk through varied vegetation and countryside – a combination of chestnut woods, bare upland hillside with stunted bushes, magnificent sweeping views and, as a finale, a really attractive path beside the Tarn river (shorter walk).

The longer walk involves another climb of 250m – the way down into the valley is reasonably steep but the views are impressive.

HOW TO GET THERE (FROM FLORAC)

Go out of the village northwards and over Le Pont de la Bessède, which joins the N106. Turn left and then shortly after right on the D998, signposted Bédouès. Almost immediately turn left over a small bridge (Le Pont du Tarn) just before the Tarn joins the Tarnon river. Take the second turning right on a road called Chemin d'Issenges (tennis courts here) where there are red/white GR splashes on a wall. Drive up this road past the entrance to a Village de Vacances and park at the top on the right.

Directions

(1) Walk to the top of the road and turn left where there are clear red/ white GR and yellow splashes, and signs indicating 'Tour de Mont Lozère' and 'Sentier de Puecheral 11km'. **(Straight on is where you come out at the end of the shorter walk.)**

Continue along this narrow paved road going steadily upwards. At first there are houses on the left. There is lovely view into the valley, left, with the Tarn river snaking below the long high ridge of the Causse Méjean, which ends in the dramatic rocky chimney of the Rocher de Rochefort above the town of Florac.

The paved road changes to a wide jeep track (10mins) and continues upwards. Ignore any turnings off, but higher up on a right-hand bend continue straight up on a narrow path where there is a GR red/ white splash – this is a shortcut across a bend (30mins). When you reach the road again turn up left.

You are walking along an ancient *draille* (pathway) taken by the flocks of sheep seeking the higher pastures of the Mont Lozère. As you get higher the vegetation changes from pines and chestnut trees on granite soil to the sparse bush land of limestone.

The track bears left round the side of a subsidiary valley and, as you come out of the woodland, you can see up left the ruin of a large house. When you reach it you notice that it is built into the hillside, facing south with a view right down the Tarn valley and hills in all directions – the builder chose his site carefully (40mins).

(2) At a crossroads, take the first right, following the smart signpost and yellow splashes. Left goes only to an unsightly rubbish dump, which is shocking to find in such a beautiful environment, and the track ahead goes to the farm at Issenges.

Continue upwards along the open hillside. Further on there are fences either side. The vegetation now consists of juniper bushes, boxwood and stunted fir trees.

Soon you see the Issenges farm down on the left nestling in the hillside in the side of a small valley with fields around. Ignore a track coming in from the right and continue until the view opens up ahead at a small cairn. In front are the rolling hills of the northern Cevennes, stretching to infinity, with the higher slopes of Mont Lozère up left – the feeling of space and isolation is breathtaking.

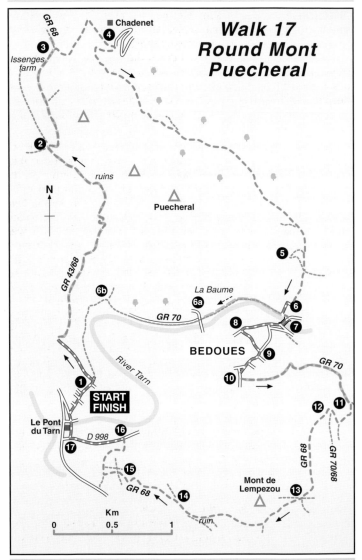

Walk 17
Round Mont
Puecheral

Chadenet ④

GR 68 ③

Issenges farm

②

ruins

N

GR 43/68

Puecheral

⑤

⑥b

La Baume

⑥a

GR 70

⑥

⑧

⑦

BEDOUES

⑨

⑩

GR 70

⑫ ⑪

River Tarn

①

START FINISH

GR 68

GR 70/68

Le Pont du Tarn

⑯

⑰

D 998

⑮

GR 68

⑭

Mont de Lempezou

⑬

ruin

Km

0   0.5   1

(**3**) Continue straight for 50m and then follow a sign and a yellow splash to the right (1hr 5mins). You are now leaving the red/white splashes of the GR68, which continue straight.

The path makes a wide bend down the bare hillside (there is a shortcut left if you wish to take it) and then flattens out alongside a bushier valley consisting of poplar, oak, ash and wild rose bushes. Keep on the main track, which crosses a barrier. It reaches the hamlet of Chadenet at a T-junction at the end of a narrow paved road (1hr 30mins).

(**4**) Turn right – **careful here,** as there are yellow arrows in both directions. If you go left you reach the larger hamlet of Malbosc. Right takes you past a tastefully renovated house (dogs barking a warning) with a beautiful vegetable garden on the slope below. Continue down by a yellow splash (do not take the path left in front of the house). This is a raised stony mule track, which descends into a wooded valley consisting mainly of chestnut trees. It crosses the top of the valley over some streambeds, and then continues down the side for what seems a long time, the trees getting larger on the lower slopes. When the path comes out of the woods you can see the village of Malbosch on the other side of the valley, left, with the road going up to it. Lower down keep to the main track and ignore any branches up to the right.

(**5**) At a T-junction turn left – there is a yellow cross to the right (2hrs 15mins). On a hillside to the right there is an attractive swathe of dark fir trees, obviously planted. The village of Bédouès appears below, dominated by an impressive church with a house attached (on visiting the site one is disappointed to find that it is 19th century, and looks more attractive from afar than at close quarters). You realise you have turned a circle when you see the original long, high ridge on the far side of the Tarn valley.

The track widens and descends, passing small stone ruins from time to time, apparently shelters of some kind. The village gets nearer down on right and the jeep track becomes paved, passing the odd house and a camping site (2hrs 25mins).

SHORTER WALK

(**6**) Before the road crosses the river look for a narrow tarmac track to the right with a 'No entry' sign, just after a sign for 'La Gardette' (2hrs 25mins). Note – there is no official walk signpost here, though there is a yellow splash further on. This wide track soon becomes grassy and is bordered by fences through the camping site called Chantemerle. After the camping it becomes an attractive raised path above the Tarn river on the left with Bédouès on the other side.

(6a) When it reaches a tarmac road (an area called La Baume on the IGN map) and a bridge across the river, left, continue straight.

The road bears away from the river, which is still on the left, along a wide, shallow valley with some large, recently constructed houses.

After the houses, the road is no longer tarmac, as it enters chestnut forest again. Follow the main track bearing left (ignore house to right with 'Propriété privé' sign). Through the trees you can still see the river, with an attractive old manor house on the further bank.

(6b) Bear left at a tarmac T-junction back to the starting point. Walk to the car park (3hrs 15mins).

Longer walk

(7) Continue down the road past the camping site of Chantemerle and turn right across the little bridge over the Tarn ignoring a track up to the left. This leads into the hamlet of La Pontèse, which is really a part of Bédouès.

(8) Just opposite the entrance to another camping site turn up left on a narrow road beside the impressive church and keep going through the little village to a T-junction (2hrs 35mins).

(9) Turn right at a corner, making for a church steeple in a further huddle of houses. At the next corner, instead of continuing round, go straight on between old houses on a narrow road until you see the red/white splashes of the GR70.

(10) Bear up left following the splashes. The track goes up the side of a hill (2hrs 45mins), past a solitary house on the left, and enters shady woodland, getting steeper as you go higher; just as you think you may not be on the right track, you see a red/white GR splash again! Down on the left is a good view of Bédouès.

The track turns away from the village and levels out, going in and around a valley.

(11) At a fork go up right on a narrower steeper track, where there is a GR splash (3hrs 10mins). You are now gaining height again through stunted chestnut trees and pines to reach a wider track.

(12) Turn right (left goes to nowhere) and continue steeply upwards to a wide pass where there are a five tracks meeting (3hrs 20mins). Take the second up right, which is the continuation of the GR68 coming in from the left. The GR70 goes off left.

Continue on the wide jeep track of the GR68, with attractive open grassland to the right and two interesting conical hills on the skyline (the Mamelons de Puech). Behind right is the Mont Puecheral that you walked around, and beyond are the uplands of Mont Lozère. Ahead right are the radio masts on top of the Causse Méjean. The track goes back into pine forest; having done a half-circle you can again see the outskirts of Bédouès. Continue around another valley on the right through pines and larches.

(13) Keep on the main upward track ignoring any branches off. When it reaches a clearing and bears round to the left, take the narrow path right where there are clear red/white and yellow splashes (3hrs 35mins). This path goes westwards, traversing down the side of the Mont de Lempezou, past a small ruin left and then over a stile.

At a fork go left where there are splashes (actually both paths go to a ruin). From the grassy hillside, dotted with bushes, you can now see the valley floor and the road going through it. The other side of the valley and the Causse Méjean look very close. The path reaches a small ruin (red/white splash) and a junction (3hrs 50mins).

(14) Turn down left (large yellow splash) where the path becomes quite steep and slippery through pines and juniper, crossing another stile. Down in the valley are the outskirts of Florac. After some old terraces, the path widens as it reaches a T-junction by a large old water tank.

(15) Turn down right (4hrs 5mins) on this wider track but, a few minutes later, look for a yellow splash on a telephone pole, which indicates a narrow shortcut down to the right. You reach the main path again where you turn down right.

Careful here – almost immediately ignore the red/white GR splashes and the yellow splashes which point down left (these lead to the main N106 road), and instead stay on the main path, which forks shortly after. Go left and continue down. As the track flattens out, bear right into the valley floor, where there are small fields, to reach the D998 shortly after (4hrs 25mins).

(16) Turn down left past a large camping site to reach the little bridge (Pont de Tarn) on the right just before the main N106.

(17) Cross the narrow bridge and take the second turning right to the parking area and the start of the walk (4hrs 40mins).

Close-up of menhir (standing stone) (Walk 18)

Walk 18

SENTIER DES MENHIRS

Difficulty:	Moderate – an uphill climb to get to the ridge
Time:	4hrs + time to explore the village
Height gain:	355m
Maps:	Cartes IGN 2739 OT Top 25 Mont Lozère 1:25,000
Start point:	Village of Les Bondons (15km from Florac)
Signposting:	No signs but green splashes and arrows all the way round. One blue splash at the inter section of La Pierre Plantée

A magnificent walk with extended views in all directions – you feel as though you are walking round the top of the world. The fantastic number of standing stones (menhirs) is an added attraction.

Why our Neolithic ancestors erected these stones over 4000 years ago is an unsolved mystery, though many theories have been put forward. In the Bondons area alone over 150 stones have been discovered, many of them lying on the ground. A programme of study and restoration has been set up in the area and most of the stones have now been re-erected and cemented in place so that they do not fall again. It is worthwhile wandering round the little village of Bondons – it has incredibly old houses with a very distinctive architecture, many of them unfortunately in a bad state of repair.

How to get there (from Florac)

Go north out of Florac, direction Mende, over the Tarn at the Pont de la Bessède, and then left on the N106. After a few hundred metres turn right on the D998, direction Bédoues/Pont-de-Montvert, and continue through the village of Bédoues before turning left, direction Bondons (4.5km from the turn-off) on the D135. Drive up this narrow winding road for 8km until you see a sign left to Bondons. Drive over a bridge and park in the first open space on the left at the bottom of the village, where you will notice a green splash on a concrete telephone pole.

N

*Walk 18
Sentier des
Menhirs*

Le Cham des Bondons

Les Colobrières

quarry

D 35

La Veissière

Combe de la Sourde

Le Bosc
Arnal

St. Martin

START
FINISH

Les
Bondons

Mont Vert

Lozerette

Le Tourel

Le Truc

D 135

Km

0   0.5   1

Ruas

La Pierre Plantée

DIRECTIONS

(1) Go back the way you came across the bridge over a stream to meet the wider road.

(2) Turn right and after a few metres look for a narrow road up left, signposted 'Lozerette' with a green arrow (5mins). This road circles round the south side of a conical hill called Mont Vert. The D135 goes through another attractive valley on the right, and there is a low ridge ahead with pine trees. On the right are the vestiges of an old uranium mine, which looks like a grassy amphitheatre, and later there are some large rocks through the trees on either side. When the road turns a corner you can see several tall stones, or menhirs, silhouetted against the sky on a higher ridge, which you will walk along later.

(3) At a fork (25mins) continue right. The road goes down over a stream on a humpbacked bridge into the hamlet of Lozerette. This is a tiny hamlet, which is mostly in ruins, though there are signs of habitation and vegetable gardens – some of the houses are being renovated.

(4) Take a grassy path up left where there is a green splash on a rock. The path is initially bushy and crosses a stream before traversing fairly steeply up the side of the hill. There is a clear view of Lozerette and, further on, Le Crouset in the valley below. If you look back you can see Mont Vert framed by the two rounded humps of the Mamelons de Puech and the village of Les Bondons; unfortunately the view is partially spoiled by large, ugly cattle sheds, which have been built higher up. You can also see and hear waterfalls. The path continues upward through a fence by the intersection at the top of the ridge called La Pierre Planté (55mins).

(5) Turn left here (there is a blue splash this time) and ignore a further blue splash on a stone, right, which is the way down the other side of the ridge to Ruas. Continue straight along the ridge following green splashes. The path goes up gently, passing another hump to the right, Le Truc (alt. 1175m), and round an impressive wide gully whose steep, bare slopes descend to trees and deep green fields. There is a path running through the gully from Lozerette. Continue along the ridge through another fence; further on, if you look back, you can see an impressive menhir on the ridge behind. The path reaches two stone menhirs standing together and a smaller one not far off (see introductory paragraph above). There are also piles of stones and remains of primitive shelters at this spot.

Continue onwards, where there is a fence to the left. Beyond, left, is another high ridge that you will be walking along later, with a solitary high menhir etched on the skyline. Ahead is a road and the village of La Veissière to the right. The path continues past more menhirs and further on you can see others dotted around – there are about 12 in all and it is a quite extraordinary sight.

(6) At a fork keep left (1hr 45mins) and descend gently through three fences to join a jeep track. You can now see Les Colobrières in a valley down on the left. The track goes upwards, passing a big, ugly quarry on the left, to reach the D35 road (2hrs).

(7) At the road turn left, going down and then up past a restored cottage to the left.

(8) After 20 minutes look for a path to the left, clearly marked with a green arrow. This is a defined jeep track with fences each side, crossing barren flat ground called Le Cham des Bondons. To the right and left are other huge stones. In springtime there are fields of white narcissi and yellow and blue orchids.

(9) Watch for a green arrow, which takes you off left and over a smart stile (2hrs 30mins). The path is not clear, but continue towards another stile ahead and then later on a third one. After going over a slight rise, the high menhir you saw from the earlier ridge comes into view, standing alone and commanding a dramatic view of hills and valleys stretching into the distance. The tall cliffs of the Causse Méjean are on the right skyline and nearer is another flat ridge separated by a gully, with the two unmistakable humps of the Mammelon de Puech beyond.

(10) Careful – from the menhir the ridge starts to slope gently downwards and the path is not evident. Follow the piles of stone and cairns, some of which have green splashes on them. On the right is a deep gully, called Combe de la Sourde on the IGN map. As the ridge drops down to the left it becomes a wide shoulder, and you can see a narrow road in the valley below. Bearing slightly right, cross a fence by a stile and green splashes just after a solitary hawthorn tree, and continue down the undefined path with the occasional cairn to guide you (look back and you can see there is a line of cairns down the shoulder). From here, you can also see exactly where you went along the ridge on the other side.

(11) Cross a jeep track, which seems to disappear into the grass at the end of the shoulder, and keep going down, bearing left until you come to another fence. Keep the fence on your right and follow green splashes until you come to a kissing gate (3hrs 15mins). After the gate, the path bears right and goes down the hill into the end of the Combe de la Sourde valley, which looks very lush. A 'combe' is a shallow valley and 'sourde' means deaf, but the author could not find out how it got such a name! Beyond is the Mont Vert hill dotted with small firs, which cast speckled shadows on the slope in the sunlight.

(12) At the bottom of the valley, go through another fence and over a dry streambed before heading gently up the other side. At a rather undefined fork in an open area go up right following a green arrow on a flat stone. The gravely track turns round the north side of the Mont Vert and you can see the village of Les Bondons ahead. As you zig-zag down again there is a large house called St Martin set in a small wooded valley and you can clearly see the road beyond. The path is sunken and bushy as it goes deeper into the lush valley, becoming very narrow, rocky and slippery at the bottom. It eventually crosses a little stream and a few minutes later meets the road by an ancient stone cross (3hrs 45mins).

(13) Cross over diagonally left onto a narrow lane (green splashes here) and a few minutes later you rejoin the road into the village. As you turn a corner there is a very old house, which is being renovated (with a possible date of 15— over the door). Bear down left by the war memorial to the parking area at the bottom of the village (4hrs).

Walk 19

WALK AROUND LE PONT-DE-MONTVERT

Difficulty:	Moderate – the way is not always clear. There is a crossing over the Tarn river on boulders (which could involve some wading after heavy rain) and 2km of road walking to finish.
Time:	4hrs
Height gain:	405m
Maps:	Cartes IGN 2739 OT Top 25 Mont Lozère 1:25,000
Start point:	Village of Le Pont-de-Montvert
Signposting:	Mediocre – the green splashes are sporadic and not always there just when you most need them.

This is a lovely walk around the area of Le Pont-de-Montvert in the Lozère region. Its resemblance to the Scottish highlands is striking – no wonder Robert Louis Stevenson loved it! The hills are covered with wiry upland grass, purple heather, broom and pine trees – there is even some bog! The ruined hamlets and working farms are an added interest, but where are the flocks of sheep?

Le Pont-de-Montvert is situated on the confluence of the Rieumalet and Tarn rivers, and the tall grey village houses line the banks of the Tarn, linked by an attractive 17th-century bridge with a quaint tollhouse at one end.

More importantly it was events here that triggered the War of the Camisards (see Introduction, 'War of the Camisards'). During the night of the 24/25th July 1702 a group of Calvinists, lead by Esprit Séguier, marched to the house of the Abbot de Chaila and liberated seven fellow Protestants held prisoner for trying to flee the country. The house was then burnt to the ground and the abbot stabbed to death and thrown in the river. Esprit Séguier was burnt alive a few weeks later on the 12th August.

HOW TO GET THERE (FROM FLORAC)

Go out of the village northwards and over Le Pont de la Bessède which joins the N106. Turn left and then shortly after right on the D998, signposted Bédouès/Le Pont-de-Montvert, into the upper reaches of the Tarnon valley. Continue along this attractive winding road until you reach Le Pont-de-Montvert (20km from Florac). Turn left between the two bridges, signposted 'Génolhac and Parking'. Then turn left on the D20, direction Mont Lozère, but also signposted to a parking area on the corner near the 'Temple' (Protestant chapel).

DIRECTIONS

(1) Go out of the parking and turn right on the D20. At the corner look for a track off right (green splash) and then go almost immediately left up a weedy jeep track where there are houses down to the right. When the jeep track ends take a narrow path up left (no splashes).

(2) After a few minutes the path reaches a jeep track where you turn very sharply left (green splash) and continue to reach a narrow road. Turn right and walk up for about 5 minutes until you see a narrow path up left and a gate **(note – this is a shortcut across a long, wide bend in the road).**

(3) Go through the gate (green splash) and up a narrow path through rocks and bushes. Go straight at a tiny crossroads and then past a ruin down on the right and a large boulder. The path levels out and goes down to the road through another gate (30mins).

(4) Go across the road and through yet another gate (green splash on post) on a bushy path. You can see a huddle of buildings ahead, which is the hamlet of Le Masel. The path bears left underneath the road, turning into an old mule track. It winds round a sombre ravine where there are poplar, ash and oak trees, and crosses two small watercourses. After the second watercourse the track goes uphill, through a gate and up a narrow path with high walls to reach La Veissière. Only one of the houses seems to have been renovated – the other buildings are ruins.

(5) Just after an attractive vaulted wash-place at the entrance to La Veissière, turn up sharp left (50mins) and then take the second track to the right (not the first as the green splash seems to indicate). The track passes behind the hamlet and you can see the ancient roofs, some of them still intact. It goes through some impressive boulders as it follows

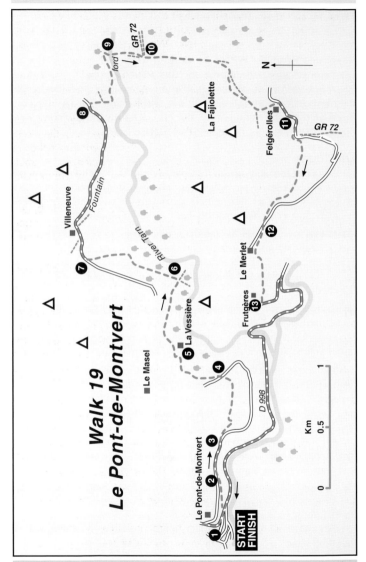

Walk 19
Le Pont-de-Montvert

the curve of the hill between the river and the road, both of which you can hear but not see. There is lots of tall bracken and several small watercourses trickle down to the river. Where you cross open areas you can see the D998 in the valley, way down on the right.

(6) The track goes through another fence before reaching a confluence of paths (1hr 5mins). Turn up left and a few minutes later go down right (green splash). You are now in attractive beech forest. Keep on this wider mule track and ignore a turning off to the right. The track crosses over a stream on a right bend and then comes out of the wood onto a grassy slope strewn with boulders. Follow the fence up to the left and along an abandoned mule track, through a wire fence. The track becomes boggy and goes along a narrow stream for a short while before crossing it and continuing to the road (1hr 25mins).

You are approaching a region of sinister-looking bare hills, the slopes almost entirely covered by boulders, the highest being the Roc de Fenêtre at 1422m. These hills are quite a contrast to the other slopes in the area, which are covered with heather, bracken or forest.

(7) Turn right, past an ugly modern barn on the left, and walk through Villeneuve, which consists of a working farm. Further on there is a sign 'La Fontaine', and it is worth going down to see an attractive old water trough, covered in thatch, with a rivulet running through it. Follow the road for about 1km, with the bare bouldery slopes left and lovely beech-covered hills right, with the Tarn winding along the valley below. Right back on the horizon are the tall cliffs bordering the Causse Méjean. You pass a sign indicating that you have entered the Parc Nationale des Cevennes.

(8) After the road crosses the river by an old stone bridge (1hr 45mins) take a path to the right (no splashes). This is a wide grassy track, bordered with barbed-wire fences, going round the hill through tufted grass, heather and bracken, with the bare stony hills still on the left. The defined track goes down into beech woods following the Tarn upstream. You can see the river down right, flowing through large flat rocks, creating little waterfalls and beautiful deep pools – there is a narrow irrigation channel between the path and the river which continues to the hamlet of Felgérolles, 2km south.

You come to an information board describing Gasbiel, which means *vieux gué* (old ford), which you are about to cross.

This crossing was used until the end of the 18th century by the Commanderie de l'Ordre de Malte, who owned all the surrounding land, to go from the village of l'Hôpital to Frutgères, both of which were important centres at the time (later superseded by Le Pont-de-Montvert – see below). In medieval times the region was a frontier between the Visigoths to the south and the Pays de Franc to the north. There are interesting pictures of how the terrain looked. In medieval times it was covered by forest, later completely denuded of vegetation as the peasant toiled the land, and is now covered with low bushes.

(9) Continue along from the information board for a couple of minutes to reach the ford at an attractive glade, crossing a wire fence just before the river (2hrs). You have to step from boulder to boulder across the river to reach a hummocky island. From here there is a further stream to cross – bigger boulders this time, which can be a problem for the short-legged! **Careful here – if the water is high you may need to wade across the first part of the ford.**

When the author did this walk for the first time she met an old couple with bags full of mushrooms of different kinds, which they had picked in the vicinity. They showed them with pride, enumerating the different culinary qualities of each type and explaining how you could tell the poisonous varieties from the edible ones. The lady said they lived in Felgérolles but when asked the way they looked puzzled. 'It is just over the hills,' they said. 'We don't take any special path!'

There are no green splashes at the ford but there is a track almost immediately on the other side, where you bear left past a grove of beech trees and then round a corner. A few metres later bear right on a narrower path (green splash) and up to meet the red/white splashes of the GR72 coming in from the left.

(10) Continue on this sandy track bearing south through heathland of heather, broom and stunted pines and then down the side of the hill towards Felgérolles. The path becomes irritatingly stony as the whole slope consists of broom and boulders – in front is the high hump of La Fajiolette 1326m.

With some relief, you go through a barrier at the bottom of the hill by the irrigation channel to reach the hamlet (2hrs 30mins). There is a *gîte d'étape* here, but little else except some very attractive ruins, a fountain and some old stone arches.

(11) Walk out of the village to join a paved road and turn down right. Just before a corner, left, watch for a small path off to the right where there is another national park sign (2hrs 40mins). The path goes round the contour of the hillside between grassy slopes, old stone walls and fences, then down across rivulets and boggy areas to reach the narrow road leading to Le Merlet.

(12) Turn right for a few metres and then go down left on a path below the hamlet. Just before a modern house turn down left (no green splash). If you want to see Le Merlet turn up right here on an old track towards the tastefully restored houses which consist of a *gîte* and *chambres d'hôtes*.

This is a sunken mule track flanked by old stone walls, where the original stones have disappeared it is extremely wet and muddy! It zigzags down the hill beside the stream and then bears right on a delightful path with lovely views into the valley. Go through yet another barbed wire barrier and you are in the hamlet of Frutgères (3hrs 10mins). There is a tiny family cemetery here with a iron fence.

It is amazing to imagine that this hamlet was once a thriving community and the centre of a large parish when Le Pont-de-Montvert was little more than a few houses. In the 12th century, the nearby village of l'Hôpital housed the important Comanderie des Hospitaliers de St-Jean-de-Jérusalem, an important religious and military order who later took the name Ordre des Chevaliers de Malte. The church was burnt by the Camisards in 1702 when the resident curé was assassinated, the day after the murder of the l'abbé du Chaila in Le Pont-de-Montvert (see introductory paragraph).

(13) Where the path meets a jeep track bear down left past a modern house to reach the paved D998 road. Follow this road for 2km, crossing a bridge over the Tarnon, where you can see deep pools amongst the boulders. Although the road is being widened (1999) there is not too much traffic, but this may depend on the time of year – there are spectacular views of the river rushing along on the left, which compensate. As you come into the village turn up right to reach the parking (4hrs).

Walk 20

SENTIER DU PIC FINIELS

Difficulty:	Easy, as the walk is short – gradual up and down on bare hillside
Time:	2hrs 30mins
Height gain:	288m
Maps:	Cartes IGN 2739 OT Top 25 Mont Lozère 1:25,000
Start point:	Centre de ski, Le Bleymard/Mont Lozère
Signposting:	Good – follow special sign for the walk (two leaves on a pedestal with a ball in the middle). For some of the way there are red/white splashes of the GR70.

This short walk in the form of a square takes you quickly, and without too much hard climbing, to the summit of Pic du Finiels (alt. 1699m), the highest point of the Mont Lozère. It is ideal for those who want an overall view of the wild, desolate upland country of the Mont Lozère region. It is popular, so could be crowded in high season. There is no shade at all, so avoid attempting it on a hot sunny day.

HOW TO GET THERE (FROM FLORAC)

Go north out of Florac over the Pont de la Bessède and then left on the N106. Almost immediately take the first turning right on the D998, direction Le Pont-de-Montvert, which winds upwards for 16km. At Le Pont-de-Montvert, do not cross the bridge but go right on the D998, direction Genolhac, and before you leave the village you will see the D20 to the left, signposted Mont Lozère/Bleymard. Go up this narrow road for 20km through desolate upland country until you reach the nondescript ski centre of Le Bleymard/Mont Lozère, where there is plenty of parking (35km from Florac).

DIRECTIONS

(1) Cross over the road you came in at the junction with the D20, where there is a sign indicating 'Sentier du Pic Finiels 3hrs'. Continue

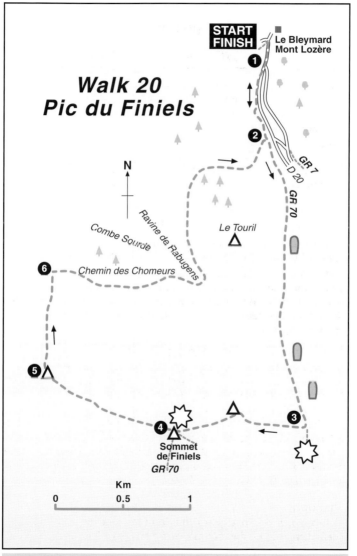

START
FINISH
Le Bleymard
Mont Lozère
❶

**Walk 20
Pic du Finiels**

GR 7
D 20
GR 70
❷

N

Ravine de Rabugens

Combe Sourde

Le Touril
△

❻ Chemin des Chomeurs

❺ △

△

△
❸

❹ △
Sommet
de Finiels
GR 70

Km
0   0.5   1

south up a wide ski track with fences each side, passing a rather strange building with a huge sloping roof.

(2) Bear slightly left where a sign indicates that the jeep track you are crossing is called Le Chemin des Chomeurs ('Road of the unemployed'). This was built by out-of-work local men in 1936 and was resurfaced in 1998. There is a wooden post and a GR red/white splash by a radio mast. Over on the right are ski tows, which make the area rather ugly.

Continue up the grassy slope bordered by heather and bilberry bushes on a defined open path. There are menhirs all the way up, the author counted 50 in all. These strange standing stones were used as markers in ancient times (see Walk 18 for further information). This path climbs up gently to the left of the hill, with the road down on the left and the summit of the Lozère on the ridge ahead. The terrain dips gently and then continues more steeply upwards.

(3) Reach a sign indicating 'Sommet de Finiels 1km', right (45mins). Go straight at this point for a few minutes over the brow of the slope, across a jeep track, to a look-out point with a dramatic view of the southern Cevennes ranges. Retrace your steps to the sign and go west up the side of the hill to the summit. There are tall sticks all the way up instead of stones, possibly for skiers.

Reach a round stone shelter at the first summit (alt. 1688m). From here there is an extensive view of the northern area of the Lozère, a wild region of rugged hills, some forested but others covered with heather and dotted with stunted coniferous trees and bushes. There is a good view of Le Bleymard in the distance (1hr).

(4) Continue on the obvious path across the ridge to the Sommet de Finiels, which is the highest point of the Mont Lozère at 1699m; there is a trigger point and another stone shelter (1hr 10mins). Here the GR70 goes off to the south (this is the route Stevenson took over the Mont Lozère*).*

Look out for stones engraved with the cross of Malta as this region belonged until 1795 to the soldiers of St-Jean-de-Jérusalem who used these stones as boundary markers.

The path goes across the ridge with cairns to guide you, though the way is obvious. It reaches a third stone shelter and then another summit at 1685m, with a fourth shelter and big piles of stones (1hr

20mins). There is a sign here indicating to the right 'Chalet de Mont Lozère 4.5km'.

(5) Turn right (direction north) and make your way down the mountain on a narrow path to reach an unpaved road (you are now on the Chemin des Chomeurs) running along the bottom of the slope (1hr 35mins).

(6) Turn right on this road (direction east) and follow it all the way back. Go past a small patch of widely spaced fir trees, with small rivulets running under the road and a larger one as the road does a U-turn and continues round another high hill called Le Touril (alt. 1575m). The Ravine de Rabugens is on the left, tree-covered as it gets lower. The road bears right round to the front of Le Touril and there are beautiful views northwards. Soon you pass into ski country as you go through a fence and over a wide ski track; there is more fir forest, probably planted to stop the wind blowing the snow away.

Go under two ski tows and across another wide ski track. Ahead, you can now see the radio mast passed on the upward climb, with the ski resort on the left. Pass another ski tow before reaching a barrier and the radio mast (no. 2 on map). From here retrace your steps down to the village (2hrs 30mins).

Walk 21

STE-ENIMIE (GORGES DU TARN)

Difficulty:	Moderate – a walk along the Tarn river and a climb to a col and down to St-Chély-du-Tarn
Time:	4hrs 45mins (plus time to explore villages of Ste-Enimie and St-Chély-du-Tarn)
Height gain:	458m
Maps:	Cartes IGN 2640 OT Top 25 Gorges du Tarn 1:25,000
Start point:	Ste-Enimie
Signposting:	You are on an official walk (some PR6 posts). The splashes are confusing, the colours ranging through yellow/green, yellow/red, green, blue and grey. It is better to ignore them as the walk is easy to follow.

A magnificent walk along the Tarn river and up to a pass on the Causse (upland plain). An added bonus is that there are no steep ascents or descents, which can be so tiring. In springtime the profusion of flowers along the banks is breathtaking and many different species of orchid can be admired.

The medieval villages of Ste-Enimie and St-Chély-du-Tarn are an added attraction, but try to do this walk out of season, as otherwise they will be packed with tourists.

Ste-Enimie, with its cobbled streets winding upwards through old houses, is worth exploring. The Roman church of Notre-Dame has some interesting ancient statues and modern ceramics illustrating the legend of Ste-Enimie. There is also a tiny museum, consisting of one room, showing the interior of a typical dwelling in the 18th century. Above the village is the ermitage (grotto) of the saint, which was converted into a church in the 12th century.

According to the legend, Enimie was a princess in the 6th century who suffered from leprosy and was cured by the waters of the nearby Source de Burle (spring). In thanksgiving for her miraculous recovery she founded a monastery and became the abbess before retiring to a nearby grotto. After her death both the monastery and the grotto became places of pilgrimage. The monastery fell into ruins but was rebuilt by the Benedictines, only to decline once again and finally shut in 1799. During the Revolution most of the buildings were destroyed.

HOW TO GET THERE (FROM FLORAC)

Take the N106, direction Mende, and after 5.8km go left, direction Ispagnac/Ste-Enimie, on the D907bis along the Gorges du Tarn through Ispagnac, Molines, Blajoux and Prades to reach Ste-Enimie (27km from Florac). Park in the centre of the village.

DIRECTIONS

(1) Walk across the bridge over the Tarn river, direction Meyrueis, passing some new houses and the cemetery – ignore a signpost to the left indicating two walks.

(2) Soon after the sign announcing the end of Ste-Enimie, take the path right signposted Draille de Lozère and Tennis (yellow/green splash). This is initially a wide undulating track with attractive views of the gorge on the right. However the Tarn river is often obscured by bushy terraces and small fields which were formerly cultivated with orchards and vineyards. On the other side of the gorge are impressive cliffs with one road snaking along beneath them and a higher road winding up to the top of the Causse.

(3) At a fork go up left on the narrower path where there are red/yellow splashes (20mins) – the right fork goes down to a tennis club, which looks out of place in such an unspoilt position, as does the garish blue of a swimming pool round the corner on the other side of the river.

(4) The path reaches a further fork with a PR6 wooden sign to Camin Ferrat and St-Chély-du-Tarn (30mins), where you go up left again. You will come out from the lower fork on your return.

The narrow path, called Sentier de Chèvres ('Path of the goats'), goes up fairly steeply through bushes, brambles and stunted woodland. The Tarn is occasionally visible through the undergrowth on the slopes to the right.

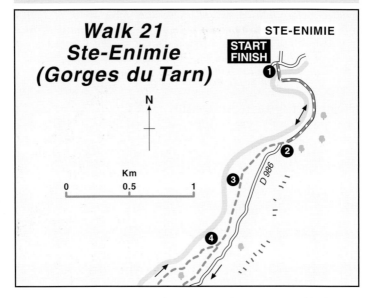

Walk 21
Ste-Enimie
(Gorges du Tarn)

STE-ENIMIE

START FINISH

N

Km
0   0.5   1

D 986

(5) On reaching the D986 road again, go right (45mins) and look carefully for a path up to the left after 140m, signposted Draille de Lozère, PR6 (yellow/red and green splashes). This is a wide stony track, which soon narrows as it goes up diagonally to the road and then steepens across a patch of scree through stunted pines, oaks, juniper and boxwood. Continue up the side of a wooded ravine, passing a high rock standing alone on the right-hand side. Later on there are occasional views of the rocky walls of the Cirque de Pougnadoire and the road along the cliffs to the village of Cabrunas, perched on the edge of the Causse.

At a bend beside a dried-up streambed, there is an empty man-made hole which could have been a watering place for goats (1hr 10mins). Enter a forest of tall Austrian pines. At the side of the path there are curious round white stones with the initials ATF chiselled on them. These are the boundary markers of the Gorges du Tarn forest from the end of the 19th century. The path continues upwards and widens as it moves away from the ravine, later flattening out over the top and round the contour of the hill.

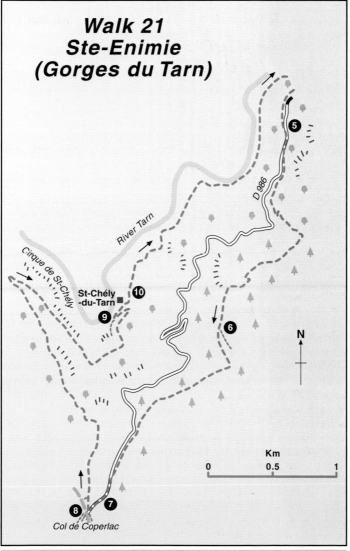

Walk 21
Ste-Enimie
(Gorges du Tarn)

River Tarn

Cirque de St-Chély

St-Chély
-du-Tarn

D 986

Km

0   0.5   1

N

Col de Coperlac

(6) At a fork go down to the right (1hr 35mins), signposted 'Col de Coperlac/St-Chély-du-Tarn' and 'Draille de Lozère' (left indicates Cabrières). Soon after there is another small man-made watering hole in the undergrowth to the right. The track undulates through the pine forest, where the trees are often tall on the right and stunted on the left. The track descends gently and runs parallel to the road for a short while before joining it where the forest stops and you emerge into open Causse scenery.

(7) At the road go up left for a few minutes to the Col de Coperlac (alt. 907m) (2hrs 10mins). It is a rather ugly col (pass), with numerous signposts (even one saying 'Esperanto – langue international'). A road to the left goes to the Mas St-Chély and ahead is signposted Caussignac/Meyruis – this is still the D986, which you crossed earlier, but now you leave it behind for good.

(8) Follow a wooden sign to the right indicating Ste-Enimie/St-Chély-du-Tarn and PR6 on a wide jeep track. Almost immediately go right again at a fork onto a narrower path (green splash on a rock), heading down the side of the gorge towards the little village of St-Chély-du-Tarn far below. Beyond the wide gully on the right, you can see the path you took through the forest of pines.

The track is open and easy, with magnificent views of the gorge and the high rocky cliffs on the other side. Descend through scattered woodland looking down on the tiny village far below with its ancient houses, Romanesque church, bridge over the Tarn and the hotel swimming pool.

The village recedes during a gradual descent round a big hairpin bend (2hrs 45mins) and appears again on the left as the path swings back above the cliffs of the Cirque de St-Chély. On the other side of the gorge you can now make out the footpath from Chély up to Cabrunas on the lip of the Causse; on the road below cars disappear into a tunnel through impressive overhanging rocks. Keep going down round a gully. You can see canoe enthusiasts picnicking on the shingle banks of the river and under the bridge. There is a further hairpin before arriving at a sign and a path to the right (3hrs 15mins).

(9) Go down right (the upper path continues along the side of the Tarn) on a stony track towards the houses.

(10) Just before entering the village there is a sign to Ste-Enimie up to the right (3hrs 20mins) after a curious display of old agricultural implements opposite an attractive old mill with old cartwheels set in a wall. This is the direction you will take to continue the walk, but first it is worth exploring the village and perhaps pausing for a drink at the Auberge de la Cascade.

St-Chély-du-Tarn is quaint and well known, often full of tourists in season. There is a rivulet running through the houses, an old stone bake-house in the centre and a Roman church with a cemetery. Look for a sign left to a 12th-century chapel, which leads you past the hotel swimming pool and along the side of a house to a huge rocky overhang. The crude, tiny building is built into the rock, and one wonders how it was constructed, especially in the 12th century!

Return to the entrance to the village and follow the sign to Ste-Enimie (see no. 10 above). The path is steep and stony up the hillside for about 10 minutes, after which it flattens out along overgrown terraces. There are again yellow/green and green splashes, starting from the village.

You are undulating back alongside the Tarn lower down than the outward path. Through the scattered woodland there are tantalising views of the deep brown waters of the Tarn below, with its banks of silvery shingle and small waterfalls – it is fascinating to watch the canoes negotiating these mini-rapids. The path continues round the contours of the hill, in and out of gullies, over scree beds, along the old stone walls of former terraces and past the occasional ruin. At a rocky look-out point there is a particularly magnificent view of the river (3hrs 45mins).

Sometimes you are near the river, sometimes higher, but never where you can actually scramble down and bathe your feet! There are camping sites on the far bank.

Just after a high wall the path meets another coming in from the left (4hrs 5mins) where there is a sign to Ste-Enimie. Continue above the river until you see the swimming pool on the left and you know you are about to rejoin the outward path.

At the fork (no. 4 on the sketch map), retrace your steps back to the village (4hrs 45mins).

Walk 22

GORGES DU TARN FROM LA MALENE

Difficulty:	Shorter walk: strenuous up and down
	Longer walk: strenuous, with uphill and downhill climbs, but flat along the Tarn and up on the Causse
Time:	3hrs 30mins/6hrs 30mins (plus time to wander around La Malène)
Height gain:	440m (shorter walk)/458m (longer walk)
Maps:	Cartes IGN 2640 OT Top 25 Gorges du Tarn 1:25,000
Start point:	La Malène
Signposting:	Adequate – follow yellow splashes to La Caze, red/green across the Causse to Rieisse, and yellow down to La Malène. On shorter walk follow intermittent yellow splashes.

The longer walk needs stamina, but is very rewarding and not especially difficult. The first part goes along the dramatic Gorges du Tarn. Then there is a stiff climb up to the top of the Causse Méjean into a desolate landscape of flat upland plains and open skies before the long descent into the gorge again.

For those with less time and stamina, the shorter walk includes part of the gorge as well as a climb up and down to the popular viewpoint at the Roc des Hourtous. The Roc overlooks the Défilé des Détroits, the narrowest part of the gorge, and there is a good view of the Point Sublime and the Cirque des Baumes.

La Malène (meaning 'bad hole') has always been a meeting place. Strategically situated at the junction of the roads crossing the Sauveterre and Méjean plains, thousands of sheep have stopped here to feed and water. In the 12th century the Montesquieu barons built a château, which gave added importance to the village. During the upheavals of the Revolution the nobility took refuge in the many caves in the surrounding cliffs. In 1793, 21 inhabitants were shot by revolutionary troops and all the buildings were burnt. On the cliff called La Barre, which dominates La Malène,

Causse Méjean, ruins of La Chabassude (Walk 25)

Walking to the edge of the gorge, Sentier de Vernagues (Walk 25)

Salamander on Mont Lozère

there is still a black mark, which it is said was made by the noxious fumes from a house full of burning nuts! It is worth taking time to wander around the attractive winding streets of the village and to visit the 12th-century church. There is also a small museum showing how the inhabitants lived until the present century. The 16th-century château is now a hotel.

HOW TO GET THERE (FROM FLORAC)

Take the D16, which winds up the side of the gorge onto the Causse Méjean. Continue on this road (crossing the D986 after 26km) until it joins the D43, direction La Malène. There is another series of hairpin bends down into the gorge again to reach the village. Park in the large car park just across the bridge opposite the Château/Hôtel de la Malène (34km from Florac).

DIRECTIONS

(1) Go back over the bridge past the tourist office and turn right at the end on a flat wide path – there is a yellow splash. The Tarn river is flowing down on the right, with the D907 beyond and the dramatic cliffs of the gorge towering above.

(2) After a few minutes, note a sign up left to Roc des Hourtous (this is the way you will return from both walks).

Continue on this wide undulating path appreciating the beauty of the river meandering below with its deep, still pools, jagged rocks and miniature waterfalls. The clear waters are bordered by shingle beaches, which look very tempting for sunbathing and swimming. On the other side of the river are several caravan parks.

In the cliffs there are the black mouths of caves, which were used for refuge by the aristocracy during the French Revolution.

At times the river is hidden by undergrowth; on the opposite side you can see a house surrounded by tiny fields sandwiched between the road and the water.

(3) Just after a rocky cut-through watch for a signpost left (40mins) indicating 'Les Vignes/Le Rozier/Toutes Directions' (yellow/green and yellow splashes). If you continue on the main track there is a large sign reading 'Defense d'entrée/propriété privé', which leads to the property called Gaujac on the IGN map.

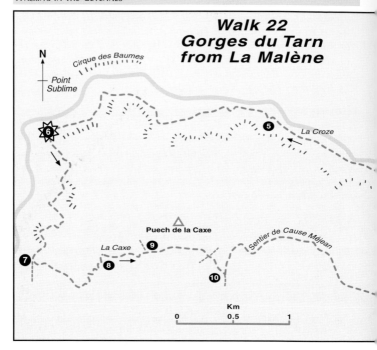

**Walk 22
Gorges du Tarn
from La Malène**

The narrow track curls up fairly steeply and carries on higher up along the side of the Tarn.

(4) After 5 minutes there is a sign left to the Roc des Hourtous. Go this way if you have chosen the shorter walk (45mins).

Continuation of shorter walk

Zigzag up the side of the gorge, mainly through boxwood and stunted oak and pine trees. Keep on the main path following the infrequent yellow splashes – the rare small branches off are shortcuts. At times it becomes quite rocky and you have to watch your feet, but it is never a difficult path and there are magnificent views all the way up.

Go under a big rock wall (1hr) and continue upward in larger zig-zags, getting nearer to the craggy rocks at the top of the Causse. Near

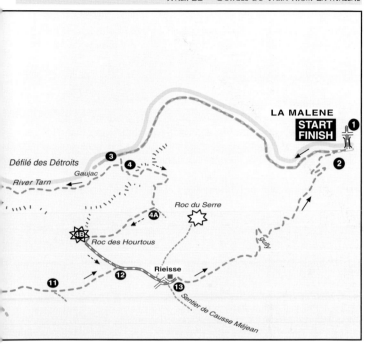

the top the vegetation opens up and the going gets easier.

(4A) Where the track forks (1hrs 35mins) keep on the main path bearing right. You are now walking along the top of the Causse through scattered woodland. There are a number of look-out points with wonderful extended views of the river far below as it meanders through the high rocky walls between the upland plains of the Causse Méjean and the Causse Sauveterre. Keep going westwards, and after a while you notice that the path is well trodden by people who drive up to see the view and take a little walk along the Causse!

(4B) Rather abruptly the path reaches a car park and a small café and souvenir shop. Beside is an entrance to the Roc des Hourtous that leads through a picnic area with tables to a look-out point. It has a big flagpole and is surrounded by a railing – there is indeed a fantastic view (2hrs).

Make your way back to the car park and down the road, which is bordered by a hedge, right, and attractive open fields. Meet the path coming in on the right from the longer walk – not easy to see but there is a rather faint yellow/red splash (2hrs 5mins).

Continue from ** below.

Continuation of longer walk
The track undulates up and down along the contour of the hill, sometimes fairly steeply, sometimes downwards, but rarely flat! The vegetation consists mainly of pines, firs, beech, boxwood and stunted bushes. There are small patches of scree, and from time to time the stony path becomes rocky – on the whole it is not difficult, but just seems to go on and on! The gorge below narrows at the Défilé des Détroits.

Without realising it you are gaining height and there is only the odd glimpse of the river far below – the path goes under overhanging rocks, and far down is the large house of La Croze in a bend of the river.

(5) The path descends to a clearing (1hr 25mins). Go up left (yellow/green splash on tree) and continue through woodland, round a gully and over a rivulet, still undulating along the hillside, often through tall pines. On the other side of the gorge the rocks become even higher and more impressive as you look towards the Cirque des Baumes and the much-visited look-out spot of the Point Sublime. The little hamlet of St Hilaire cowers beneath these towering yellow cliffs. There are frequent glimpses of the road winding between the river and the cliffs, disappearing in and out of tunnels. Through the bushes to the left you can now see that you are walking under a high perpendicular rock face and by a huge detached rock with a lone tree on its summit. The river gradually turns south and you do the same on the rock above.

(6) At a rocky outcrop, there is a superb view down the valley (2hrs 40mins). The path continues past other look-out spots. As you head southwards the vegetation is gentler and the valley opens up and become less rocky and oppressive. In front is the village of Les Vignes with its little bridge (the first bridge across the Tarn since the one in La Malène). Descend round a ravine and continue towards Les Vignes.

(7) Watch for a path up to the left (3hrs 20mins) with a green/yellow splash on a tree; the word 'Caxe' is inscribed on a rock in the path,

Roc des Hourtous

but it is difficult to decipher. If you continue there is a signpost to this 16th-century farm and a yellow splash indicating up right, so you know the turning is correct!

This is a stiff climb of about 400m up the rocky gorge – at first it goes up the side of a tree-covered ravine with rocky outcrops. As you gain altitude the path becomes much steeper through bushes and large boulders, with round high crags at the very top.

Before you arrive at the top of the Causse at La Caxe take a last look back at the breathtaking gorge with its magnificent cliffs – the contrast between the gorge and the flat, windswept upland plains is amazing (4hrs 10mins).

(8) Go towards the magnificent 16th-century farm, in the process of renovation, and veer right, following a yellow splash walk along a narrow jeep track bordered by stone walls.

A few minutes later turn left off the jeep track and go straight ahead on a narrower path following the sign 'Riesse' and the red/yellow splashes of the Causse Méjean (do not go left where there are crosses). Keep on the main path going slightly upwards.

(9) At a fork go right following the red/yellow splashes (the blue splashes go left).

The wide sandy track meanders through stunted pine and fir woods with lots of open spaces. After the magnificence of the gorge, this section seems rather tame (or a relief) – there are places where you can see the wide sweeping landscape, but most of the time the trees obscure the view. The path crosses a jeep track and widens momentarily before going down right at another fork. The way becomes poorly defined down through stunted pine trees and open areas – keep on the main path and follow the red/yellow splashes carefully, ignoring all tracks off.

(10) Carry straight on when the path merges with a jeep track (4hrs 30mins) – there is a large open field on the right. It continues for quite a while through pinewood with no open views.

(11) At a fork turn left off the jeep track on a narrower track which becomes momentarily rocky and rather messy. There is a view to the left, the first for a long time. After 10 minutes the path meets a road (5hrs 10mins).

(12) Turn right – **note:** this is the road to the look-out point of the Roc des Hourtous.

**Shorter walk joins the longer walk here.

Walk towards the hamlet of Rieisse, which you don't see from afar. Just before, there is a large sign left indicating the Roc du Serre, which is another well-known look-out point (there is an old stone cross here). **The walk to the Roc du Serre takes about 10 minutes through woodland, so leave 30 minutes for the round trip, with time to appreciate the view (route not done by author).**

(13) Almost immediately, just before a *gîte d'étape*, turn down left by a grassy patch with another stone cross and walk into Rieisse past a beautiful old house with enormous arches. Follow the yellow splashes past an old bake-house and then go straight at a wooden sign for La Malène, ignoring a yellow/red cross. Then turn right, and shortly after left, at stone indicators which are not easy to read (2hrs 20mins shorter walk/5hrs 25mins longer walk). **Note** – at Rieisse you turn off the Sentier de Causse Méjean (red/yellow splashes) and follow yellow splashes to La Malène.

The path out of the village is wide and grassy between old stone walls. It narrows into a lane and starts to go down off the Causse through oak trees and bushes down the side of a big gully. Far below you can see the village of La Malène.

The path becomes stony as it descends, crossing the gully and continuing along the other side. As you get lower the woods become denser and there are numbers of beech trees.

Continue downwards past a large rock to the right and then rocky walls. After what seems like an endless descent you arrive at the jeep track and the Roc des Hourtous sign (item no. 2 above) that you passed on the outward journey.

Turn right and then left over the bridge to the village (3hrs 30mins shorter walk/6hrs 30mins longer walk).

Walk 23

SENTIER DES COURONNES

Difficulty:	Moderate – a lot of up and down but nothing difficult
Time:	4hrs 30mins
Height gain:	548m
Maps:	Cartes IGN 2640 OT Top 25 Gorges du Tarn 1:25,000
Start point:	Centre of Florac
Signposting:	Follow sporadic green splashes and occasional posts (black arrow with green square below)

This is a delightful walk, which enables you to see the magnificent pinnacles bordering the Causse Méjean and dominating the town of Florac. There are also the added attractions of the prehistoric dolmen at the Col de Pierre Plate and walking by the working farm of Le Pradal. The views of the Tarn valley and the Lozère region to the north are outstanding.

How to get there (from Florac)

The walk starts from the car park at the top of the village, signposted 'Parking Parc Nationale des Cevennes'. In the château is the administration centre of the national park, which is worth visiting. Here you will find a wealth of information concerning the region and a wide selection of maps, videos and books.

Directions

(1) Go up to the end of the car park and over Le Pont de la Draille bridge, where there is a *pisciculture* (fish farm) on the left. Go straight up some steps and along a narrow street to reach the D16 road.

(2) Turn left and shortly after, at the entrance to the Parc Paul Arnal, there is a board indicating the name of the walk and other relevant information.

    Careful – do not walk through the park, but continue on the road round the corner, left, where there is a black arrow with a green

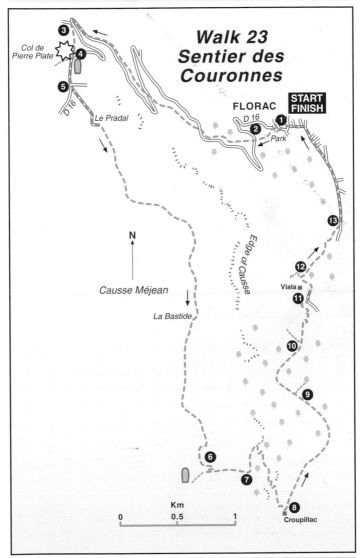

Walk 23
Sentier des Couronnes

Col de
Pierre Plate

FLORAC

START
FINISH

Park

D 16

Le Pradal

N

Causse Méjean

La Bastide

Edge of Causse

Viala

Km

0   0.5   1

Croupillac

square underneath on a post, and a narrow path up right signposted 'Sentier des Couronnes' (10mins). Where the path forks go up right following the signpost. It crosses the road for the first time. Continue upwards following yellow arrow and green splashes. **Be careful, the yellow arrow then points to the left, but this is for another walk.** Ignore it and continue ahead following green splashes which are not so evident.

At the second road crossing (20mins) turn right round the corner for about 100m and look for the green splash on a path up left. There is a lovely view of Florac and the river below as you traverse along the top of the valley. As you get higher you can see the villages of Bédouès and Cocurès in the Tarnon valley to the right, with the high plains of the Mont Lozère in the background. The path goes through stunted nut trees, boxwood and beech. At the fourth road-crossing the path comes out under a new wall. Look for a green splash on a telephone pole and go right for a few metres until you see a steep path to the left. This cuts off a hairpin bend and very shortly you arrive at the D16 again and the top of the Causse (1hr 10mins).

(3) Go straight across the road (this is the fifth crossing) and up a wide jeep track (signposted Rouchet/le Tomple) for around 100m. Look for a tiny cairn and a green splash left on a narrow path, which crosses the hill diagonally and reaches the road again at the Col de Pierre Plate.

(4) Turn up right past a dolmen, which looks like a long flat stone and was thought to be an ancient burial site. When we did the walk for the first time a family were using it as a picnic table! There is a good view here of the Tarn valley, the Méjean Causse and surroundings.

(5) After 120m bear left, signposted 'Le Pradal 0.8km', onto a narrower tarmac road. Up on the hill to the left are ugly TV and radio masts. Ignore any branches off and continue southeast on this straight, level road across the Causse. You are now walking through the rather bleak scenery of these upland plains, with patches of green cultivated fields, grazing cows and rare flocks of sheep to break the monotony.

Walk through the solitary buildings of La Pradal, which is a large working farm with some huge sheds (1hr 30mins). Continue on the undulating jeep track, following the occasional green splashes and ignoring any minor paths branching off. The track goes over the brow and again there are good views of the Tarn valley and the ruined buildings of La Bastide (alt. 1080m) (2hrs).

The track goes in front of the ruins and past a large cultivated field on the left. Continue onwards past a junction back right which goes to the radio masts behind La Bastide. After about 15 minutes the jeep track becomes stony and goes down through a rocky area with box bushes before bearing right round the perimeter of a large green field. There is a fence on the left for a while and then the path veers away and zigzags up towards two menhirs (tall rocks) on the horizon.

(6) Before you reach them there is a rather undefined fork where you bear up left (green splash on a post) and through a barrier. Turn down left, and continue with the large field now beyond the fence on your left and the edge of the Causse further over right.

(7) The path bears away from the fence to a small cairn right at the edge of the Causse, where there are green splashes (2hrs 35mins). Turn down left, traversing north down the front of the slope, then bearing right and underneath superb rocky crags and pinnacles which stand out like sentinels. The terrain becomes rockier past a high isolated needle of rock on the right, which dominates the valley far below.

(8) As you get lower the path becomes sunken and bears left (green splashes) just before reaching the hamlet of Croupillac (3hrs).

This is an easy path along the side of the Causse across open hillside and through bushes – to the right are meadows, and you can see a lower path going through them. Pass through two barriers.

(9) Where the path forks go up left following a green splash – the track is rather eroded and narrow for a little while, so care should be taken. Again the views are extensive, and especially the flat top of the Sentier de Cans (Walk 31) on the other side of the Tarn valley, with hamlets standing out on the rugged hillside and the reddish rocks of the Mimente valley coming in on the right. North are the twin humps of the Mamelons de Puech and the rolling uplands of the Mont Lozère.

The path goes in and out of stunted woodland, becomes rocky in places and continues downwards. It passes round the edge of a tree-covered gully, through another barbed-wire fence and bears round to the right (green cross straight ahead).

(10) Go right at a fork (3hrs 35mins) and around a small promontory – the town of Florac and the river come into view again as well as the

D907 wending its way through the valley.

The path now zigzags down fairly steeply, bearing right, and you can see the abandoned terraces ahead around the hamlet of Viala, where there is a huge indentation in the side of the gorge. Continue downwards through a wooden gate (green splash) and round the side of a small gully to reach the road at an intersection (4hrs).

(11) Bear up left, following the green splash and ignoring the downward road ahead. Go up a short hill in front of Viala, which consists of a large ramshackle honey farm. Pass in front of the building and ignore the turning down to the right.

(12) At the next fork go down right at a sign into a busy gully and underneath an overhanging rock. The path is overgrown and bushy for a short while and goes up for a few minutes before descending again through a small forest of pines, passing a small ruin. It becomes overgrown, with an old wall to the left, before it finally reaches the road just before the sign indicating Florac (4hrs 15mins).

(13) Turn left, cross the road and go down stone steps with railings onto a path above the river. Soon you reach the roundabout on the outskirts of Florac, where you go straight into town (4hrs 30mins).

Walk 24

SENTIER DE TARN AND CAUSSE MEJEAN

Difficulty:	Moderate – some up and down to reach the Causse
Time:	4hrs 30mins
Height gain:	488m
Maps:	Cartes IGN 2640 OT Top 25 Gorges du Tarn 1:25,000
Start point:	Village of Salièges (3km from Florac)
Signposting:	Not very good, as this is a combination of different walks. Yellow/green along the Tarn – yellow until the crossroads. Green up the side of the gorge and to Le Tomple. Red and green across the Causse. Signposts on the way down.

A walk with contrasting scenery and dramatic vistas – the path goes along the side of the Tarn valley, with occasional views of the river below, and then climbs up to the top of the Causse Méjean, where the high sweeping plains of this austere upland region seem to go on for ever. The sudden arrival of the road at the lip of the gorge again and the view of Florac far below is breathtaking. Although there is a climb up and down it is not too demanding and worth the effort!

How to get there (from Florac)

Go north from the centre of town and turn left at the police station. Then take the first turning right at a sign for Salièges/Monteils and continue for 2km until you get to the hamlet. Parking is limited here, so go through the houses and up left at a fork (the walk starts to the right); park almost immediately beside the road in a field opposite a modern house. **Note:** this is not a legitimate parking place, so make enquiries at the house. The lady of the house is very friendly and will merely ask you to park your car in her drive if they are working in the field.

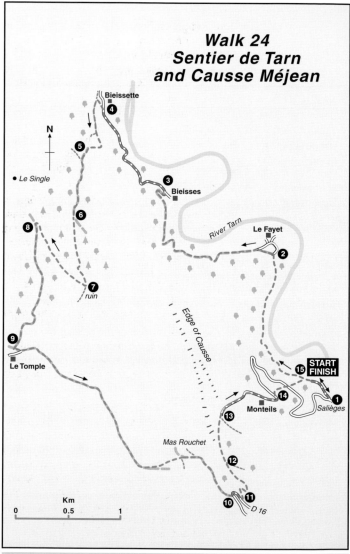

Walk 24
Sentier de Tarn
and Causse Méjean

Bieissette
④

N

● Le Single

⑤

Bieisses
③

River Tarn

Le Fayet
②

⑥

⑧

⑦
ruin

⑨
Le Temple

Edge of Causse

START
FINISH
⑮

⑭
①
Salièges

Monteils

⑬

Mas Rouchet

⑫

⑩ ⑪
D 16

Km
0   0.5   1

DIRECTIONS

(1) Walk down to the fork and go left between two buildings where there are yellow/green splashes on a telephone pole. This is a narrow descending paved road, which shortly turns into a jeep track. There are open fields and you cannot immediately see the river as you are crossing a spur. Just after a stream there is a path coming in from the left, which is the way you will return (see no. 15). Keep to the main track through magnificent chestnut woods, climbing gently and crossing two more streams.

Later on you can catch glimpses of the Tarn river in the valley below, with the road beyond. The track passes some beehives to the right and undulates high above the river – there is an unsightly factory with two chimneys on the other side of the valley.

(2) Just before the track goes down to the hamlet of Le Fayet (30mins) turn up left following a sign to Bieisses and a 'No entry' sign. There are also faint yellow/green splashes on a telephone pole. Continue along the track – on a bend by a large rock there is a lovely view of Bieisses and the Tarn in the valley below. Shortly after, there is a turning down to the hamlet (50mins), an attractive huddle of houses on a hill overlooking the river. Keep on the main track (there is a sign to Biesses by the side of the road), which zigzags down towards the village. There are open views here and you can see two parallel roads on the other side of the valley.

(3) When the track comes to a tarmac road (the one going to Bieisses), turn down left (1hr). The road undulates over the same streams crossed higher up towards the hamlet of Bieissette, which consists of only two houses (1hr 20mins).

(4) Take the first narrow path up left before the first building, ignoring a red/yellow cross, past a water trough and a bread oven. This is a shortcut to meet the main track coming up from the right. Turn left up the hill for about 100m. Go through a gate, and where the path seems to split into three, take the middle one (splashes here) and keep on the more defined grassy path all the way. It goes above some old terraces, past large clearings and bushes, traversing the hillside rather than climbing steeply. Keep going across three small crossroads on the main path up by a low stone wall on the right with intermittent yellow splashes (also some green); at some points the path is not clear.

(5) Reach a T-junction at a jeep track where there are signposts (1hr 35mins). Turn left (right goes to Ispagnac/Quézac). The jeep track goes up quite steeply through scattered woodland and then traverses upwards, going through a gate and nearing the overhead wires of a telephone pole.

(6) **Careful** – a few minutes later turn up to the right at the pole, marked by a green splash. This is a narrow path winding upward fairly steeply through stunted pine forest and bushes. There are beautiful views into the valley below.

(7) Where the path bears right at a big boulder ignore a path on the left and continue upwards to the top of the Causse by a small ruin (2hrs 10mins).

   Careful – just before you reach the ruin take a narrow path up to the right, where the green splash is not immediately visible. A few metres later you are on the top and you can see a defined path going up right onto a wide grassy ridge where there is a small cairn (2hrs 20mins). From here there are magnificent views of the rolling upland plains of the Causse Méjean and you can see where the Tarn gorge cuts a swathe through the Causse. Nearby ahead is the radio mast of Le Single. Walk towards the radio mast following intermittent green splashes.

(8) The path goes down to meet a wide jeep track, where you turn left through scattered woodland with a number of dead trees. It meets the narrow road along the top of the Causse near the tiny hamlet of Le Tomple, where there is a sign left to Florac (2hrs 45mins).

(9) Turn left on the stony road where there are yellow/red splashes of the Tour de Causse Méjean. Continue on the road stretching before you as it meanders over the undulating empty landscape of grass and scrubs, although there are some fields planted with grain; the road seems to go on for ever! Later there are two tracks left leading to the isolated farm buildings of Mas Rouchet. Suddenly you are on the edge of the Causse and you can see Florac in the valley far below. There are some impressive rocky peaks, sticking out at the top of the gorge like a series of stalagmites, which are extremely photogenic.

(10) The stony road meets the paved D16 winding up from Florac at a hairpin bend (3hrs 30mins). Turn down left.

Looking down the valley to Florac

(11) After the first bend look for a path to the left at a small sign with a black arrow, green band and a picture of a camping site – you will follow this sign most of the way down. This stony path zigzags down fairly steeply northwards across the front of the ridge. In front you can see the narrow road far below leading to the hamlet of Monteils.

(12) Careful – where the path goes down right go straight on (3hrs 45mins) by a sign. At a fork a few minutes later continue on the main path (the lower one is a shortcut), which descends through attractive beech wood and becomes stonier.

(13) When the path meets a gravel road (3hrs 55mins) turn left down into Monteils passing an isolated cemetery to the left. Walk through this charming little hamlet, which looks as though it is in a picturesque time warp.

(14) Ignore a turning to the right (Impasse de Ferradou) just after this house and continue to the next fork. Take the right-hand fork, and immediately there is a narrow path down right (no splash here). It goes down through chestnut woods (at a fork go left) and crosses another paved road. At a further fork keep on the main path to the left down to the jeep track taken on the outward journey.

(15) Turn right and retrace your steps to the car (4hrs 30mins).

Walk 25

SENTIER DE VERNAGUES

Difficulty:	Moderate – quite a climb up to the Causse Méjean; very little shade
Time:	3hrs 15mins
Height gain:	330m
Maps:	Cartes IGN 2640 OT Top 25 Gorges du Tarn 1:25,000
Start point:	Below the village of Vernagues (7km from Florac)
Signposting:	Sporadic but adequate – posts with a picture of a house. No signs along the top of the Causse but the way is evident.

This is a dramatic short walk to the top of the Causse Méjean, and the contrast between the valley, the rocky crags and the sweeping plain of the Causse is startling. It is recommended not do this walk on a hot day as there is little shade. For further information on the Causse Méjean see Introduction, 'Northern Cevennes'.

How to get there (from Florac)

From Florac take the D907 signposted, St-Jean-du-Gard/Barre-des-Cévennes. After 5km, where the road forks, continue up right on the D907. After 2km look for a narrow road to the right signposted Sentier de Vernagues. Go up here for around 100m and park in a space on the left – it makes the walk about 20 minutes shorter if you drive up to the hamlet, but there is limited space for parking.

Directions

(1) On the other side of the road to the parking is a sign for the Sentier de Vernagues. Take this narrow path, forking right almost immediately, going up fairly steeply. When you reach the road turn right and then go up again to cross the road a second time. At an intersection of paths keep straight on upwards. When you reach the road a third time turn right and walk into the village (15mins).

Walk 25
Sentier des Vernagues

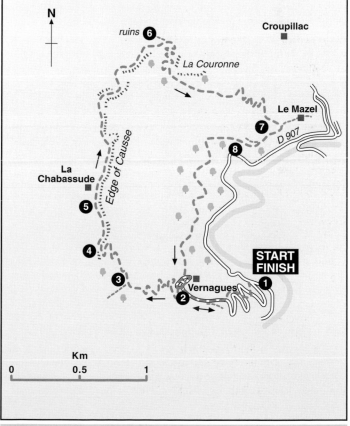

N

ruins ⑥

Croupillac

La Couronne

Le Mazel

⑦

D 907

La
Chabassude

Edge of Causse

⑤

⑧

④

③

START
FINISH

Vernagues ①

②

Km
0   0.5   1

(2) At the entrance to the village turn up left on a concrete track at a signpost. Avoid a track to the left a few metres later and continue round a corner which takes you above the village, bearing left at another sign.

Keep upwards on the wider main track, which crosses a jeep track and passes the entrance to a concrete water tank on the right. It continues upwards past ancient terraces, going alongside a fence and becoming grassy, hedged with bushes. Ignore the entrances to small attractive meadows. Higher up the terrain becomes rocky again and there are lovely views of the roofs of Vernagues and the Tarnon valley with the flat open ridge of the Sentier des Cans (Walk 31) on the other side. The path crosses a jeep track again (45mins).

(3) Bear right following the sign, when a jeep track joins from the left (55mins). At the first corner go right off the track (well signposted).

As you climb higher you approach the rocky crags bordering the upland plain of the Causse Méjean and eventually you bear left underneath them. The path makes a left hairpin before doubling back; just before getting back to the crags it arrives at the top of the Causse at a signpost (1hr 10mins).

The top of the Causse is a surprise – suddenly, stretched in front and to the left, are rolling grasslands of an empty, treeless land, stretching into infinity.

(4) Almost immediately the path reaches a jeep track where you bear right. Up on the left are the ruins of La Chabassude. These buildings, consisting of barns and sheep pens, were never permanently inhabited, but used by the villagers of Vernagues only in the summer.

(5) As you approach the ruins you will see a signpost over on the right. Follow this sign, which directs you across the top of the line of crags. There is no defined path but follow the fence for a while. Keep going slightly upwards across the grassland, sufficiently away from the edge of the Causse. Ahead you can see the path you will take down to the valley towards the hamlet of Le Mazel, with the ruins of the *bergerie* (sheep farm) at the top of the slope, so keep that in view.

On the top there are good places for a picnic, though there is no shade on a hot day. The view is impressive in all directions – over the flat, desolate fields of the Causse, the rocky crags bordering the gorge, the deep narrow valley far below and misty blue ridges rolling to the horizon.

Start to descend and go through a barrier in a fence. After a few minutes you reach a defined path, which continues all the way to the ruins (1hr 45mins).

(6) Take the wide rocky path, which goes down in huge zigzags underneath imposing rocky crags – on a sunny day the heat reverberates off the rocks and it can be very hot.

As the path goes lower it gets stonier, going through a barrier (2hrs) and then out on a grassy ledge overlooking the village of Le Mazel. It becomes a stony mule track between high bushy banks eventually bearing right (sign here) through a gate to reach the cultivated fields of the village.

(7) Just before the path reaches Le Mazel, turn right at a signpost (2hrs 35mins). If you look back you can see the hamlet of Croupillac on the hill above and the narrow road winding up to it.

(8) You are now walking along the hillside on the raised path of an old terrace with the valley down on the left. Go down left at the next two forks (no signs) – the village of Vernagues looks discouragingly far away but this is an illusion. The path loses height through taller oak trees round the head of a narrow ravine (Valat de Coumbes) and then starts to go up again and round the flank of the hill. It is a delightful stretch bordered by bushes, chestnut trees and old stone walls. At a fork after a lovely field to the right keep to the top path round another indentation, over a dry riverbed and through a barrier. The path becomes sunken, with an old wall, and then goes into the open. As you near the outskirts of Venagues there is a delightful view of the Tarnon river winding through the valley.

Ignore any branches off on the last short climb up to the village (3hrs). In the village turn right to rejoin the road you took on the outward journey. From here retrace your steps down the hill to the car (3hrs 15mins).

Walk 26

LE CHAOS DE NIMES LE VIEUX
(Causse Méjean)

Difficulty:	Easy – very slight height gain
Time:	3hrs
Height gain:	120m
Maps:	Cartes IGN 2640 OT Top 25 Gorges du Tarn 1:25,000
Start point:	Hamlet of Le Veygalier, Causse Méjean
Signposting:	None, although the open country makes it fairly easy to find your way – through the Chaos follow wooden posts with black arrows on a yellow background

This walk gives you the opportunity to really appreciate the scenery and vastness of these fascinating upland areas – the jumbled rocks of the limestone-riddled Chaos de Nîmes are geologically interesting. It was a pastor, Paul Amal, in 1910 who gave them the name Nîmes Le Vieux to distinguish them from another site (Chaos de Montpellier le Vieux) on the Causse Noir. The Michelin Guide states that during the prosecution of the Protestants in the 16th century, the Royalist troops saw the word 'Nîmes' and thought they had arrived at the town of the same name – the story does not fit the historical facts, however, as the name wasn't given to the area until 1910!

HOW TO GET THERE (FROM FLORAC)

From Florac take the D907, signposted St-Jean-du-Gard/Meyrueis. Where the road forks keep up right on the D907, signposted Meyruies, and continue until the village of Vebron (13km). At Vebron turn right before a café on a small road, signposted Villeneuve/Route du Causse, which winds up the side of the gorge to the Causse Méjean. Once on the Causse go through the hamlet of Villeneuve and follow the sign Col de Perjuret to Le Veygalier, which is a huddle of houses with a small museum explaining the geology of the Chaos de Nîmes Le Vieux. Continue to the end of the hamlet and park your car opposite the museum, which is part of an old house.

The museum is only open from Pentecost (mid-June) until September, or possibly at the whim of the caretakers! There is an entrance fee.

Directions

(1) Go back to a large modern barn on the road you arrived by, and turn up left on a jeep track with signs 'Propriété privé' and 'No through road'. Where this track bends round left to a house, go straight up on a narrower path.

(2) This quickly joins a jeep track coming in from the right by a large round man-made pond. Continue on the track, which curves left and goes through a barrier. You can see the village down on the left and the hamlet of L'Hom beyond. There are lots of rocks here, which are part of the complex called the Chaos de Nîmes.

   You are now walking through typical Causses scenery – low rolling hills stretching into infinity with occasional small fields of crops (mostly clover) ringed with fences. The slopes are strewn with rocks and low bushes – this is a wild and desolate country.

   Walk along the defined jeep track (direction north) through a long metal gate (20mins). You can see the track undulating through this austere scenery towards a fir forest on the horizon – it passes a small watering place, made out of black plastic, which is used for the flocks of sheep that inhabit this upland area. There is often a fence on the left and then later on to the right. Keep to the main track and ignore faint jeep tracks branching off. **Note:** on the IGN map this track appears to be straight but it has been re-routed so now there are a number of bends.

(3) Wind round to the left (35mins) just before reaching the rather sinister-looking pine forest, which has a fence bordering it – the scenery is not unlike the highlands of Scotland. Continue on the track to reach a large ploughed field and a gate (direction northwest).

(4) Careful – when you come to the fence round the large ploughed field (50mins), turn your back to it and make for the lowest point of the forest which sticks out in a sort of V-shape on the horizon with a low hill behind it – the direction is southwest (worth checking if you have a compass). There appears to be no path as you turn down over a rather rocky area, but on looking back you can see the faint outlines

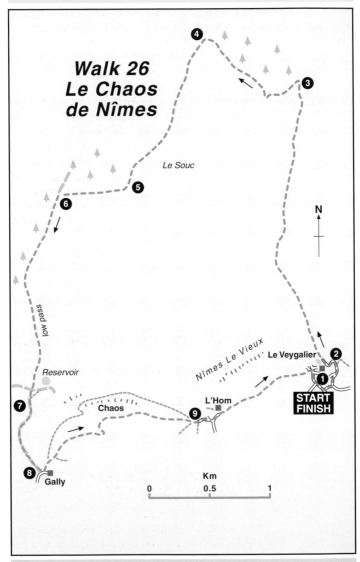

Walk 26
Le Chaos
de Nîmes

Le Souc

N

❹

❸

❺

❻

low pass

Reservoir

Nîmes Le Vieux

Le Veygalier

❷

❶

START
FINISH

❼

Chaos

L'Hom

❾

❽
Gally

Km

0   0.5   1

of one. Go to the right of a large fenced-off field, planted with clover, and then another field. After a slight rise you can see the large ruin of the Le Souc *bergerie* (sheepfold). Climb over a fence and continue. If you go over to look at this sheepfold you find that the buildings are still used for sheltering the sheep although the obvious dwelling has fallen into ruins.

(5) When you arrive at the point where the forest sticks out, turn right round the side of it (1hr 15mins) and up a slight slope dotted with boulders and bushes. There is no defined path, but keep the trees near on the right. There are lovely views of higher hills on the horizon, direction southeast.

(6) At the top you reach an overgrown jeep track, where you turn left (1hr 25mins). The grim firs are still on the right with a fence on the left and cultivated fields beyond in a shallow depression. The track bears left away from the forest and makes for a small fold in the slopes ahead, called a *collu*, meaning a low pass.

Look back here and appreciate the incredible scenery – a wide expanse of undulating grass-covered slopes sprinkled with rocks and bushes and ringed with the dark, brooding fir plantation.

(7) At the *collu*, which you cross by a barrier in a fence, continue on the track past some cultivated fields to a low crest. Then turn down right at a T-junction by a wooden post – up left goes to a reservoir. The jeep track is now well defined and curves right around masses of jumbled rocks, the start of the Chaos.

Reach the hamlet of Gally (2hrs 5mins), which is really one large farm with a big modern barn. There is a large information sign here marking the start of the official path through the Chaos de Nîmes Le Vieux, which is one of the most dramatic places to visit in the Causse Méjean.

(8) Bear up left past a shed marked 'Buvette' (café) and follow the yellow signs upwards and through a gate. There is now a clear path marked with posts through these weirdly shaped rocks – there is always a fence to the right. You come to another information board entitled 'L'abri' (shelter) which explains that this small area is sheltered from the severe climate of the Causse; there are also descriptions of the local trees and flowers. The path goes down into a little dell where the vegetation is quite luscious (long grass, oaks and nut

Chaos de Nîmes Le Vieux

trees) – what a welcome change to the severe upland scenery of the surrounding Causse.

Continue round the jagged limestone rocks, following the yellow signs until you go through a kissing gate. Walk on for a few metres and then turn left at a sign. This takes you past yet another information board entitled 'A L'Assaut' (attack) in front of a tall rock covered with different plants and lichen. The board explains the different plants that grow in the rock crevices. Continue down to a board with a shepherd's song on it (one side in French and the other side in patois). The path bends to the left and, just before it reaches the narrow road, there is a yellow sign indicating left, which you ignore. Go straight on by a board entitled 'Produits de Causse'.

Note – you are on a circular path from Gally, and if you wish to see more of the Chaos continue up to the left still following the posts and splashes. You will then have to re-walk part of the same path you have just completed.

(9) At the road (2hrs 40mins), where there is another board explaining the life of the flocks and shepherds, turn down right past a huge modern barn; at a T-junction bear left into the old hamlet of L'Hom. Go through the houses until you see a *gîte d'étape* on the left and continue onwards to a sign 'Tour de Causse Méjean' (red/yellow splashes). This is a grassy path to the village of Le Veygalier, which you can see ahead.

There are still lots of jumbled rocks to the left, and the old buildings of Le Veygalier blend in so completely that they are difficult to distinguish!

You are initially on a sunken path with bits of wall on both sides and then on an open path – there are two difficult stiles to cross. All along here are yellow signs with arrows in the opposite direction, as this is an official walk into the Chaos de Nîmes. Soon you reach the village and the parking (3hrs).

Walk 27

SENTIER DE FOURQUES

Difficulty:	Medium – no great height gain
Time:	3hrs 15mins
Height gain:	367m
Maps:	Cartes IGN 2640 OT Top 25 Gorges du Tarn 1:25,000
Start point:	Village of Fraissinet-de-Fourques
Signposting:	Adequate – two posts with the name of the walk, yellow splashes and red/white splashes on the GR.

A really delightful walk which enables you to enjoy a lovely wooded valley and the wild upland plains of the Causse, including the fascinating jumbled boulders of the Chaos de Nîmes, with a gradual climb to the top rather than a grinding slog! The views in all directions from the side of the Causse are breathtaking.

HOW TO GET THERE (FROM FLORAC)

Take the D907, direction St-Jean-du-Gard/Meyrueis, which winds along the Tarnon valley. Where the road forks keep up right on the D907, signposted Meyrueis, and continue to the village of Vanels. Stay on the principal road, which becomes the D996, still signposted Meyrueis. Continue to Fraissinet-de-Fourques (19 km from Florac).

DIRECTIONS

(1) Park in the centre of the village near the war memorial and the river. Walk over the river by the little bridge near the parking and go up left towards the church.

Before you get to the church turn up right between two houses (yellow splash) on a narrow paved track. Go left just before the track bends to the right before a big ruined house – (indications on rock). Go up the grassy track and continue straight past an iron cross (the path coming in from the right is where you will return at the end of the walk). Go down between two houses to meet a jeep track and continue straight. Ignore the first track off to the right.

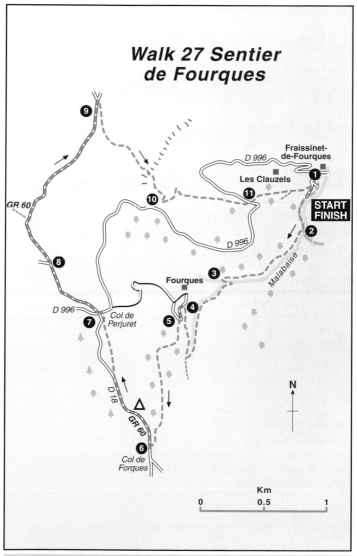

Walk 27 Sentier de Fourques

(2) Careful – look for yellow splashes indicating right where there is an old cross called Croix de Salgas (10mins). This path takes you into a delightful narrow leafy valley – the Malabaise stream flows down on the left and there are attractive little fields between you and the water. Later on you can hardly see it because of the numerous bushes and trees, but you can often hear birdsong. At a fork keep up right and ignore any other paths branching off.

(3) Cross the river at a little double bridge called the Pont du Coutel (20mins) – do not go immediately right, where there is a wooden sign with a wren indicating a special bird-walk around this valley, but bear left round a corner and walk upward with the stream now down on the right. It becomes very bushy and enclosed along this path.

Cross the river again (40mins) at a *gué* (ford) and reach a T-junction where you turn right and then climb out of the valley to a paved road just before the hamlet of Fourques.

(4) Turn left up the road and continue to the first hairpin bend.

(5) Take the jeep track to the left as the hairpin bend goes right (50mins), ignoring the yellow cross on a tree. You are now off the official walk with yellow arrows until you arrive at the Col de Perjuret. (If you want to omit this part of the walk continue on the road, which goes directly to the col.) The wide jeep track climbs fairly steeply up the tree-covered valley, through beech and oak wood. Ignore any paths branching off to the left. Eventually you come out of the woods and can hear the road up to the right before you reach it at the Col de Fourques (alt. 1040m) (1hr 20mins).

The view from here is magnificent – you can see the jagged cliffs of the Causse to the left, with Fourques ahead and Fraissinet-de-Fourques, with the lovely valley you have been through, in the foreground. Beyond are range after range of purplish hills. On the other side of the col is a different country – the high empty upland plains of the Causse, sprinkled with bushes and boulders rolling bare to the horizon and no habitation in sight.

(6) Turn right on the D18 road joining the GR60. Go off right at the beginning of a left-hand bend and continue on this grassy, sometimes undefined, path, which is a shortcut, until it reaches the Col de Perjuret (alt. 1028m) (1hr 35mins).

(7) At the col the D18 becomes the D996 and goes left to Meyrueis and right to Florac. Cross over and go straight up a narrow road sign-posted Nîmes Le Vieux. There is also a sign for Sentier de Fourques, which is encouraging. Although still on the GR60 you follow intermittent yellow splashes from now until the end of the walk.

(8) Follow the road up over the Causse and keep right at the first junction where there are yellow splashes (1hr 45mins). Further on the road bends round to the right where the GR60 goes off to the left. As you walk along the top of the Causse you can see lots of big boulders ahead (the Chaos de Nîmes – see Walk 26) and then the few buildings of the hamlet of l'Hom. The road arrives at a fork (left goes to l'Hom and right to Le Veygalier). There is also a yellow sign indicating Sentier de Fourques (2hrs 10mins).

(9) Double back right off the road as directed. There is no defined track so you have to follow the intermittent yellow splashes, which are on stones, very carefully. Keep the fence on your left until it veers off left and then go slightly left and then right on a rather undefined path round the edge of a depression and down by yellow splashes on the rocks. On a mound in front is a large cross (worth going up for the view); keeping this as a target, make your way over to a field down right (splash on the fence post). Before you get to the cross there is a path going into a narrow gully. This is irritatingly stony and eroded as it goes down the hillside, widening out further down. Ahead is a delightful green shoulder dotted with bushes, and you can clearly see the road and the village of Fraissinet-de-Fourques in the valley below.

(10) At the bottom of the slope go left by a round watering hole (2hrs 35mins). **Careful here** – go under telephone wires, through a kissing gate in a fence, and straight on until you see a path veering sharp right – there is a yellow splash but it is not easy to see. If you continue on, the path becomes a narrow sheep track so you know you have missed the turning!

The wide track goes diagonally down the side of the hillside, bordered with boxwood, to reach the D996 (3hrs).

(11) Cross the road and go down another past a lovely glade of big old chestnut trees and then down through woodland between old walls, crossing a jeep track and continuing towards the village – you can see the clock on the church steeple coming nearer and nearer. The path comes in by the iron cross seen at the start of the walk. Retrace your steps through the village to the car park (3hrs 15mins).

Walk 28

SENTIER DE POMPIDOU

Difficulty:	Easy – down to start with and then up to a pass, but the height gain is gradual. There is a shorter variant (see map) – not done by author.
Time:	3hrs + about 45mins to visit the Romanesque church of St-Flour-du-Pompidou
Height gain:	From 772m down to 510m and then up to 850m
Maps:	Cartes IGN 2740 ET Top 25 Corniche des Cevennes1:25,000
Start point:	Village of Le Pompidou on the D9
Signposting:	Little signposting. Some yellow splashes and yellow PR posts.

A delightful walk with lots of shade from chestnut trees on a hot day – the pass has one of the most extensive views of the Cevennes countryside and is a good illustration of the division of granite and limestone layers.

The village of Pompidou is situated on the Corniche des Cévennes ridge which separates two valleys (the Borgne and the Vallée Française). It is protected from the north winds by the limestone upland plain of the Can de L'Hospitalet. On the top of the austere Protestant church is a charming weathervane in the form of an angel.

If you do the longer walk, take time to visit the 12th-century chapel of St-Flour-du-Pompidou, formerly dedicated to the Cevenese Pope Urbain. It will take you about 45 minutes on foot (it goes down the hill so there is an uphill walk back) or a few minutes by car. Abandoned in 1746, the church was used to house hay, and chickens were still scratching around inside it until 1955. It has since then come under the auspices of the Cévennes National Park authorities and the départment of Lozère, who have done a tasteful restoration. Because of its incredible acoustics it is the venue for a number of concerts. Ursula Hirsch designed the modern stained-glass windows in 1973.

The young Tarn river on the third day of the Mont Lozère circuit

The bell tower at Auriac on the fourth day of the Mont Lozère circuit

Entering the hamlet of Les Combettes on the fifth day of the circuit

On the D983 between Florac and Pompidou is the hamlet of St-Laurent-de-Trèves, situated on a rocky outcrop with magnificent views. Dinosaur prints have been discovered here, dating back 200,000 years when the region was a limestone swamp. it is worth taking the short walk round the site to see the footprints, which are amazingly clear.

HOW TO GET THERE (FROM FLORAC)

From Florac take the D907, signposted St-Jean-du-Gard/Barre-des-Cévennes, the scenic road over the Corniche des Cévennes. After 5km bear left onto the D983. At the Col du Rey go straight on the D9 (the D983 goes off left to Barre-des-Cévennes). The road goes over the Can de L'Hospitalet (a small Causse) before winding down to the little village of Le Pompidou (23km from Florac). Park in the centre of the village.

DIRECTIONS

(1) Walk past a display panel, which shows interesting maps and information. Take the first signpost left on the D61 to Biasses and Ste-Croix-Vallée-Française.

(2) A few metres later turn right at a crossroads indicating Le Masaout which is the hamlet you are making for. Straight on is a yellow/red splash and a sign to Eglise de St-Flour 14th-century church (see above). This is the point to which you will return if you take the short cut.

Continue on this narrow road (D61), initially with a high wall to the right and beautiful open views and green fields to the left. It passes a disused tennis court, an old stone edifice and later a small cemetery hidden in the grass before reaching a junction (10mins).

(3) Turn left following the sign to Le Masaout. This is still a narrow paved road winding down through chestnut woods and bracken. Later on there are some open fields and orchards. Ignore two tracks going off left.

(4) When the road winds right, follow the sign left to Le Masaout where you are out of the trees and can already see the houses (35mins). The narrow tarmac road takes you through the tiny hamlet where there are lovely vegetable gardens to the right, with the main huddle of houses up left. There are also two tiny cemeteries. The track passes in front of a house and deteriorates to a grassy path on the top of an old terrace. Take a few minutes to explore this hamlet, which has a number of *gîtes* (holiday houses), which can be rented out.

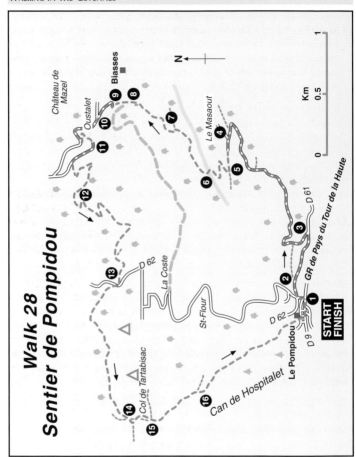

Walk 28
Sentier de Pompidou

(5) When the path splits, after a few minutes, go down right. The narrow track becomes wider as it descends into chestnut trees and then passes an old stone building. As it nears the bottom of the ravine you can hear the sound of water. Soon the path crosses the stream on an old grassy bridge, with the tall ruin of a mill on the other side. You have descended 262m from the start of the walk (55mins).

(6) Bear right (sign back to Le Masaout) along the side of an ivy-covered wall onto a flat man-made path above the stream down on the right. In early summer this path can be quite lush and overgrown. The vegetation has changed from chestnut trees to Mediterranean type bushes such as Kermesse oak, box, broom, holly and heather. There are occasional views of the chestnut forest on the slopes you have descended. Walk along until you reach a T-junction (1hr).

(7) Turn up left (there are wooden signs here with nothing on them!). Now you start to climb up and there is a remarkable bevy of about 50 beehives up on the left. Stay on the wide path as it flattens out again. You are walking through chestnut woods once more and starting to descend to reach an intersection (1hr 10mins).

(8) Continue straight down despite the yellow cross on a tree. **To shorten the walk, turn left here and follow the yellow splashes which will take you back via St-Coste and the church at St-Flour.** The track goes down towards the Vallée Française. On the slope on the other side of the valley you can see the Château de Mazel with four little towers. This was built in the 18th century and modelled on a château in the Loire.

(9) Ignore an overgrown path up left with a sign 'Propriété Privé' on a tree and follow the narrow road down. On a right hand hairpin there is an entrance flanked by two stone pillars to a large house, partly renovated. It has a sign saying 'Bar' over one door and a tumbledown tomb on the left with a rather curious new plaque in front which reads (English translation) 'Here lies Hélène Treille, née Souillet, in thanks to someone I have never known but who gave me Suzette' – one can interpret this in several ways! The road continues down round a left hairpin below the house to meet another road with an old stone temple opposite ('temple disinfecté' on the map) (1hr 20mins).

(10) Turn left on the road into the hamlet of Le Soulie passing a large property on the left. After a left hand bend and just before a ruin on a right hand bend, turn up left (no sign here) on a grassy track, wide at first and then narrow. This goes steeply up with a fence on the left and a large concrete water tank, to reach another renovated house called Oustalet (name on the front) on a narrow road. Turn down right on this pebbly road, which soon starts to gain height past more houses and vegetable gardens. Continue along until you see a jeep track going up left (1hr 30mins).

(11) Take this track as it winds up steadily through tall chestnut trees which become more stunted as you gain height; there are branches to left and right but stay on the main path. At a more prominent fork, ignore the branch down to the right which leads to a private house, barely visible through the trees, and continue uphill (1hr 40mins).

(12) The track goes in and out of the woodland and through dense fir trees. Keep winding up until it reaches the D62 road (2hrs 5mins).

(13) Cross the road and follow the track round the hillside. It soon comes out into the open where there is a beautiful view of the Vallée Française down to the right and a number of small villages, including Barre-des-Cévennes, up on the hillside. Continue in and out of woodland and soon you see ahead the ridge of the Col de Tartabisac where the slopes are covered with heather. The track goes round the side of a ravine, but before the end watch for a path up to the left (with no sign) leading to a low pass (2hrs 20mins).

(14) The narrow path goes directly to the top of the Tartabisac pass (alt. 845m), where there are spectacular views to the south. To the immediate left is a rocky granite hill, and on the right is the limestone plateau of the Can de l'Hospitalet – the granite and limestone regions meet at this pass. You can see Le Mazel down on the left in the woods and Le Pompidou up right on the ridge. In front are the blue misty mountains of the Cévennes rolling to the horizon and the top of Mont Aigoual. This is an ideal spot to stop for a picnic and appreciate the wonderful panorama! (2hrs 30mins).

(15) Follow the wide track to the right on a delightful balcony path. After 50m ignore a sign left to La Roquette and continue round the bottom of the Can de l'Hospitalet ridge. You can see the D9 going up and over a hill in front and the D61 in the valley. There is a wooded valley to the left with bouldery granite cliffs beyond. The path now has yellow PR posts and soon merges into a wide gravel road descending from the right. Follow this track down to an obvious fork (2hrs 40mins).

(16) Go up right at a PR post and continue on the main track past two small ruins on the right and between bushes, chestnut trees and fields beside old stone walls. In springtime there are masses of orchids at the side of the path. You drop into the village from above with the Mairie on the left. Turn down left past the church to where you parked your car (3hrs).

Walk 29

ROUND BARRE-DES-CEVENNES

Difficulty:	Easy walk with no great ups and downs
Time:	3hrs 30mins + about 1hr to look round Barre-des-Cévennes
Height gain:	About 100m
Maps:	Cartes IGN 2740 ET Top 25 Corniche des Cévennes 1:25,000
Start point:	Col du Rey (alt. 992m) – at the junction of roads D9 and D983
Signposting:	Very good – wooden posts with PR and black arrow, yellow splashes and red/white splashes of the GR

A truly delightful, easy walk through curiously gentle countryside, in contrast to the usual austere scenery of the Cevennes uplands. At times it resembles southern Scotland and even Devon! There is the added attraction of visiting one of the most authentic villages in the region. Barre-des-Cévennes is a typical example of villages-rues, with a single long main street, strategically built to be the economic hub of a wide area. They were gathering places for the transhumance (large flocks of sheep moving to upper pastures) and had a lively weekly market.

The Place de la Loue ('louer' meaning 'to rent'), the open area at the northwest entrance to the village, was the market place for hiring in spring and autumn. Hundreds of people gathered to obtain work as shepherds, chestnut gathers, domestic servants or casual labourers. These markets attracted thousands of people, some of whom came from as far away as the Var and Vaucluse regions.

Barre-des-Cévennes was one of the important centres of the Camisard movement (see Introduction, 'The War of the Camisards'), and on the wall of an old house by the present Protestant church is an inscription: 'Qui est de Dieu ait la parole de Dieu, 1608' ('Who believes in God hears the word of God, 1608').

How to get there (from Florac)

From Florac take the D907, signposted St-Jean-du-Gard/Barre-des-Cévennes. After 5km bear left onto the D983 and stay on this dramatic road along the Corniche des Cévennes for 11km. Turn off left at the Col du Rey on the D983, signposted Barre-des-Cévennes. At the col there are uninhabited buildings and a small parking area.

Directions

(1) From the col, start along the D983, where there is a yellow sign to La Can Noire (a *can* is a small upland plateau); open fields border the road. After a few minutes turn up left by a PR wooden post with a black arrow. This undulating sandy path goes through open pine forest with a number of glades and patches of heather. The Vallée Française is down on the right, with the D983 running through it to the village of Barre-des-Cévennes.

The path goes along the side of a fence with lovely fields beyond. Soon two large barns appear down on the right attached to an old farm (25mins). This is called Balmégouse on the IGN map and you can see the narrow road leading to it.

The path goes above the barns and undulates around the hill through pinewoods. Turn right at a junction as indicated by a yellow PR marker on a wooden post, and continue through tall pine trees to reach the road from Balmégouse (40 mins).

(2) Turn left, and then right after 30 metres onto a wide track with a PR marker. The track is flat at first and then starts to descend, with a clear view ahead of the rear of the characteristic cliff (or Barre) above Barre-des-Cévennes (45 mins).

(3) Continue down to reach the D20 road at a big oak tree (50 mins).

(4) Turn down right for a few metres and then left onto a smaller road. There is an old signpost to les Bastides and le Bouquet, but do not be put off by the yellow cross!

If you prefer to take a shorter route to Barre-des-Cévennes ignore the left turning and follow a wooden PR sign down the D20 road, cutting across a bend as indicated. At the junction with the D983 turn left into the village. To continue the walk go back to the junction with the D20 (and follow the route from no. 12 below).

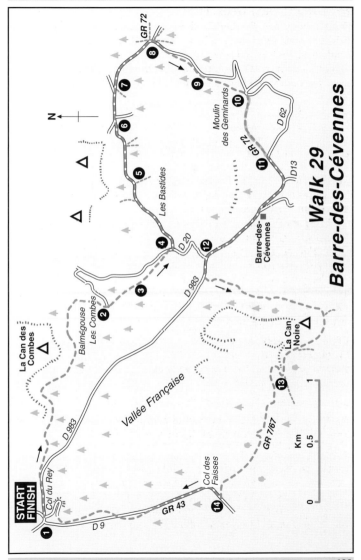

Walk 29
Barre-des-Cévennes

The narrow paved road goes up fairly steeply to a large renovated house, which used to be a farm (Les Bastides). It has a lovely view down the valley, ringed by gentle hills and two curious rocky escarpments, the same ones which dominate the village of Barre-des-Cévennes on the other side. The road curls round behind the house and then becomes a jeep track as it continues upwards past another house (1hr).

(5) Where the road becomes paved again by a sign to a house up left called Le Fromental (1hr 10mins), continue straight to a small col at 969m (no name on the IGN map). The views from this low pass are magnificent. Ignore a sign to the left to Le Bramedou.

(6) Continue along the road, ignoring a branch to the right marked 'Voie sans issue' ('no entry'), back into pleasant open pine forest.

(7) At a fork go straight – left goes to Le Bouquet, which is a *gîte* for horse riders (1hr 15mins).

(8) About 6mins later, at a large intersection called Les Quatre Chemins on the IGN map, ignore all left turns and continue on the road sign-posted 'Barre-des-Cévennes 2km'. You are now on the GR72, which has come in from the left.

(9) After another solitary house on the right called Balaurie, take a narrow path off to the right (1hr 30mins). There are red/white splashes on the pine trees as it goes down into an idyllic mini-valley with a tiny stream (could be dry depending on the time of year) and joins a jeep track coming in from the right. Continue down to a big building and a sign bearing 'Moulin des Geminards'. It is an interesting old mill in a lovely setting; in the grassy field in front are some solitary graves surrounded by iron fencing.

Behind the building is a high man-made waterfall tumbling into a large pool, the perfect spot for a refreshing dip as the water is so clear. There are many out-buildings, some in ruins, but part of the mill appears to be inhabited. On the bank behind are some original Cevenese beehives made out of hollowed-out chestnut-tree stumps with large flat stones as roofs.

(10) Cross the old stone bridge beyond the mill (1hr 40mins) and turn right by red/white splashes up a wide jeep track out of the valley. You can see now that the old mill is at the confluence of two small valleys. The track passes some barns to reach the D62 road at the top.

Barre-des-Cévennes

(11) Turn right on the road (no signposts) passing a *gîte d'étape* and a camping area. At a junction with the D13 (2hrs), keep straight on into Barre-des-Cévennes (left goes to Plan de Fontmore). Go down the long village street, which is narrow with no pavements.

At the end of the street, on the right, is an information booth, which offers a leaflet (also in English) with a numbered plan of the interesting places, including a 12th-century Romanesque church and an old fountain. It is worth taking one of these and following the numbers – the plan is somewhat confusing, but it does give you an overview of the history of this Cevenese village. It takes about an hour to fully explore.

At the end of the main street continue straight out of the village on the D983 passing a hotel/restaurant on the right and an iron cross left.

(12) Ignore the D20 going right to St-Julien-d'Arpaon and continue for 100m until you take a path off left with a number of yellow signs – 'GR

7/67', 'L'Hospitalet 5.5km – Aire de Côte 23km' (2hrs 15mins). This is a wide sandy balcony path, quite flat at first – there is a lovely view of the village on the left with the cliffs above and, further on, the modern houses of a *village de vacances*.

The track starts to go up gently round the base of La Can Noire, with green fields on all sides. It passes a radio mast on a promontory with sweeping views of smoky grey hills; the higher ridge of Mont Aigoual is clearly visible (2hrs 35mins).

(**13**) Here the track bends right (northwards). After 10mins go up to the right on a narrower track over a rather smart stile by a gate (PR sign). The stony track winds up through scattered pines and another gate in a clearing to the top, where there is a large flat meadow of waving grass (2hrs 45mins). Bear left across this wide meadow (look for red/white splashes on a stone) and then continue through heather, stunted bushes and pines. Watch out for red/white GR splashes and a PR sign when entering the woods. Continue to another barrier just before reaching the D9 road at the Col des Faisses (alt. 1018m).

(**14**) Go right just before the road where there is a wooden post with a yellow sign which takes you on a narrow path – you have now joined the GR43. At a fork a few minutes later go up to the left (there is a sign). The sandy path becomes somewhat undefined, with stunted bushes in all directions, but keep near the road on the left and the way becomes clearer. The wooden PR posts appear again. Fork right away from the road at a PR sign (3hrs 20mins). Soon you get your first view of the Tarn valley and the huge cliffs of the Causse Méjean. Continue until you see the parking just below at the Col du Rey (3hrs 30mins).

Walk 30

ROUND FONTMORT FOREST

Difficulty:	Moderate – no significant height gains but the walk is quite long
Time:	4hrs 20mins
Height gain:	370m
Maps:	Cartes IGN 2740 ET Top 25 Corniche des Cevennes 1:25,000
Start point:	Relais Stevenson Hotel/Restaurant off the N106, direction Cassagnas
Signposting:	Good – follow the red/white splashes of the different GR long-distance routes and white splashes where indicated

A lovely long walk, part of which is on the famous Stevenson Trail. It is good to do on a hot, sunny day as much of it is through the forest of Fontmore.

In Travels with a Donkey (written 1879) Stevenson mentions the village of Cassagnas as being 'a cluster of black roofs upon the hillside in this wild valley, among chestnut gardens, and looked upon in the clear air by many rocky peaks'.

He also mentions that in the rocky caves near the village was one of five Camisard arsenals (1702–04), where 'they laid up clothes and corn and arms against necessity, forged bayonets and sabres, and made themselves gunpowder with willow charcoal and saltpetre boiled in kettles. To the same caves, amid this multifarious industry, the sick and wounded were brought up to heal; and there were...secretly nursed by women of the neighbourhood.'

Stevenson goes on to say that the wildness of the region and the loyalty of the Cassagnas villagers was such that the Camisards could camp without sentries in the surrounding hills. The village was subsequently devastated in 1703 by Loyalist troops when 'four hundred and sixty villages and hamlets were, with fire and pickaxe, utterly subverted'.

How to get there (from Florac)

Take the N106, direction Alès, that winds along the beautiful Mimente valley. After a sign, left, to the hamlet of Les Crozes Hautes the road crosses a bridge and there is a sign to the right indicating Relais Stevenson Hotel/Restaurant on the D62. Take this narrow descending road for 1km and park just before the hotel (17km from Florac). This hotel has been built on the site of the former railway station, as evidenced by a round black water tank nearby with 'Gare de Cassagnas' written on it.

Directions

(1) Walk back down the road you arrived on (do not go over the bridge, which is where you come out on your return).

(2) Take the second turning down to the right underneath telephone wires and opposite a house (old station hotel) where there is a faint red/white GR splash (GR72). Along this track some wooden railway sleepers are still visible, as this used to be the railway line from Alès to Florac. The Mimente river is down on the right, but it is difficult to see because of the trees and bushes. Occasionally you catch a glimpse of attractive pools of dark water and rocks. Keep on the main track as you continue through mixed woodland of mainly oak, ash, larch, conifers and beech.

You are still on the railway track as it crosses the river, which is now far below on the left hidden in undergrowth. Continue through woodland and then out into the open across attractive grassy meadows and rocky areas with the occasional old stone building. On the other side of the valley is the village of Cassagnas, scattered rather haphazardly across the hill (see introductory paragraphs above). The track re-enters woodland and passes through old stone walls, presumably part of the former railway.

(3) Where the GR72 goes down left and across a small wooden bridge, follow the sign up to the right indicating Col des Laupies (do not go straight on) – at this point you leave the old railway line. Follow the white arrows and splashes until you reach the col (pass). You are now climbing fairly steeply round the hill on a sometimes rocky track through delightful beech forest, crossing rivulets and a stream.

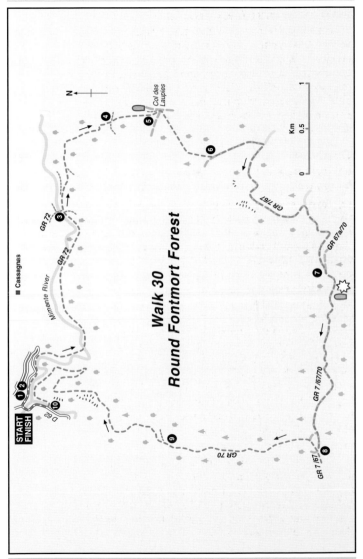

Walk 30
Round Fontmort Forest

■ Cassagnas

Mimente River

GR 72

GR 72

Col des
Laupies

GR 7/67

GR 67&70

GR 7 /67/70

GR 70

GR 7 /67

START
FINISH

D 62

N

Km
1
0.5
0

(4) When the path meets a wider track (1hr 5mins) turn up right, gaining height steadily. Later on ignore a track off to the left. There is a stream on the right, which you eventually cross. At a small clearing bear up left where there is a post and a white/blue splash on a large flat stone (1hr 20mins). The track goes by a charming wooden water trough by a rivulet. As you gain height there are tall Austrian pines and larches.

Just before a very large clearing, there is a menhir in the trees to the left. You have reached the Col de Laupies (alt. 1001m) which is an important intersection as there are seven different paths you can take from here (1hr 35mins)!

(5) Look for the red/white splashes of the GR7/GR67 to the right of the clearing, indicating Barre-des-Cévennes, and take this defined track.

(6) After 15 minutes it reaches another open area at a T-junction with a wide smooth jeep track. Go left, following the GR red/white splashes in a southerly direction off the side of the hill and round a big bend through scattered pine wood and then mixed woodland. Keep on the main track with the GR splashes. Just after a track branches right, cross a stream round a shallow indent in the contour of the slope (2hrs 15mins) and wind to the right.

(7) Keep straight on the track where the GR67A/GR70 comes in from the left (2hrs 30mins). You are now walking part of the famous Stevenson Trail. The forest thins and there are lovely open views. Shortly after there is a sign left indicating a menhir. Take this small path and after 50m you see a majestic stone with a curious marble sheen standing on its own – it must have been dragged here to honour a chieftain. Further on is a big flat rock and promontory which overlooks a wonderful view the of Gardon valley below. Beyond are the blue hills of the Cevennes National Park with the higher crest of Mont Aigoual on the horizon.

This is a perfect place for a picnic – there is an air of mystery and holiness about this spot which in former times was an ancient burial ground. There is a curious indentation in the ground surrounded by slabs of stone, which may well have served for some pagan ceremony.

Retrace your steps to the jeep track, which is covered with flat slabs of stone for a few hundred metres. The track goes down through sparse

The view from the Cassagnas-Fontmore forest over the Gardon valley

woodland bracken and heather and continues round the south side of the hillside, with views into the valley and the road snaking through it. Keep on the main jeep track, ignoring any lesser tracks coming in from right or left, passing the old stone wall of the Reservoir de Fontmort and an attractive wooden water trough (3hrs). There are now woods on both sides, so the views disappear.

(8) At the next intersection go sharp right (3hrs 5mins) on the GR70 (the GR67 and GR7 go off left). There is a signpost indicating 'Reservoir Boubeaux 2km' and 'Cassagnas 5km'. You are now heading north towards the valley you started from. A few minutes later, at another intersection, go straight on the middle track following a GR splash (cross on tree to right). The track starts to go down gently, flattens out across another open area and then goes down again through woodland.

(9) At a further fork go left (3hrs 30mins), still losing altitude. Ignore a path off to the right and continue on the main track, which comes out of the forest with broom bushes up on the left and fir trees to the right. There are lovely views as you continue downwards towards the valley and the Mimente river. The track goes back into dense pine forest and then through mixed woodland down the side of a ravine on the right where you can hear the river. Cross a small grassy bridge leading to a road (4hrs 10mins).

(10) Turn down right, signposted Cassagnas 3.5km, and continue past a little house on the left. On the other side is the river and a low weir in a rather charming grassy area; you feel you want to dash down to the shoreline and bathe your feet in the cool water. Cross the iron bridge just beyond to get back to the Bar/Restaurant Espace Stevenson (4hrs 20mins).

Walk 31

SENTIER DES CANS

Difficulty:	Medium, with a long steady climb at the start. Much of the walk is along the flat top of the Can de Tardonneche and on a paved road.
Time:	4hrs 30mins
Height gain:	517m
Maps:	Cartes IGN 2740 ET Top 25 Corniche des Cevennes 1:25,000
Start point:	Le Pont de Barre on the D907, direction St-Jean-du-Gard, 1.5km from the centre of Florac
Signposting:	Not always there when you need it – follow yellow splashes and occasional signposts. Note: For part of this walk (nos. 3, 4 and 5) the path indicated on the official IGN map is inaccurate.

A really delightful walk up and along a can. A can is a small limestone plateaux, of which there are a number in the area with specific names, such as Can de Tardonneche. They were separated from the larger upland plateaux of the Méjean and the Sauveterre by the river courses of the Tarn, le Tarnon and the Mimente. There are wonderful views in all directions and especially down into the narrow valley of the Mimente.

This walk is not recommended on a very hot day, as there is little shade at the top. The two hamlets of La Rovière and Ventajols are added attractions.

How to get there (from Florac)

Take the D907, signposted St-Jean-du-Gard, and go left at Le Pont de Barre (approximately 1.5km from the centre of Florac) over a small arched bridge. Continue for about 200m and you will see a minuscule parking area (room for two cars only) on the left. Above it there is a sign for the Sentier des Cans and GR43.

DIRECTIONS

(1) Follow yellow splashes on the narrow path up the hillside, bordered by bushes and a stone wall on the left-hand side. The path goes up medium steep along old terraces called *bancels* and then through a gate. These small terraced fields, bordered by stone walls, permitted maximum use of the land. There are lovely views into the Tarnon valley below, with the Tarnon river and D907 road winding through it. You pass an old house hidden in the trees to the left (5mins).

The path continues upwards along the top of an old terrace and then through oak woodland. After another gate, the vegetation becomes denser as you get nearer to the hamlet of La Rouvière, a mere huddle of houses, some of them in ruins (20mins).

(2) At the entrance to the village the GR43 goes down to the right (this is not indicated on the IGN map, so it must have been re-routed). However, stay on the Sentier des Cans, marked with yellow splashes going straight through the houses on a weedy tarmac road. The road continues round a left hairpin, so you can see the hamlet clearly down on your left. The tarmac finishes at the entrance to a house, which has a gorgeous view down the valley. The stony track continues upward, bearing right, and becomes rockier. The view opens out, and you can see the ridge with its dramatic chimney which dominates Florac, though the town is hidden in the fold of the hills.

The rocky track zigzags along the side of the hill, with a huge quarry on the other side of the valley. You climb steadily upwards, bearing away from the valley edge round the side of a ravine and crossing a landslide at the top (50mins).

(3) A few minutes later ignore a path to the left, and shortly after keep left at a fork; a few metres further on go right and then right again at the next fork – all very close and clearly marked with yellow splashes. Continue on the main path along the side of the valley. It makes a bend to the left, where you go through a fence (yellow splash on a post), and then crosses patches of shale; above is a rocky outcrop. There is a fence to the right on the way round the top of the hill.

(4) Here the path bears left with wooden posts with yellow splashes as you continue to the top, heading north to the top of the Can de Tardonnenche. A *can* is a small flat place (a larger area would be called a Causse) (1hr 10mins).

Walk 31
Sentier des Cans

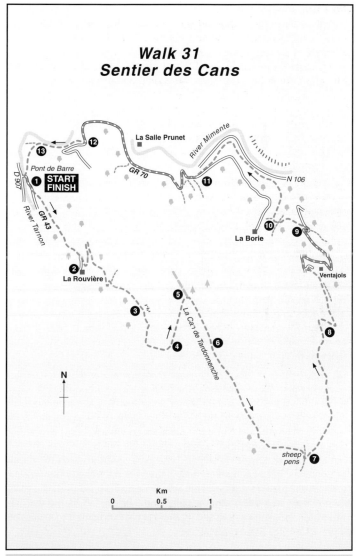

(5) From now on the wide track is flat as it goes through fields of wheat, cattle fodder and grassland – there are also herds of cattle. The track is not always well defined so follow the wooden posts carefully. When they cease you are parallel to a rough jeep track, which you join and go right (1hr 15mins). **There should be a yellow arrow here but when the author repeated the walk it had disappeared!**

(6) Go slightly upwards for about 5 minutes to a T-junction and another jeep track. Bear right following the yellow splash (ignore a small sign-post straight ahead indicating Florac par la Borie). The track continues through cultivated fields and pastureland, often with a fence to right or left to keep in the cattle. Keep straight and ignore a jeep track leading to an isolated farm on the right (1hr 30mins).

The track starts to go down gently, becoming slightly sunken with a fence to the left and blackberry bushes to the right (delicious to pick in September).

(7) At some sheep pens the track bears sharply left – this is not at all obvious from the yellow splashes (1hr 50mins)**.** Continue on, with fences both sides, and ignore a gate and smart stile to the right. The track goes through a gate and passes an attractive grove of maple trees – there are also hawthorn, broom and boxwood bushes. Over on the right is an old building and then a *bergerie* (sheep farm) with piles of old stones and shale (these could have been dumped while clearing the land for planting). Keep to the main track, which goes through another gate and follows a fence on the left. Further on there is a high fence to the left to keep out the deer.

(8) Where the high fence ends, leave the jeep track and turn left (clearly marked with yellow splashes). The high fence is still on the left as you go through another wooden barrier and there is a lower fence to the right. There is a magnificent view to the right of the Mimente valley with the river winding through. The track continues round by the high fence on the left and then zigzags round the hill before straightening out and descending fairly steeply on a grassy path towards the hamlet of Ventajols. Ignore a path coming in from the right and continue along the top of an ancient terrace into the village (2hrs 35mins). (From the map it looks as if this incoming path should be the GR70, but there are no red/white splashes. It could be that the GR has been re-routed since the map was printed, as the splashes do not appear until much later.)

Dolmen lookout point (Walk 30)

Follow the yellow splashes through the rather untidy huddle of houses – it is interesting to see the individual graves of people in private gardens and beside the road out of the village. The road becomes tarmac at the entrance to the village, where there is a good view left of the village of La Borie on the hillside.

(9) Follow the road down until the third hairpin bend and take a path off to the left – there is a yellow splash on a tree (2hrs 50mins). This narrow path traverses fairly steeply round the side of a hill through chestnut woods and open patches with lots of heather.

(10) Turn right at a T-junction with a jeep track (3hrs). After 5 minutes the track reaches a bend where you do not go straight but bear left (yellow splashes). This is where the red/white splashes of the GR70 finally appear and you are now on part of the trail taken by Robert Louis Stevenson in 1879 and still walked today by many tourists. A few minutes later the path crosses a stream round the top of a ravine (ignore a path up left) and then goes along the side of the ravine with the stream down on the right. Keep straight and ignore a track off to the left in a clearing (yellow and red/white crosses).

The track winds down (ignore two more branches to the right) and almost reaches the N106 in the Mimente valley. Beyond the road is the river and then the abrupt steep slopes of the red tinted cliffs on the other side.

The path then merges with a wider track coming in from the right and running parallel to the road. Keep straight on this wider track high above the road which goes round the hill and soon you can see the long high ridge above Florac. Down on the right is an old bridge over the river and you can see where the N106 crosses on a modern bridge – there is another narrow road above. The defined jeep track goes round the hill on a balcony through chestnut trees to meet a tarmac road coming down from the hamlet of La Borie (3hrs 40mins).

(11) Go right here and round a bend, where you can see the village of La Salle Prunet down on the right on the N106. Keep to the main paved road which seems never-ending, passing a water cistern on the right and then reaching the outskirts of the village at a large new house up on the left. On the other side of the valley is the Château de Montvaillant, which housed the dragoons of Louis XIV during the wars of the Camisards (1702–05).

(12) On joining another road, go left at a sign to Les Fouzes and a 'No through road' sign (there is also a yellow splash). Cross an old bridge where you go down to the right at a further sign to Les Fouzes and another no through road sign (4hrs 5mins). As you continue, the river, which at this stage has attractive deep rocky pools, is very near on the right. As you approach the D907 to St-Jean-du-Gard, the rock ridge on the other side seems very close.

(13) Just before another house, look for yellow splashes, red/white GR splashes and big blue arrows on the road (someone really wants you to go this way!) which direct you onto a narrow track up left (4hrs 15mins). You climb up through chestnut woods (ignore a path right with more blue arrows), round the last hump of a hill and then go down where you can see little Pont de Barre bridge ahead.

On reaching the bridge turn up left to the small parking area and the start of the walk (4hrs 30mins).

TOUR OF MONT LOZERE – 5 days

Difficulty:	Strenuous rather than difficult, as there are no great height gains. Days 3 and 4 are long, so it is best to start early.
Times:	Day 1: Florac to Mijavols (3hrs 45mins)
	Day 2: Mijavols to Les Bastides (4hrs 45mins)
	Day 3: Les Bastides to Le Bleymard (6hrs 20mins)
	Day 4: Le Bleymard to Les Laubies or La Fage (6hrs or 6hrs 15mins)
	Day 5: Les Laubies or La Fage to Florac (4hrs 15mins/4hrs)
Maps:	Cartes IGN 2739 OT Top 25 Mont Lozère 1:25,000; Cartes IGN 2740 OT Top 25 Corniche des Cévennes 1:25,000
	(most of the route is covered by the Mont Lozère map, but short parts of the walk on Day 1 are covered by the second map)
Start point:	Florac – middle of town
	Good, though not always obvious – follow the red/white splashes of the GR68 and GR7

Mont Lozère is a huge granite upland area covered with tough grass, stunted bushes and, in some places, big boulders. There are also a number of fir plantations. Although there are no high peaks to climb or tricky rocky summits to negotiate, this is nevertheless a strenuous five-day walk across wild countryside where there are few villages and even fewer people. Don't count on stumbling on many comforting wayside inns or cafés! This area could be mistaken for the highlands of Scotland, such is the similarity of the landscape!

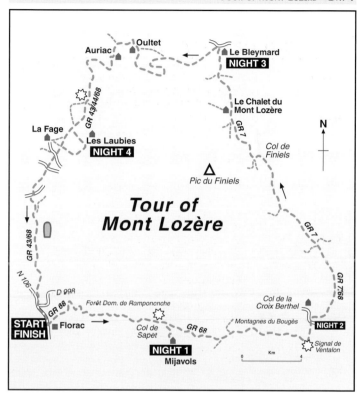

DAY ONE: FLORAC TO MIJAVOLS

Time:	3hrs 45mins
Height gain:	534m to Col de Sapet then 180m down to Mijavols
Overnight stop:	gîte at Mijavols

(1) Walk out of Florac northwards on the D316, direction Mende, over the Tarn at the Pont de la Bessède to reach the N105. Cross over the road and by a stone wall you will see the red/white splash of the GR68 Tour de Mont Lozère path and a sign Col de Sapet. Take this path,

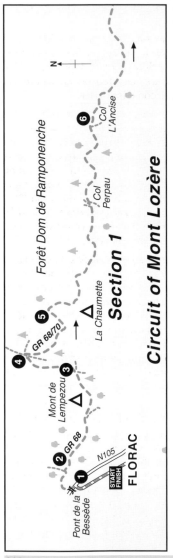

Forêt Dom de Ramponenche

Col
L'Ancise

Col
Perpau

Section 1

La Chaumette

GR 68/70

Mont de
Lempezou

GR 68

N105

START
FINISH

FLORAC

Pont de la
Bessède

Circuit of Mont Lozère

which climbs up quite steeply (at a fork keep right on the main path) to reach a jeep track (20mins).

(2) Turn right on the main track and continue upwards through pine and chestnut trees. After a few minutes go up left following GR splashes – the jeep track continues to a water tower. The path goes into the open and you get your first view of Florac down on the right.

At a T-junction go up right (splashes here) and a few minutes later through a barrier. Look for the red/white splashes carefully as they are few and far between (there are also yellow and blue splashes). Keep up left at a fork and then go up left above a ruin (50mins).

Look back and you get a good view of the gorge cliffs and the flat summit of the Méjean Causse. Continue upwards over bare hillside dotted with bushes – the path becomes less steep as you bear right northwards round the southern flank of the Lempezou. The path crosses another barrier and enters woodland, past a small hut, to reach a jeep track at the Col de Lempezou (1hr 5mins).

(3) Turn up left following a sign for GR68 Le Sapet and continue round the hill going slightly downwards – up to the left you can see a long straight ridge with the twin humps of the Mamelons de Puech and in the valley, right, the village of Bédouès. The track reaches a big intersection 838m (1hr 20mins).

(4) Turn right on the main jeep track following the GR68 – this is now also the GR70, which comes up from the village of Bédouès and is part of the famous Stevenson Trail until the Col de la Planette. The track goes round the side of a wide tree-covered ravine where the Tarn valley and the village of Cocurès come into view.

(5) Turn right at a further intersection at the end of the ravine (1hr 30mins) indicating straight 'Les Bastides 20km/Pont-de-Montvert 19km/Mijavols 8km', which is encouraging. The wide jeep track continues round the side of La Chaumette (alt. 1031m) and another wide ravine with continuing views left of the Tarn valley. It goes by the reservoir de la Chaumette and through a denser patch of pine forest, where there is a small hut, to reach another intersection at the Col de Perpau (2hrs 10mins). Keep on the main track upwards, ignoring other paths branching off as you wind around a number of smaller tree-covered ravines, traversing the large Forêt Dominiale de Ramponenche.

(6) Just after a track going up right you cross the Col de L'Ancise (2hrs 30mins) though there is no indication – you can see the hamlets of Rampon and Saliège nestling on the slopes below. The track continues through beech and pine and then through broom bushes onto open slopes curling round the left of a small hill. You can see the château of Grizac ahead on the other side of the valley. The track goes round the north side of Le Sapet (alt. 1114m) and reaches the Col de Sapet (alt. 1080m), where the D20 road crosses, linking St-Julien-d'Arpaon to Le Pont-de-Montvert. There are two menhirs here and lovely views in all directions (3hrs 10mins).

(7) Leaving the GR go down right, direction Mijavols 3km (eastwards) – you can see the path curling down the hillside ahead and the hamlet of Pierrefort on a hump down to the right but you cannot see Mijavols until you reach it round a corner. The track descends round a gully at the head of which there is an attractive gathering of beeches and a stream. Avoid a path up left signposted La Bastide (this is a bridle path and an alternative route back up on Day 2, though you would then miss the attractive balcony path). Continue downwards to the hamlet – the *gîte d'étape* is the first building on the right (clearly marked), and if you go round to the front and push hard the door will open (3hrs 45mins).

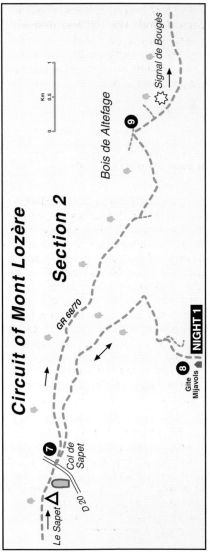

To find the owner, Mme Chaptal, go down to the farm, which you can't miss (there is a sign saying 'Acueil gîte'). This is where you will also eat later.

Gîte d'étape, Mijavols, 48400 Florac (20 places). Mme Chaptal, tel. 04 66 45 09 04. Dinner, bed and breakfast 26 euros – this includes a roaring fire, which is a blessing if your clothes are wet. If it is very cold ask Mme Chaptal to put on the central heating! She will also provide sheets at no extra cost.

Mijavols is one of the few surviving working villages and is basically one large farm and a small cluster of houses. There are 16 people who live there all the year round. If you are the only people in the gîte you will eat 'en famille' in the disorganised old farm with Mr and Mrs Chaptal and their two adopted African children. If you can speak French they will tell you about their life raising sheep, agricultural conditions in the Cevennes and the history of the region. An interesting snippet of

*information is that there is a dearth of women and lots of elderly
lonely farmers – during the Second World War this area sheltered
many refugees and was also one of the centres of the Maquis (resistance movement). The women preferred to marry them and leave
rather than endure the hard life of a farmer's wife! This caused a
population crisis, which has not yet been reversed.*

Day Two: Mijavols to Les Bastides

Time:	4hrs 45mins
Terrain:	undulating
Height gain:	236m up (short stiff climb to Mont Ventalon) and then down 279m to Les Bastides
Overnight stop:	Auberge des Bastides

(8) From Mijavols retrace your steps to the Col de Sapet (40mins).

At the col turn up right following the GR68 splashes and the sign
for Col de Berthel 14km/La Bastide 15km. This is a narrow sandy/
pebbly balcony path, going through Scottish-type scenery with slopes
of heather, broom, scattered firs and bushes. It goes steadily upwards
to a low pass at 700m (1hr) and continues on the northern side round
a gully through delightful beech forest – you can hear the odd car as
the D20 is quite near at this point. The path goes up and out onto a
grassy slope, where you can see a cairn of stones ahead on the lower
slopes of the Signal de Bougès. You pass a small wooden hut, called
the Chalet de Loirs, which used to serve as a refuge for the shepherds
but is now all boarded up (1hr 15mins).

Soon after the hut there is a sign to the right, 'Mijavols 3.5km' (this
is the bridle path coming in). Continue upwards along the ridge with
beech wood left, which you enter again to reach an intersection in a
clearing (1hr 35mins).

(9) Go up right where there is a GR sign on a tree (not straight on,
marked as a horse trail). There is a medium steep climb on a wide track
for some time with a wood on the left, passing four cairns. The first
cairn, off to the right, is the one seen earlier and is a wonderful viewpoint. The third large one with a nearby borne is the Signal de Bougès
(alt. 1421m) (1hr 55mins), with the fourth one just beyond to the right.

From here the path drops slightly onto a flat ridge with a fence to
the left shutting in the Bois de Altefage. There are extensive views of

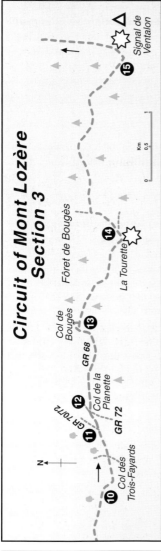

Circuit of Mont Lozère Section 3

mountain ridges on both sides. To the north the landscape looks wilder, harsher and more inhospitable than the gentler tree-covered scenery to the south.

The track starts to go up again as it enters a rather grim forest to reach a clearing where there are a number of cairns.

(10) Bear left going steeply down to reach a crossroads in another clearing, which is the Col des Trois-Fayards (2hrs 15mins).

There are notices along here asking walkers to be quiet and listen for the sound of the Grand Tetras (capercaillie), which has been recently introduced into the area with great difficulty.

(11) Go down left on the GR68, direction east (the splashes are rather confusing and the map is not clear), through scattered pine forest where there is a hut with a small TV aerial on the left, to arrive at a crossroads with a menhir and signposts.

There is a monument here to the memory of Raymond Senn, a native of Alsace who loved the area and created the Tour du Mont Lozère.

Here the GR72 goes north to the Pont de Monvert. The GR70, which met the GR68 at the Col de Lempezou, now joins the GR72 northwards. Follow the GR68 signs and a few minutes later you reach

Signal de Bougès

the Col de la Planette (alt. 1292m), where the GR72 goes hard back right (southwards).

(12) Do not take the track ahead straight up the hill but continue on the main wide jeep track (GR68) slightly to the right. Continue gently down through pleasant mixed forest until the track turns hard left and then merges with another track coming up from the right. Soon after bear right at a junction (GR signs on a tree). After 200m go right (down) at a T-junction – left goes up to the nearby Col de Bougès (2hrs 45mins).

(13) Continue down through pleasant but rather monotonous forest until the road bends right, levelling off and then merging with a track coming up from the right (signposted 'DFCI Rochecourbe') in a clearing (3hrs). Very soon you get a good view of the enormous forest of Bougès with a number of jeep tracks crossing it.

In this forest we saw an unusual number of parked cars – later we found out that this was the mushroom season, and locals and non-locals were collecting, as this area is well known for its mushrooms. Later, in front of the Auberge des Bastides, we saw a parked van and a queue of people with their baskets selling what they had gathered. Probably they were then winged away to the best restaurants in the world – hopefully there were enough left over for the local people, as we were rather disappointed that we got none for our dinner!

The path undulates through the forest, which is rather gloomy at this point, and as it rounds a corner there is a look-out point, La Tourette, with a lovely view southwards (3hrs 10mins).

(14) A few minutes later go up left and through a wooden barrier ('DFCI La Draille') where there are GR markings, and do not go straight to the Col de Jalcreste. Continue on the main path and at a fork go right, signposted 'Signal de Ventalon' (left is signposted 'DFCI Retenue de le Goudesche/Les Bastides'), climbing steeply to the summit, which you can see ahead with a TV aerial on it. **Note** – about 15 minutes before the summit there is a left fork, which may be a welcome shortcut for those too exhausted to do the last steep climb up and down – however, you will also miss the extended views at the top!

From the Signal de Ventalon (alt. 1350m) (4hrs) there are views in all directions of magnificent forest-covered hills with hardly a house in sight. There is a little building here, and also three maps giving the location, names and altitudes of the peaks to the north, south, east and west. This crest also stands at the division of the waters – all waters flowing north go to the Atlantic, and those flowing south go to the Mediterranean.

(15) Take the narrow rocky path hard back to the left that goes steeply down to a junction where the GR7 comes in from the right. Continue left, undulating down the long wide slope with forest either side. Go past a junction left, where the shortcut joins, and then right where the GR du Pays branches off. The track becomes steeper and stonier, past a road loop on the left and finally down to the main road at the La Croix de Berthel, a crossroads where the D35 and D998 meet (4hrs 30mins).

(16) Take the D998 straight, signposted Pont de Montfert. You are now off the GR68, which goes right. Walk along the road in the valley, where there are lovely green fields with a stream running through. The road rounds a corner over a bridge and on the right is the *auberge* (4hrs 45mins).

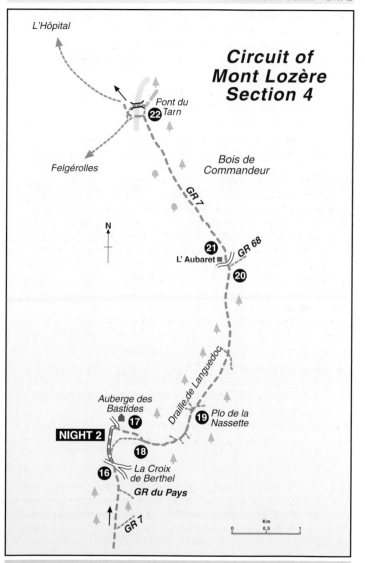

L'Hôpital

Pont du Tarn
22

Circuit of
Mont Lozère
Section 4

Bois de Commandeur

Felgérolles

GR 7

N

21
L' Aubaret
GR 68

20

Draille de Languedoc

Auberge des Bastides
17

NIGHT 2

18

19
Plo de la Nassette

16
La Croix de Berthel

GR du Pays

GR 7

Km
0   0.5   1

Auberge des Bastides, gîte d'étape 20 places, tel. 04 66 45 81 25, Mme Dubois. Dinner, bed and breakfast 26 euros (gîte). 31 euros pp. double room with washbasin only.

The auberge was shut so it was dinner in the bar, which was much more fun. The mushroom gatherers came in for a snifter, and when not serving drinks the owner was feeding the baby and supervising two little girls. Later on a hunter arrived and gave a dramatic description, along with appropriate noises and getting to his knees, of being caught between two fighting stags and not knowing what to do, which generated much volatile discussion!

DAY THREE: LES BASTIDES TO LE BLEYMARD

Time:	6hrs 20mins
Height gain:	470m up to the Col de Finiels and 473m down to Le Bleymard
Overnight stop:	Hôtel La Remise, Le Bleymard

(17) Go back up the road, and as you round the corner by the bridge turn to the left through a wooden gate by a sign 'Sentier de Rouvières'. There are a *gîte equestre* and sheep sheds up left beyond the stream and a fence to the right. You soon enter tall pinewoods where you follow bird signs up the main path to a defined jeep track (10mins), which is the Draille de Languedoc (long-distance sheep track).

(18) Turn left and continue along the track through sparse mixed forest and glades (Le Fôret de Rouvieres) to reach an intersection. Go straight on and continue upwards to the Plo de la Nassette (alt. 1151m). At signposts go right ('DFCI Retenue de Rientort') then up left off the jeep track where there are GR splashes. This is a steep wide slope, cut like a swathe through the trees. At the top, where there is a low cairn, all you can see is forest in all directions and a low ridge in front (40mins).

(19) The track goes down gently to more signposts in a big forest clearing.

Continue straight up again to reach open heathland with heather and broom bushes. You are now out of the forest proper, walking through boulders towards the hamlet of l'Aubaret (alt. 1250m), which is essentially one large farm. There are attractive open fields round the cluster of houses, which you enter at an idyllic little bridge over the clear, shallow l'Alignon stream to reach the road (1hr 5mins).

(20) Just before the road, the GR68 that you have been following since the start of the walk goes off to the right, and you now join the GR7, signposted 'Pont de Tarn/Le Bleymard 6hrs'. Cross the road and go up the side of a big old house which has been renovated (GR splashes) – round the back of the building is a large square of flagstones surrounded by a wall which is where the farmers used to thresh the corn.

Don't go to the left beside a wall behind the house but up right (north-wards) into a big bouldery slope ('chaos' in French), where you have to watch carefully for the GR splashes and cairns or miss your way – you cross and re-cross a little stream which could be dry in high summer.

(21) Bearing slightly left you reach the top and a defined path, where you bear right. Look back here for an exceptional view of the rolling Cevenese hills. On the left you can even see the top of the Gorges du Tarn and the Causse Méjean. The path continues through boulders, heather and stunted firs, and over a few streams, cutting a wide swathe through the Bois du Commandeur to arrive at a big clearing at the Pont du Tarn (alt. 1326m) (1hr 55mins).

(22) Go right (left is Felgérolles) on a wide track which reaches more signposts. Follow the sign left to 'Chalet de Mont Lozère GR7' and cross over the Tarn bridge. This is where this well-known river becomes more than just a stream – it is wide and shallow with an incredible clarity. The path goes left immediately after the bridge, then loops away from the river becoming wider, direction northwest, through open moorland consisting of heather, broom and rocks. On both sides there are ranges of stony hillsides, the Roc de la Tarabelle and La Baume du Monsieur on the left, and Le Cap Francais (1400m) ahead to the right. There are old marker stones all the way along this path, flanked by fences, because you are still on the Draille du Languedoc – there is a huge patch of flat moor land on the left which is named Cham Redon (*cham* is a local name for a low, flat area which can often be boggy), presumably good for grazing sheep.

(23) Go off to the left (GR splashes), which is just a shortcut to reach the unpaved road and soon becomes a sunken, narrow overgrown path between broom bushes with a stone wall on the left. At the road turn left towards the remote hamlet of l'Hôpital (right goes to a parking and information centre at the Mas Camargue, which is the start of a short circular 'Sentier Decouverte' walk).

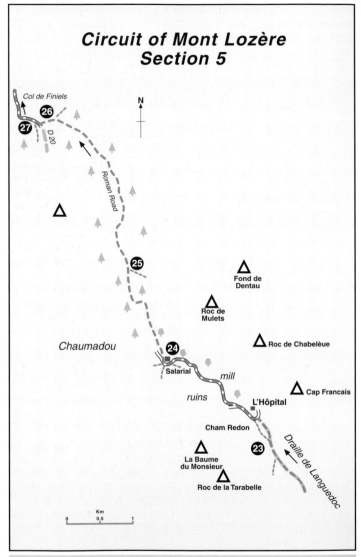

Circuit of Mont Lozère
Section 5

Col de Finiels

N

26

27

D 20

Roman Road

25

Chaumadou

Fond de
Dentau

Roc de
Mulets

Roc de Chabelèue

24

Salarial

mill

ruins

Cap Francais

L'Hôpital

Cham Redon

23

La Baume
du Monsieur

Roc de la Tarabelle

Draille de Languedoc

Km
0   0,5   1

The GR goes below the hamlet and reaches a T-junction (2hrs 30mins). Go up right, signposted 'Chalet de Mont Lozère 11km GR7' (left goes to Le Pont-de-Montvert).

It is worth taking a few minutes to have a look round l'Hôpital, which is a cluster of attractive old houses, most of them shuttered. It is here that the knights (chevaliers) of the order of Saint-Jean-de-Jerusalem had their headquarters. They owned most of the land in the Lozère region until 1795, and stones with a carved Maltese cross, which was the emblem of the order, marked their boundaries. Some of these stones can still be seen, especially on the Pic du Finiels.

Continue past a small disused mill on the right, with a dilapidated thatched roof and a stream rushing through the building to disappear under the road. There are more ruins down on the left, so L'Hôpital clearly used to be much bigger. You can see the unsurfaced road on the left, which goes to Le Pont-de-Montvert. Straight ahead is a curious formation of rocks. Up to the right is the rocky summit of the Roc de Chambelève and, beyond, the Roc des Mulets. The road goes through a small beech forest. Further on there is a sign right indicating Croix de Malte 50m (one of the boundary stones mentioned above). The road gets flatter and winds along to the tiny hamlet of Salarial (2hrs 50mins), which consists of only two houses, but also has a small cemetery with the graves of the Servière family (some of them quite recent).

This family were probably (and maybe still are) the only people who live here – what a wonderful thing to have your own private family cemetery in a place far from the madding crowd!

(24) At Salarial you go off the road to the right (signposted 'Chalet de Mont Lozère'). This is a narrow path going up the side of a gully with the tree-covered Chaumadou left and the rocky Roc des Mulets to the right. Look for the GR splashes carefully. You go over a stile, and at a fork go either way (they meet up) through some woodland and over rocks to the head of the gully. Here you cross small rivulets and an embankment of boulders – there is a lovely view southwards over sweeping, bare moor land with mountains beyond (3hrs 15mins). Continue upwards through stunted woodland with the stream on the right – there is a good view, right, of the jumbled rocky summit of the Roc des Mulets.

(25) Turn left at the next T-junction (3hrs 30mins) as the path levels out, skirting the forest and becoming straight and wider with stunted woodland each side – this is an old Roman road and is still the Draille de Languedoc. Where the forest thins there are lovely extended views. You gently gain some height as the track goes past an old Roman reservoir on the right to reach a sign for Piste du Col, where there is also a wooden barrier across

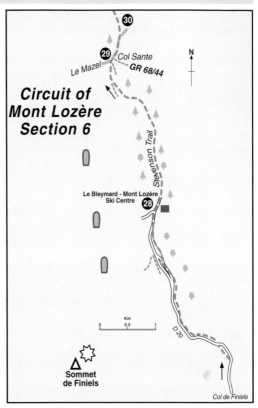

the road. You are now in an area of cross-country skiing and you can see the bare slopes of the Mont du Finiels (the highest part of the Mont Lozère) on the left.

(26) Turn left at a further T-junction onto a jeep track, which meets the road at the Col de Finiels (alt. 1541m). You meet civilisation again, as there are often cars at this junction, which is near the nearest point to the Mont Lozère (4hrs 10mins).

(27) Turn right following the sign 'Chalet de Mont Lozère 4km' and walk along the road for about 10 minutes (there is a stone along here with a Maltese cross on it) – the path then goes off left and alongside the asphalt to cross it again and continue on the other side. There is now a long gradual descent on a narrow grassy path with the road never far away. You can soon see the spread-out ski resort of Le Chalet de Mont Lozère ahead and, far right, the hamlet of Lozeret. You pass underneath a ski lift by fences and reach the old road, where you turn right and continue down into the resort (5hrs 5mins) – the main road comes in on the left.

(28) Walk right through this conglomeration of modern buildings on a wide road and look for the signs of the GR where the road comes to an abrupt end by a large building on the right, UCPA (a sort of youth centre). You are now on the Stevenson Trail, where he came south from Le Bleymard to go over the Pic du Finiels – it must have been much prettier then, with no ugly buildings and ski lifts! This is a wide descending jeep track, which forks left in a wide clearing (5hrs 15mins), with lovely open views. A few minutes later go straight on, ignoring two left forks. The track descends steeply through woodland for about 10 minutes and then becomes gentler for a while.

The path becomes narrower as it steepens again towards the Col Sante at an intersection and the start of cultivated fields (5hrs 50mins). Two paths come in from the right, one the GR44/68, and the road left goes to Le Mazel.

(29) Continue straight, following sign 'Le Bleymard 2km' on a wide jeep track through open country – if you look back you can appreciate the steep descent you made through the woods.

(30) Where the path forks a few minutes later go left (there is a red/white GR cross ahead). Soon you reach the outskirts of Le Bleymard, which is a long straggly village with a few small housing estates and modern buildings. The path goes along the side of the hill on a wide grassy path, and Le Bleymard is down to the left in a valley. You eventually reach the road, which bears left and takes you all the way into the village (6hrs 10mins). Bear right at the bottom, by a statue of Henri Rouvière (1875–1952, a local man who became an anatomist and Professor at the Faculté de Médecine in Paris), and walk down to a bridge over the Lot river. Continue to a crossroads (the D901 crosses the D20) and the hotel is in front (6hrs 20mins).

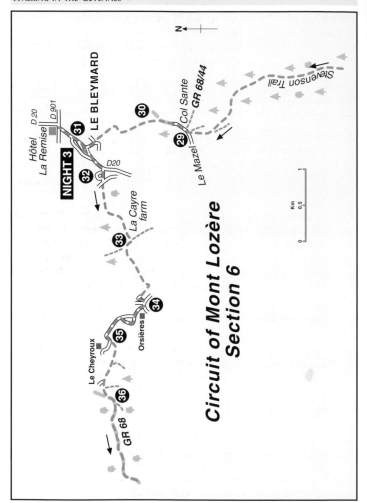

Hôtel La Remise, 48190 Le Bleymard. Mme Haubenque, tel. 04 66 48 65 80. Dinner, bed and breakfast – 190FF. Room with bath – 215FF.

DAY FOUR: LE BLEYMARD TO LES LAUBIES OR LA FAGE

Time:	6hrs/6hrs 15mins
Height gain:	368m up and 224m down to La Fage
Overnight stop:	Auberge des Laubies or Gîte d'étape La Fage

(31) Go back into the village and take the middle of three roads (the one by the monument) and walk through the main street where there are some little shops. Go past the post office, ignoring the road immediately left, and continue to the D20 which goes over a bridge bearing left. Shortly after turn up right on a narrow road (there is a GR splash further up and a sign for 'Sentier de Chantduc 2hrs', with an owl symbol, which indicates a local walk). This road goes to a *village de vacances*, a conglomeration of small holiday houses (10mins).

(32) Continue round the road and then take a grassy path up right and, following the owl signs, immediately left up a steep narrow stony path. Cross a small road and continue up until the path flattens and becomes very overgrown through long grass. It sinks between bushes and a fence and low stone wall as you continue gaining height. Keep straight until you arrive at the flat top of the hill (35mins).

(33) The path then widens into a grassy jeep track with fences each side and descends to a paved intersection where there are GR splashes (40mins). Turn right, passing by the farm of Le Cayre and through gates made out of cartwheels. Continue past a beautifully restored house on the right; keep left of the buildings, down a leafy lane.

At a fork go right (GR splashes) and keep to the main path, crossing a jeep track and descending to the pretty little village of Orsières (55mins) nestling in a valley. You are off the harsh, windswept plateau of the Lozère; the landscape is softer here and looks curiously English.

(34) Go left in the village, then right over the bridge and right again at a fork (there is an *auberge* on the left, which looks inviting). The road goes up towards the hamlet of Mas. Go left by a house to pass a farm and continue right on the road to reach a beautifully restored old church with a huge bell (like most French churches it was shut). Pass to the left of the church and then onto a track up left (GR splashes), which is just a shortcut off the road (1hr 10mins). When you rejoin the road go up to the left and you can soon see the hamlet of Le Cheyroux over on the right.

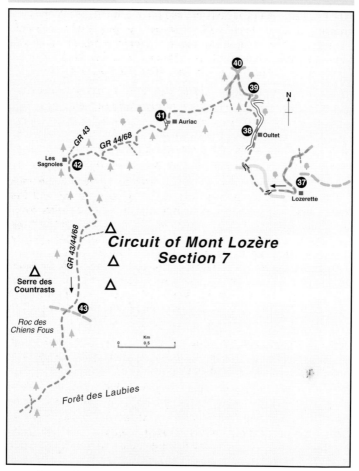

Circuit of Mont Lozère
Section 7

(35) The road bends left and then right. Just where it bends right go straight on a wide path where there is a cross on a tall stone, going upwards through cultivated fields.

(36) Continue up and over a brow, past a track to the left, to reach an unpaved crossroads where you can see the village of Oultet ahead (1hr

30mins). Turn left (if you go right there is a menhir at 100m). The track goes in and out of a large beech forest – ignore any paths branching off.

There is now a big detour round a hairpin bend, down the side of a valley to reach Lozerette (1hr 55mins), and then back round the other side to Oultet, which appeared so near at the start!

Lozerette is one of those sad little deserted hamlets one discovers so often in this region – a cluster of ruined houses left to die. We noticed that many of the stone barns still carry notices saying they were condemned because of contamination by tuberculosis, and you will see this notice in many of the old villages in the area. Where there are still working farms, new barns have been constructed.

(37) Going out of the hamlet, bear down to the right into an attractive wooden valley – at first the path goes through open slopes and then enters woodland down to the valley bottom to cross the Oultet stream on a primitive slatted bridge. Continue along the other side through trees, glades and small fields, past a small ruin to the left and cross the river again on another wooden bridge (2hrs 15mins).

The path crosses little rivulets as it starts to climb out of the valley and levels out before coming to a paved road where you go right to the hamlet of Oultet, another cluster of old houses, some of which are being tastefully renovated. It also has a picturesque bell tower, which is an feature of many of these remote Lozère villages.

(38) On leaving the village go up to the left by a concrete water trough (2hrs 35mins) on a jeep track – there is a road through the valley down on the right and woods up on the left.

(39) At a crossroads go up round a hairpin to the left. On the horizon to the right you can see the towers of a ruined castle dominating the village of St-Julien-du-Tournel. As you gain height there are extensive views (the tree-covered slope of La Felgère is up left). Go left at a junction by a menhir into woodland (GR sign) and continue to a junction with signposts (3hrs).

(40) Go left following the signs 'GR44/GR68' and 'Auriac, La Fage l2km'. The path goes up through forest – at a fork go up right off the main jeep track and continue to another fork at the top of the hill. Go right (GR splash hidden here) where the path flattens somewhat by a large field to the left and then starts to descend round the side of

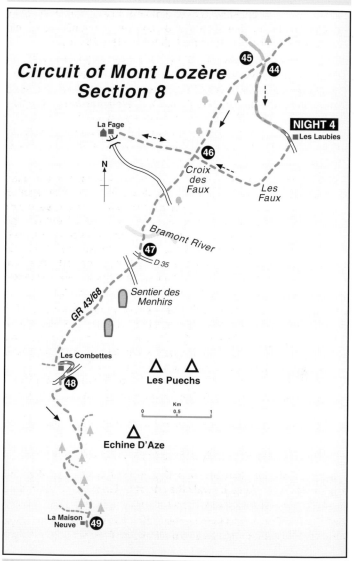

*Circuit of Mont Lozère
Section 8*

45 **44**

La Fage

NIGHT 4
Les Laubies

N

46

*Croix
des
Faux*

*Les
Faux*

Bramont River

47
D 35

GR 43/68

*Sentier des
Menhirs*

Les Combettes
48

Les Puechs

Km
0   0,5   1

Echine D'Aze

La Maison
Neuve **49**

the hill, with a lovely view right of jumbled valleys, the hamlet of Le Bouchet and the outline of the Col de Loubière. Continue down into Auriac, passing another attractive bell tower (3hrs 25mins).

(41) Turn down right in the hamlet and then up left (GR splashes here). The road soon degrades to a jeep track as it gains height round the contours of a tree-covered hill, goes round a gully and crosses a stream on a little bridge (3hrs 40mins). It continues round a further gully and then steadily upwards though low woodland. Eventually you reach a T-junction, where you turn right for about 5 minutes to the intersection of Les Sagnoles (alt. 1325m) at a large clearing (4hrs 20mins), where the GR43 comes in from the north.

(42) Go left here, southwards, and this is where you feel you are at last on the homeward stretch (La Fage is now 8km). You have joined another long-distance sheep trail. Continue climbing gently on a stony track over the plateau for 3km, initially through pine forest with attractive glades and then over open moorland with low sweeping slopes dotted with stunted firs and rocks on all sides. There is a junction to the left where the bridle path joins from Auriac. The wide sandy track skirts the east side of the Serre des Countrasts at 1474m, the slopes covered with bilberry bushes, heather and boulders. Keep right on the main track at a fork.

(43) Make for a junction with signposts you can see ahead (5hrs 5mins). Follow GR splashes and a sign, left, 'La Fage 5km/Florac 17km' on a poorly defined grassy path. The jeep track continues right to Lac de Barradon 1.5km (a popular fishing lake) and Florac 23km, and left to the Chalet de Mont Lozère (15km).

Continue gently upwards on a very wide path through a fir plantation, passing the rocky summit of the Roc des Chiens Fous ('Rock of the mad dogs') on the right.

The Forêt des Laubies seems to go on for ever, but at least you are starting to descend.

(44) The path reaches a wide unpaved road and signs (5hrs 35mins).

Note – the official Mont Lozère path goes via La Fage, but when the author was rechecking the walk the *gîte* at La Fage was not providing food – hence the deviation via Les Laubies.

Deviation off the GR Mont Lozère official path – Turn left down towards Les Laubies (right goes to the Etang de Barrandon and straight on to La Fage). After about 10 minutes descending through forest, there are extensive views in all directions. As the road bends left the Mamelons de Puech come into view on the right. Walk along to Les Laubies joining a surfaced road at the entry to Les Laubies Hauts. Go down right to Les Laubies Bas, past the church and a bridge over the Bramon stream until you see the *auberge* on the left just after a left-hand bend (6hrs).

Auberge des Laubies, 48000 St-Etienne-du-Valdonnez (Famille Romain Salles), tel. 04 66 48 01 25. Dinner, bed and breakfast (double room with shower down the passage) 25 euros.

For those who prefer to stay on the official route and go via La Fage, see below.

(45) Continue straight (left is signed 'Les Laubies 2km' and right goes to the Lac de Barradon). The stony path winds downwards through stunted pines, and for the first time the landscape opens and there is a magnificent view southwards – the Mamelons de Puech come into view on the left, with the cliffs of the Causse Méjean above Florac on the right. The path becomes bouldery as it drops fairly steeply through heather and broom bushes with cairns to guide you. Later it turns sandy and eroded before reaching a crossroads at the Croix des Faux (alt. 1258m), an iron cross on a stone plinth.

(46) Turn right following sign 'La Fage 1.5km' – the GR goes straight on to Florac and you will rejoin this later. The path goes through broom bushes with some cultivated fields beyond. Soon La Fage comes into view, and you get to the road which crosses the Bramont stream by a bridge. On entering the village there is a sign left to *gîte d'étape* (6hrs 15mins).

***Gîte d'étape* La Fage, 48000 St-Etienne-du-Valdonez. M. Meyrueix, tel. 0466 43 82 80. Dinner, bed and breakfast 31 euros (*chambre d'hôte* – room with bath).**

Take time to look around La Fage, which is a good example of the traditional village architecture of this region – it has a bell tower, a bake-house, covered fountain, a ferradou *(place where they shoed bullocks) and an iron cross. The bell tower served as a rallying point in times of crisis and rang out to announce important happenings, such as births, marriages and deaths. All has been painstakingly renovated without making the hamlet look artificial. It is still very much a remote farming community, and at the present time it has 16 permanent inhabitants, belonging to five families, and eight secondary holiday residences.*

Day Five: Les Laubies or La Fage to Florac

Time:	4hrs 15mins/4hrs
Descent:	666m

From La Fage: Retrace your steps to the Croix des Faux (no. 46) and then turn right at the signpost 'Florac 13km' (20mins).

From Les Laubies: Go out of the *auberge*, turn right and go over the bridge. Then turn immediately left and go straight on a jeep track, which meanders through fields with superb rural views, to the farm of Les Faux (20mins). Go by Les Faux to the right, above the buildings on a paved road. Just after a stone cross where the road bends left to a T-junction, go off right on a jeep track, and soon after fork right at a junction. Keep straight, going slightly uphill and finally down to the intersection with the GR43/44/68 and the Croix des Faux (35mins), where you turn left.

From no. 46: At the Croix des Faux the GR44 goes off to La Fage. Follow the sign 'Florac 13km and GR 43/68', which is a sandy path through bushes and scattered woodland with cultivated fields beyond, going down steadily (you can see the La Fage on the right), flattening out before coming to a narrow road (45mins/30mins). Ahead is the tree-covered ridge of the Echine d'Aze.

Cross the road and continue following the red/white GR signs along a flat path, which becomes a lane with a stone wall (you are still on a *draille*) and later fences on both sides. Ignore any turnings and keep straight as the path narrows.

There is a short rocky scramble as you descend into an attractive shallow valley and cross a stream. A few metres later stepping stones take you across the Bramont river and then the path goes up past a large cultivated field to meet the D35 road, where there are signposts (1hr 5mins/50mins).

(47) Cross the road and continue straight over large fields to the brow of the hill, crossing a lesser road. You come to a signpost indicating that this is the Sentier des Menhirs and Pierre des Trois Paroisses as the path goes up between a number of these old marker stones (see

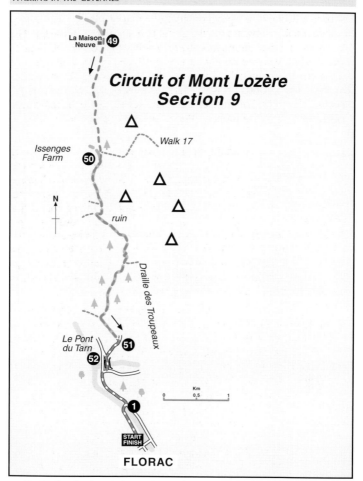

**Circuit of Mont Lozère
Section 9**

La Maison Neuve **49**

Walk 17

Issenges Farm **50**

N

ruin

Draille des Troupeaux

Le Pont du Tarn **51**
52

Km
0   0.5   1

1

START FINISH

FLORAC

walk 18 for further information) along a wide, high, exposed ridge where there are views in all directions, particularly down ahead, of the Gorges du Tarn around the village of Ispagnac.

The path descends the wide ridge, with a good view of the Mamelons and the Echine d'Aze to the left, through scattered pine and bare hillside. At a T-junction bear down left into a shallow valley to a jeep track, just before the delightful hamlet of Les Combettes (1hr 40mins/1hr 25mins). There is a small stone building on the left, which is the original bake-house with an interesting chimney and a lovely stone archway on the right. There are also several sundials on display outside one of the houses, and an inscription above another which we could not decipher. Continue up out of the valley where the road does a U-turn, crossing the Brenou stream before reaching another road (1hr 45mins/1hr).

(48) Go right on the road and then almost immediately off left on a steep jeep track, following a GR splash on telephone pole. Look back and you get a good view of the ridge you walked over and the hamlet of Les Combettes. The track goes up steeply round the contours of the hill. Keep on the main path as you enter a forest, skirting round the Echine d'Aze ridge (1233m) and passing a sign ('Sentier des Menhirs, Echine d'Aze') opposite a track up to the left which obviously goes to the summit (2hrs 5mins). On the right are white stones with AF markers which indicate the forest boundary. The jeep track starts to go down towards a house in a dip with a long ridge to the left. There are some attractive green fields on the right.

(49) Continue straight past La Maison Neuve, which is a solitary house in a lovely position with glorious views (2hrs 30mins/2hrs 15mins) – the track right goes to the hamlet of Mont Méjan. There is a short stiff climb to the top of the ridge, where you come to an area of hillside streaked with black and bluey grey markings which indicate that the limestone area has given way to granite. You are now on top of the ridge on a wide stony track – down on the left is the hamlet of Malbosc. At a right junction there is a menhir and a sign 'Sentier des Menhirs – terre bleu'. The track continues to a pass where there is a small cairn (3hrs/2hrs 45mins). Right is the farm of Issenges, and left is the path you take for Walk 17 (Sentier du Tour Puecheral). Look back for a last extended view of the Mont Lozère uplands, the rolling hills disappearing like waves into the horizon.

(50) Continue straight, and at a further intersection keep on the main track. It becomes wider, passing a solitary ruined house to the left with a magnificent view as it curls round the top of incoming valleys. It continues down in wide curves, the limestone bushland vegetation

Les Combettes

giving way to a granite soil of pine and chestnut forest. The Tarn valley is straight ahead and there is a good view of the town of Florac. Watch for a shortcut (missing a hairpin) on a narrow path down to the right (GR sign). Later on ignore a track round to the left. The jeep track becomes paved before it reaches a T-junction, where there are signs 'Tour de Mont Lozère/ Tour de Puecheral' (3hrs 50mins/3hrs 25mins).

(51) Turn down right and continue past a large *village de vacances,* where there are playing fields, a swimming pool and tennis courts further down. There is a housing estate on the right.

(52) At the bottom of the road turn left and cross a small bridge (Le Pont du Tarn) to the D907, going to Le Pont-de-Montvert. Turn immediately right to the wider N106 road, where you turn left. Walk for 500m until you reach the Pont de Bessède, where the circular walk started. Cross the bridge and continue into the centre of Florac (4hrs 15mins/4hrs).

Appendix A

A GLOSSARY OF LOCAL WORDS

aven	in Occitan Avenc – a hole or cave caused by erosion in a limestone soil; found on the upland plains in the Cevennes. Swallow hole or sinkhole in the dictionary
bastide	house or farm – also a fortified town (12th century)
bouges	variety of broom
camin ferrat	stony path – the animals that used these paths were shoed so they did not slip
can	small upland plateau
cassagnes	oak grove or plantation
causse	from the Celtic word cala, or calso, meaning a limestone plain or plateau
cham	flat, low-lying area
chaumette	shady place
collu	low pass
combette	narrow valley
draille	a long-distance track taken by the shepherds with their flocks when going to upland summer pastures
échine	spine or ridge
estrade	road
faisse	ash tree
felgere	fern or bracken
ferradou	place to shoe bullocks
loubière	place planted with white poplar trees
mas	conglomeration of farm buildings housing extended families – often self-sufficient
mazel	small *mas* or farm
méjean	in the middle
meyrueis	large field
planette	small plain or pass
plo	large pass
pradal	natural grassland
sapet	fir wood
serre	long mountain or hill ridge
tarn/tarnon	rapid-flowing water
tomple	large hole or cave
sapet	fir wood

Appendix B

TABLE OF WALK TIMES

SOUTHERN CEVENNES

1.	Circuit de L'Arre	1hr 45mins+	42
2.	Circuit des Maures	3hrs 15mins	46
3.	Roc de L'Esparon	3hrs 30mins	52
4.	Pic d'Anjeau	2hrs 45mins/4hrs 20mins	58
5.	La Cirque de Navacelles	4hrs 15mins+	65
6.	Sentier de la Trescoulade	4hrs 45mins	72
7.	Sentier des Ruisseaux	2hrs 45mins	78
8.	Circuit des Camisards	5hrs 45mins	82
9.	Le Sentier des Anes	3hrs 30mins+	89
10	Truc de Montaigu	3hrs 30mins	95
11.	La Draille de la Transhumance	3hrs 45mins	100
12.	Les Cascades d'Orgon	3hrs 15mins	105
13.	Lac des Pises	3hrs 10mins+	109
14.	Circuit de St-Guiral	2hrs 45mins	114
15.	L'Abîme de Bramabiau	4hrs/5hrs+	118
16.	Vallée du Bonheur	5hrs	125

When two timings are given they refer to shorter and longer circuit options. A + sign indicates that extra time should be allowed for visiting historical sites or villages.

Appendix C

MAPS

The maps referred to in this guide are as follows. They are at a scale of 1:25,000 (1cm = 250m) unless otherwise indicated.

Southern Cevennes

Cartes IGN 2641 ET Top 25 Mont Aigoual/Le Vigan (Walks 1, 2, 3, 6, 7, 10, 12, 13, 14, 15, 16)

Cartes IGN 2741 ET Top 25 St-Hippolyte-du-Fort/Anduze/St-Jean-du-Gard (Walks 8, 9, 11)

Cartes IGN 2642 ET Top 25 St-Guilhem-Le-Désert/Cirque de Navacelles (Walks 4, 5)

Northern Cevennes

Cartes IGN 2740 ET Top 25 Corniche des Cevennes (Walks Nos. 28, 29, 30, 31, and Tour of Mont Lozère)

Cartes IGN 2739 OT Top 25 Mont Lozère/Florac (Walks Nos. 17, 18, 19, 20, and Tour of Mont Lozère)

Cartes IGN 2640 OT Top 25 Gorges du Tarn et de la Jonte/Causse Méjean (Walks 21, 22, 23, 24, 25, 26, 27)

Other useful maps

Parc National des Cevennes IGN – 1:100,000 (1cm = 1 km): gives an overall view of both regions

Carte Routière et Touristique Michelin No.240 Languedoc/Roussillon – 1:200,000 (1cm = 2 km)

Specialist shops

Stanfords, 12-14 Long Acre, London WC2E 9LP, tel. 0207 836 1321, website www.stanfords.co.uk, email (orders & queries) weborders@stanfords.co.uk, email (general, sales & enquiries) sales@stanfords.co.uk. The largest selection of guides and maps in England: anything not in stock can be ordered (delivery 2–4 weeks).

The Map Shop, 15 High Street, Upton-upon-Severn, Worcs WR8 OHJ, tel. 01684 593146, fax 01684 594559, e-mail Themapshop@btinternet.com, website www.themapshop.co.uk. A wide selection of maps and guides.

Other **websites** from which IGN maps can be ordered:

    www.map-world.co.uk
    www.maps2anywhere.com
    www.ign.fr (this is the official IGN website)

Otherwise local newsagents and bookshops in the Cevennes stock maps and guidebooks (the latter mainly in French). The big supermarket chains in most towns also stock local maps (often cheaper than in UK).

Appendix D

TOURIST OFFICES AND SYNDICATS D'INITIATIVE

(Note: If you have internet access, you can just type the name of the area or town you are interested in into a search engine (such as Google) and get full information (in English) about such things as where to stay and what to do.)

Many of these tourist offices speak English and/or have English documentation. When phoning from outside France the prefix is 0033 + 9 digits (omit first zero).

Parc National des Cévennes (Offices)
Maison du Parc
6bis Place du Palais, 48400 Florac
Tel (33) 466.49.53.01
info@cevennes-parcnational.fr
www.cevennes-parcnational.fr

Maison du Parc
Boulevard des Châtaigniers, 30120 Le Vigan
Tel (33) 467.81.20.06
info@cevennes-parcnational.fr
www.cevennes-parcnational.fr

For general information on the different departments in the Cévennes, contact the tourist offices below:

Gard region	3 Rue Cité Foulc, BP 122, 30010 Nimes Tel (33) 466.36.96.30 contact@tourismegard.com www.tourismegard.com
Herault region	30 Allée Jean de Latte de Tassigny, Esplanade Comédie 34000 Montpellier Tel (33) 467.60.60.60 www.herault-tourisme.com
Lozère region	14 Bd.Henri Bourillon, BP 4, 48001 Mende Cedex Tel (33) 466.94.00.23 cdt@lozere-tourisme.com www.lozere-tourisme.com

Southern Cévennes Tourist Offices

LE VIGAN
Maison de Pays
Place du Marché
30120 Le Vigan
Tel (33) 467.81.01.72
contact@cevennes-meridionales.com
www.cevennes-meridionales.com

VALLERAUGUE
Maison de Pays
7 Quartier des Horts
30570 Valleraugue
Tel (33) 467.82.25.10
office.tourisme.valleraugue@
wanadoo.fr
www.aigoual-cevennes.com

L'ESPEROU (Mont Aigoual)
Col de la Serreyrède branch
Maison de L'Aigoual
30570 L'Esperou
Tel/fax (33) 467.82.64.67
office-du-tourisme-causse@
wanadoo.fr
www.causse-aigoual-cevennes.org

ST-JEAN-DU-GARD
Place Rabaut Ste.Etienne
30270 St-Jean-du-Gard
Tel (33) 466.85.32.11
www.otsi-st.jeandugard.com
www.tourismegard.com

ST-HIPPOLYTE-DU-FORT
Place Casernes
30170 St-Hippolyte-du-Fort
Tel (33) 466.77.91.65
ot.sthippolyte@cevennes-
garigue-tourisme.com
www.cevennes-garrigue-
tourisme.com

Northern Cevennes Tourist Offices

FLORAC
*incorporating Ispagnac, Tarn, Tarnon
and Mimente*
47 Avenue Jean Monestier
48400 Florac
Tel (33) 466.45.01.14
otsi@mescevennes.com
www.mescevennes.com

LE PONT-DE-MONTVERT
(Mont Lozère)
Rue du Quai
48220 Le-Pont-de-Montvert
Tel (33) 466.45.81.94
montlozerecevennes@free.fr
www.cevennes-montlozere.com

MEYRUEIS
Tour de l'Horloge
48150 Meyrueis
Tel. (33) 466.45.60.33
office.tourisme.meyrueis@wanadoo.fr
www.meyrueis-office-tourisme.com

MENDE
(Lozere)
BP 83, Place du Foirail
48000 Mende
Tel (33) 466.94.00.23
informations@ot-mende.fr
www.ot-mende.fr

STE-ENEMIE
Information on Gorges du Tarn-
Grands Causses Village
48210 Ste-Enimie
Tel (33) 466.48.53.44
contact@gorgesdutarn.net
www.gorgesdutarn.net

Appendix E

MARKET DAYS

As the Cevennes is a remote region with a dispersed population, the local markets play a more important community role than in other areas. The farmers and people from outlying villages make market day their weekly day out, when they come into town to do shopping, see friends and do other important business. Generally, the markets in the Cevennes are less colourful than those of Provence because they are not geared to year-round tourism. Out of the summer season, you will find stalls offering cheap household goods, clothes and farming equipment rather than expensive souvenirs such as woodwork and pottery. There will be baskets of rabbits, ducks, geese, guinea fowl and chickens – I have even seen dogs and cats for sale!

Nevertheless a market is still a fascinating place to stroll around, and the ones in the Cevennes are no exception. There are lots of fresh vegetables brought in from the surrounding countryside, mushrooms and nuts (particularly chestnuts) in season. It is worth buying the *raiolettes* onions, which are grown on the local terraces – they are big, especially tasty and can be stored for a long time. Also look for the local goat's cheese called Le Pélardon, which is made in springtime and can be bought in dry or creamy varieties. You will also find produce made from chestnuts such as chestnut honey, jams and flour.

Below is a list of markets in the principal Cevenese towns. They mainly start early and finish around 13.00. There are three types of market – *marché traditionnel,* which is a normal market offering a wide range of goods and produce; *marché paysan,* where the local farmers sell their home-grown produce; and *marché nocturne*, which are held in the tourist season and are geared to the holiday-maker. From time to time there are also *foires* in the larger towns, which are trade fairs, with a range of farming and industrial equipment. The larger ones include exhibiting and judging livestock, and often have a fairground.

CEVENNES MARKETS
These are *marché traditionnel* unless otherwise indicated.

Monday:	Alès, Lasalle, Malène (summer only)
Tuesday:	Ganges (*marché paysan*), Anduze (evening in summer), Marvejols, St-Jean-du-Gard, St-Hippolyte-du-Fort, Bagnols les Bains (summer only), Ispagnac
Wednesday:	Bagnols/Cèze, Mende, Meyrueis, Le Pont-de-Montvert (summer only), Ste-Enimie, Sumène, Vallerauge (evening in summer), Le Vigan (evening in summer)
Thursday:	Anduze, Florac, Marvejols (evening in summer), St-Jean du Gard (evening in summer), Ste-Enimie (evening in summer)
Friday:	Bagnols Les Bains (summer only), Ganges, Meyrueis, Pompidou (summer only), St-Hippolyte-du-Fort
Saturday:	Barre-des-Cévennes (July to September), Ispagnac, Le Blemard, Le Vigan, Marjevols, Mende, Meyrueis, Ste-Enimie, St-Jean-du-Gard (*marché paysan*), Camprieu (July and August), Sauve, Uzès, Sommières
Sunday :	Bréau (July and August), L'Espérou (July and August), Florac (summer only)

LISTING OF CICERONE GUIDES

For full and up-to-date information
on our ever-expanding list of guides,
please visit our website:
www.cicerone.co.uk.

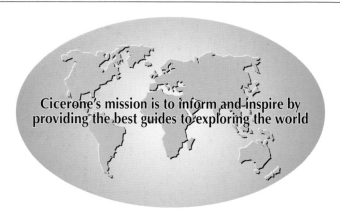

Cicerone's mission is to inform and inspire by providing the best guides to exploring the world

Since its foundation 40 years ago, Cicerone has specialised in publishing guidebooks and has built a reputation for quality and reliability. It now publishes nearly 300 guides to the major destinations for outdoor enthusiasts, including Europe, UK and the rest of the world.

Written by leading and committed specialists, Cicerone guides are recognised as the most authoritative. They are full of information, maps and illustrations so that the user can plan and complete a successful and safe trip or expedition – be it a long face climb, a walk over Lakeland fells, an alpine cycling tour, a Himalayan trek or a ramble in the countryside.

With a thorough introduction to assist planning, clear diagrams, maps and colour photographs to illustrate the terrain and route, and accurate and detailed text, Cicerone guides are designed for ease of use and access to the information.

If the facts on the ground change, or there is any aspect of a guide that you think we can improve, we are always delighted to hear from you.

Cicerone Press
2 Police Square Milnthorpe Cumbria LA7 7PY
Tel: 015395 62069 Fax: 015395 63417
info@cicerone.co.uk www.cicerone.co.uk

CICERONE